Client Interviewing, Counseling,
and Decision-Making

Client Interviewing, Counseling, and Decision-Making

A Practical Approach

SECOND EDITION

G. Nicholas Herman

Adjunct Professor of Law
Campbell University School of Law
North Carolina Central University School of Law

Melissa A. Essary

Professor of Law and Dean Emerita
Campbell University School of Law

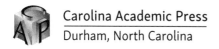
Carolina Academic Press
Durham, North Carolina

Library of Congress Cataloging-in-Publication Data:

Names: Herman, G. Nicholas, author. | Essary, Melissa A., author.
Title: Client interviewing, counseling, and decision-making : a practical
    approach / G. Nicholas Herman, Melissa A. Essary.
Description: Second edition. | Durham, North Carolina : Carolina Academic
    Press, LLC, [2020] | Includes index.
Identifiers: LCCN 2020052061 | ISBN 9781531017910 (paperback) |
    ISBN 9781531017927 (ebook)
Subjects: LCSH: Interviewing in law practice--United States. | Attorney and
    client--United States. | Counseling--United States.
Classification: LCC KF311 .H466 2020 | DDC 340.023/73--dc23
LC record available at https://lccn.loc.gov/2020052061

CAROLINA ACADEMIC PRESS
700 Kent Street
Durham, North Carolina 27701
Telephone (919) 489-7486
Fax (919) 493-5668
www.cap-press.com

Printed in the United States of America.

This book is dedicated to:

Brady and Jennifer
— GNH

Amber and Rachel
— MAE

Contents

Chapter Five

Chapter Six

Preface

This book, as its title states, provides a "practical approach" to client interviewing, counseling, and decision-making. These are practical skills, not theoretical ones. Thus, the overall pedagogical approach taken by the text is to explain to students *what to do* and *how to do it* when engaging in interviewing, counseling, and decision-making with a client. This accords with new American Bar Association Accreditation Standards 303 and 304 that mandate experiential learning opportunities for law students, including "real-life" simulation courses such as Client Counseling. Based on the guidance and techniques provided in the text, students will best learn the skills of interviewing and counseling by applying them in various role plays contained in the *Teacher's Manual* or through other role plays developed by the professor.

Three other features of this book are worthy of mention. First, the book is deliberately designed to be short—to "get to the point," without unnecessary palaver. Second, the book provides an extensive discussion of the most pertinent provisions of the *ABA Model Rules of Professional Conduct* relating to client interviewing, counseling, and decision-making (see Chapter 6). This is essential not only to ensure that these skills are applied with the highest standards of professionalism, but because many of the Rules are instructive about the lawyer's specific obligations when engaging in interviewing, counseling, and decision-making with the client. And third, the book discusses interviewing witnesses (see Chapter 7) and counseling in certain special contexts, including counseling about settlement, counseling through the writing of opinion letters, counseling the client as a deponent, and counseling the criminal defendant (see Chapter 8).

In light of these features, the book is designed for use not only as the primary text for a stand-alone course in Client Interviewing, Counseling, and Decision-making, but also as an affordable ancillary or companion text in all Clinical Programs, or in courses such as Pretrial Litigation, Trial Practice, Negotiation, or Mediation.

This second edition expands on the first in three ways: (1) the text is updated to reflect changes to the *ABA Model Rules of Professional Conduct*; (2) new sections emphasize the importance of emotional intelligence and values in counseling; and (3) new sections address counseling about mediation and counseling about transactional matters.

—GNH
—MAE

Acknowledgments

The parties gratefully acknowledge the assistance of Erin Barker in updating the text to reflect changes in the *ABA Model Rules of Professional Conduct.*

The authors also acknowledge the permissions granted to reproduce excerpts from the following:

ABA Model Rules of Professional Conduct, 2019 Edition. Copyright © 2019 by the American Bar Association. Reprinted with permission. Copies of ABA Model Rules of Professional Conduct, 2008 Edition are available from Service Center, American Bar Association, 321 North Clark Street, Chicago, IL 60654, 1-800-285-2221.

Client Interviewing, Counseling,
and Decision-Making

Chapter One

Learning Client Interviewing, Counseling, and Decision-Making

SYNOPSIS

§1.01 The Importance of Client Interviewing, Counseling, and Decision-Making

Courses in practical skills such as client interviewing, counseling, and decision-making are viewed by some law professors as "soft" courses in contrast to harder courses in doctrinal or statutory law such as constitutional law, torts, property, civil procedure, criminal law, contracts, and the like. This may be true in the sense that, while courses in substantive law require you to learn complex legal rules whose proper application to myriad factual situations often depends upon rigorous legal analysis and an appreciation of nuances in the law and the facts, courses in client interviewing, counseling, and decision-making generally do not focus on these matters. Instead, the focus is on learning and applying the processes and techniques (including pertinent ethical and legal considerations) that effective lawyers use in advising their clients and helping them to make good decisions. As such, client interviewing, counseling and decision-making courses are sometimes thought of as being heavy on "how to" mechanics and light on intellectual substance.

However, it is a mistake to think that client interviewing and counseling involve purely mechanical skills that are separable from knowledge of the substantive law and intellectual legal skills. This is because your knowledge of the law and ability to engage in legal analysis largely shape the content of your advice to a client and your representation. Client interviewing, counseling, and decision-making courses thus do not intend to downplay knowledge of the law and legal-reasoning skills, but are taught with the assumption that you will actively use the intellectual skills you are acquiring in substantive-law courses as you learn the practical skills of effective client interviewing and counseling. In this way, a client interviewing and counseling course brings the practical application of these intellectual skills to the actual practice setting. The intent is, as it is often said, to help "bridge the gap between theory and practice."

Finally, it is important to bear in mind that the skills of interviewing and counseling constitute the heart of client representation. This is so because your fundamental function as a lawyer is to help your client with a potential or existing problem or situation by (1) understanding that problem or situation, (2) advising the client about options for how to deal with it, (3) formulating a preferred plan for dealing with it, and (4) implementing that plan. All other practical skills of the lawyer flow from the foregoing—i.e., what law to research; how the situation might be resolved through negotiation, mediation, or by some other means; what transactional documents to prepare; or how the matter should be litigated at trial or on appeal. Thus, the importance of these skills cannot be overemphasized.

§1.02 "Learning by Doing" and the Role of This Book

In broad terms, "client interviewing, counseling, and decision-making" involve establishing a counseling relationship with your client, obtaining information relevant to the decision to be made by your client, analyzing the decision to be made, advising your client about the decision, and implementing the decision. The best way to learn these skills is to "just do it," under the guidance and critique of your professor and fellow students. This "learning by doing" approach, also used in teaching trial practice and other practical skills such as taking depositions, has achieved widespread recognition, particularly from the success of programs sponsored by the National Institute for Trial Advocacy,[1] a non-profit educational organization that conducts continuing legal education programs in practical skills for lawyers throughout the country.

This book is designed for use in connection with this "learning by doing" approach. The main text will provide you with the processes, concepts, and techniques involved in client interviewing, counseling and decision-making, along with illustrations of how various concepts and techniques may be applied. Then, you will be able to develop your own effectiveness in these essential practical skills from your experiences in a Clinical Program or in conducting simulated interviewing and counseling sessions based on role plays provided by your Professor.

---

1. National Institute for Trial Advocacy (NITA), 361 Centennial Parkway, Suite 220, Louisville, Colorado 80027-1284; 877-648-2632; Web site: www.nita.org.

Chapter Two

Overview of the Counseling Process and Decision-Making Models

SYNOPSIS

§ 2.01 What Is "Counseling"?

Clients come to lawyers for all sorts of reasons. A client might want you to prepare a will, handle a closing on the purchase of a home, or incorporate a new business. A client might ask you to draft a piece of legislation, a contract, or an employee handbook. A client might be in trouble, as when she has been charged with a crime, has been fired from her job, or faces a bitter divorce. A client might seek your services because she has been sued, or because she wants to file a lawsuit to seek redress for personal injuries or some other damages she has sustained. A client might want to hire you to serve as her agent in a transaction, negotiator in a business deal, or spokesperson before a city council or other public body. Or a client might simply want to talk with you about the potential legal ramifications of a particular situation or plan of action. In short, a client might call upon you to serve in any number of roles — as draftsman, advocate, litigator, agent, dealmaker, negotiator, mediator, spokesperson, or general advisor.

Regardless of the particular services you are called upon to render for a client, you will always also serve as a "counselor" to your client. That is, in the course of every representation, you will engage in an ongoing process of advising and consulting with your client to the end of helping her understand and deal with her legal situation or problem. This is what is meant by "counseling" and by the designation used on the letterhead of many attorneys that identifies them not only as "Attorneys" but also as "Counselors At Law."

§2.02 An Overview of the Counseling Process

Generally speaking, the process of counseling is a five-step process of decision-making. It also includes the process of orally gathering information from your client through interviewing. The overall process involves five interrelated functions that culminate in taking a course of action on behalf of your client. In outline form, these functions call upon you to:

(1) Establish a Professional and Interpersonal Relationship with Your Client by:
- Establishing rapport with your client through a relationship of trust, confidence, and comfort;
- Establishing the nature and scope of the representation;
- Understanding the division of authority between you and your client in making decisions affecting the representation;
- Establishing attorney's fees for the representation, or financial eligibility for unpaid legal services.

(2) Obtain Information Relevant to Your Client's Situation and Potential Courses of Action by:
- Interviewing your client about the facts of the situation and her underlying interests, needs, concerns, and feelings;
- Understanding your client's views about the issues involved;
- Exploring your client's objectives, and potential legal theories;
- Conducting any necessary factual investigation;
- Conducting any necessary legal research.

(3) Analyze Potential Courses of Action by:
- Identifying potential courses of action for achieving your client's objectives;
- Evaluating the legal and non-legal pros and cons of each potential course of action;
- Comparing the various courses of action and your client's objectives in light of the risks and costs involved.

(4) Advise Your Client about Potential Courses of Action by:
- Explaining your client's legal rights and the legal ramifications of each potential course of action;
- Advising your client about the relative benefits, risks, and costs of each potential course of action;
- Discussing with your client the probabilities of the various outcomes and the legal and non-legal consequences of each potential course of action.

(5) Decide Upon the Course of Action to be Taken and Implement the Course of Action by:
- Arriving at a decision with your client about what course of action will be taken;
- Explaining the means and process by which you will implement the course of action;
- Explaining your client's responsibilities and role in implementing the course of action;
- Consulting with and advising your client throughout the process of implementing the course of action.

It is important to bear in mind that this counseling process continues throughout the entire representation. Although in some situations all five functions outlined above might be covered in a single meeting with a client (e.g., as where a client hires you merely to prepare a boilerplate instrument in a routine transaction), in the majority of cases you will be counseling your client over a period of time. Counseling often occurs through numerous meetings and phone conversations with your client, and through opinion letters, other correspondence, and e-mail.

In most cases, and particularly where litigation is involved, there will be numerous decisions that will have to be made during the representation. Changes in circumstances will present additional courses of action to be explored, analyzed, explained, decided upon, and implemented. Decisions or courses of action that were previously agreed upon may have to be modified or abandoned altogether, and courses of action that were rejected earlier may have to be reevaluated as the facts develop. In sum, your role as counselor to your client spans the entirety of the representation—from the time of the initial client meeting to the conclusion of the representation.

§2.03 Decision-Making Models

Studies have shown that clients give the highest ratings to lawyers who have a high level of interpersonal skills.[1] Clients consistently rate lawyers who have excellent relational skills as being more competent, effective, and worthy of recommendation to future clients than lawyers who have poor interpersonal skills. Indeed, clients consider the interpersonal skills of a lawyer as being a more important measure of lawyer effectiveness than knowledge of the law, advocacy skills, or even the results of the representation.[2]

In part, the extent of your interaction with your client and the interpersonal skills you employ with your client in counseling and interviewing are shaped by how you strike the balance between your client's control over the legal representation and your control over it. In other words, who should be in charge of the representation? Who should be responsible for making which decisions? Who should control the objectives of the representation? Who should control the means? To what extent should control over the representation be shared between you and your client? The answers to these questions turn upon what decision-making model of counseling the lawyer chooses to adopt.

In his 1974 book, *Lawyer and Client: Who's in Charge?*, Douglas Rosenthal sets forth two models about the distribution of control in legal representation. One model, which he calls the "traditional" model, vests primary control with the lawyer. The other model contemplates a sharing of control between lawyer and client over most decisions affecting the representation. Since the publication of Rosenthal's book, academicians have variously identified and debated different models of lawyer counseling from the standpoint of legal ethics and practical-skills instruction. Out of this discourse, essentially three models or approaches have emerged. For purposes of clarity, these approaches may be called the "Lawyer-Centered Model," the "Client-Centered Model," and the "Collaborative Model."[3]

---

1. *See* Stephen Feldman & Kent Wilson, *The Value of Interpersonal Skills in Lawyering*, 5 Law & Hum. Behav. 311 (1981).

2. *Id. See also* Robert F. Cochran Jr. et al., *The Counselor-At-Law: A Collaborative Approach to Client Interviewing and Counseling* 2, 58–59 (1999).

3. For other general discussions about counseling models, *see* Robert F. Cochran, Jr. et al., *The Counselor-At-Law: A Collaborative Approach to Client Interviewing and Counseling*,

[1] The Lawyer-Centered Model

Under the "lawyer-centered model" of counseling, the client essentially delegates to the lawyer primary responsibility for problem solving and decision-making in the representation.[4] The lawyer has broad autonomy and authoritarian control over the professional relationship, and the client's role in the representation is largely passive.[5] Some scholars have likened the lawyer's role under this model to that of "Guru," where the client is a disciple of the lawyer-master, or to that of "Godfather," where the lawyer parentally shoulders the entire burden of the client's legal situation.[6] The somewhat dogmatic nature of this approach to counseling is exemplified by the remarks of Judge Clement Haynsworth who told a law school graduating class:

> [The lawyer] serves his clients without being their servant. He serves to further the lawful and proper objective of the client, but the lawyer must never forget that he is the master. He is not there to do the client's bidding. It is for the lawyer to decide what is morally and legally right, and, as a professional, he cannot give in to a client's attempt to persuade him to take some other stand.... During my years of practice, ... I told [my clients] what would be done and firmly rejected suggestions that I do something else which I felt improper[7] ...

The lawyer-centered model has been widely criticized as being inconsistent with client dignity and the intrinsic value of client self-determination. It has also been criticized as being inconsistent with studies that have shown that active client participation in the representation may lead to results more sat-

---

Chapters 1 and 9 (1999); Paul J. Zwier & Anthony J. Bocchino, *Fact Investigation: A Practical Guide to Interviewing, Counseling, and Case Theory Development*, Chapter 6 (2000); Thomas L. Shaffer & Robert F. Cochran, Jr., *Lawyers, Clients, and Moral Responsibility*, 3–54 (1994); David A. Binder, et al., *Lawyers as Counselors: A Client-Centered Approach*, Chapter 2 (1991); Judith L. Maute, Allocation of Decisionmaking Authority Under the Model Rules of Professional Conduct, 17 U.C. Davis L. Rev. 1049 (1984); John Basten, Control and the Lawyer-Client Relationship, 6 J. Legal Prof. 10 (1981).

4. *See* Paul J. Zwier & Anthony J. Bocchino, *Fact Investigation: A Practical Guide to Interviewing, Counseling, and Case Theory Development* 143 (2000).

5. Douglas E. Rosenthal, *Lawyer and Client: Who's in Charge?* 2 (1974).

6. *See* Thomas L. Shaffer & Robert F. Cochran, Jr., *Lawyers as Strangers and Friends: A Reply to Professor Sammons*, 18 U. Ark. Little Rock L. J. 30–39, 5–14 (1995); Thomas L. Shaffer & Robert F. Cochran, Jr., *Lawyers, Clients, and Moral Responsibility* 3–54 (1994).

7. Clement F. Haynsworth, *Professionalism in Lawyering*, 27 S.C.L. Rev. 627, 628 (1976).

isfying to clients.[8] In addition, a rigid application of the lawyer-centered model may run afoul of Rule 1.2(a) of the American Bar Association's Model Rules of Professional Conduct, which mandates that "a lawyer shall abide by a client's decisions concerning the objectives of representation and ... shall consult with the client as to the means by which they are to be pursued." (*See* § 6.03). Finally, from the standpoint of interpersonal relations, lawyers who adopt an inflexible lawyer-centered approach to counseling may be viewed by many clients as being dogmatic, paternalistic, condescending, and overbearing. In addition, interpersonal interaction between the lawyer and client is often circumscribed because of the lawyer's largely unfettered control over decision-making.

On the other hand, in many circumstances, the lawyer-centered model is entirely consistent with the expectations that clients place upon lawyers. After all, clients seek out lawyers for their expertise in the law and their objective professional judgment about what legal rights and remedies are available in a particular situation. If a legal course of action is available, many clients expect—and will even direct—that their lawyers "take charge of the case" and assume responsibility for critical decision-making during the representation. In short, it is as common for clients to grant to their lawyers broad control over the representation, as it is common for patients to grant to their physicians broad control over the most appropriate course of medical treatment. When this allocation of decision-making control over the professional relationship is made with the informed consent of the client, whether out of the client's deference to the lawyer's expertise or by virtue of the client's express directive to the lawyer, there is nothing wrong with taking a *limited* lawyer-centered approach to counseling, so long as that approach is not taken to extremes and does not violate the Rules of Professional Conduct.

[2] The Client-Centered Model

The "client-centered model" may be viewed as being at the opposite end of the theoretical spectrum from the lawyer-centered model. According to the leading proponents of the client-centered approach,

> the client-centered conception 'fills in' the traditional [lawyer-centered] approach by stressing that problems have nonlegal as well as legal aspects, and by emphasizing the importance of clients' expertise,

---

8. *See* Douglas E. Rosenthal, *Lawyer and Client: Who's in Charge?* 36–46 (study showed that plaintiffs who were actively involved in their cases obtained higher settlements and verdicts than plaintiffs who allowed their lawyers to control the representation).

thoughts and feelings in resolving problems. In a client-centered world, [the lawyer's] role involves having clients actively participate in identifying their problems, formulating potential solutions, and making decisions.[9]

Accordingly, under this model, the lawyer (1) helps identify problems from the client's perspective, (2) actively involves the client in the process of exploring potential solutions, (3) encourages the client to make those decisions which are likely to have a substantial legal or non-legal impact, (4) provides advice based on the client's values, (5) acknowledges the client's feelings and recognizes their importance, and (6) repeatedly conveys a desire to help.[10] The approach expressly requires that the lawyer develop and employ a high level of interpersonal skills and interpersonal interaction with the client.

Because the client-centered model places a premium on "the autonomy, intelligence, dignity and basic morality of the individual client,"[11] the model espouses a professional relationship that is distinctly client dominant and aimed at providing the client with "maximum satisfaction."[12] The client is given primary decision-making power throughout the representation, and the lawyer is obligated to make every reasonable effort to accede to the client's decisions about the ends and means of the representation. Some scholars have likened the lawyer's role in this relationship to that of a "hired gun," where the lawyer's primary job is to achieve the autonomous wishes of the client regardless of the effects of the representation upon third persons.[13]

In terms of how legal advice should be given, although the client-centered model does not eschew giving legal advice, it discourages lawyers from "taking the lead" in rendering opinions about the proper decision the client should make.[14] Instead, the model calls upon the lawyer to engage the client, somewhat like a psychotherapist, in an advice-giving dialogue, through which the client is psychologically encouraged to "find herself" in the representation and arrive at decisions that she feels and comes to believe are her own. For example, the leading text on the client-centered model illustrates this approach in the following counseling dialogue:

---

9. David A. Binder, et al., *Lawyers as Counselors: A Client-Centered Approach* 18 (1991).

10. *Id.* at 19–22.

11. *Id.* at 18.

12. *Id.* at 261.

13. *See* Thomas L. Shaffer & Robert F. Cochran, Jr., *Lawyers, Clients, and Moral Responsibility* 15–29 (1994).

14. *See* David A. Binder, et al., *Lawyers as Counselors: A Client-Centered Approach*, Chapters 15 and 20 (1991).

Lawyer:

Next Diana, why don't we turn to the question I asked you to think about, whether to insist on a personal [financial] guarantee from the officers [of the company]?

Client:

I've been thinking about it a lot, and I'm still not sure what to do. What do you suggest?

Lawyer:

I hate to sound like a lawyer, but there's not one right answer. A lot depends on the unique circumstances of your situation. What I suggest is this. Let's discuss the likely pros and cons both of having and not having personal guarantees. We'll even prepare a chart of the likely consequences. If you still want my opinion after we've done that, I'll certainly give it to you. But by postponing my view, I'll be able to take what you say into account in giving you my opinion. Does that sound all right?

Client:

That sounds like it'll take some time, and frankly I don't want to devote the time or money to it. You're a lawyer, and I'm sure you've come across these situations lots of times. I'll go along with what you think is best.

Lawyer:

I'm not sure that I know what's best. But you tell me if I'm wrong. My sense is that your primary objective is for this deal to go through and that you feel the company itself is pretty solid. If I'm right about those things, probably you're better off not insisting on personal guarantees. Is that a decision you're comfortable with?

Client:

[I don't know.] I know we've gone round and round on this, but I just can't decide. What do you think I ought to do?

Lawyer:

Well, I agree that it's time to cut bait on this one. In the abstract, either decision might be proper, so primarily my advice grows out of what you've said as we've talked. I know your accountant has advised you to get personal guarantees, and I don't want to come between you and her. You can tell me if I'm wrong, but what you've indicated is that your primary objective is for this deal to go through, and that you feel the company itself is pretty solid. Also, you have some fear that insisting on guarantees might sour this deal and soil future business opportunities. Based on these feelings, I think you'd be best off not insisting on personal guarantees. Does that seem sound?....[15]

The principal features of the client-entered model—considering problems from the client's perspective, involving the client in exploring potential solutions, encouraging the client to participate in the decision-making process, and recognizing the importance of the client's views, values, and feelings—are certainly essential to effective counseling and effective representation. On the other hand, if the client-dominant *process* of the client-centered approach is taken to an extreme, it may deprive the client of the very *substance* she seeks from her lawyer: an objective and candid assessment of her situation, uninhibited advice as to what she can do about it, and—consistent with her expectations and informed consent—an appropriate level of attorney control over the representation.

[3] The Collaborative Model

The "collaborative model" of counseling represents a middle ground between the lawyer-centered model and the client-centered model but still leaves primary decision-making control with the client. The leading proponents of this model explain its features and benefits as follows:

> We believe that the authoritarian [lawyer-centered] model provides too small a role for clients, the client-centered approach provides too small a role for lawyers, and that clients will be best served when lawyers and clients resolve problems in the law office through collaborative decision making. Under this model, the client would control decisions, but the lawyer would structure the process and provide advice in a manner that is likely to yield wise decisions.
>
> This model would be likely to avoid the problems of the authoritarian [lawyer-centered] model. The client's control of the decisions would ensure client dignity. It would also be likely to yield superior results to the authoritarian [lawyer-centered] model. [Douglas] Rosenthal found that the more varied forms of client participation and the more persistently the client employed them, "the better his chances of protecting his emotional and economic interests in the case outcome." We share Rosenthal's call for lawyers and clients to engage in "mutual participation in a cooperative relationship in which the co-

---

15. *Id.* at 348–349. *See also* David A. Binder, et al., *Lawyers as Counselors: A Client-Centered Approach* at 368–371 (2d ed. 2004).

operating parties have relatively equal status, are equally dependent, and are engaged in activity 'that will be in some ways satisfying to both [parties].'"

A collaborative client counseling model would also avoid the weaknesses of the client-centered counselors. It would provide the lawyer and client with an opportunity to consider the effects of their decisions on other people. It would provide the flexibility to counsel the client in a wide variety of ways. Finally it would enable the client and lawyer to engage in a collaborative deliberation that would be likely to yield practical wisdom.[16]

Some scholars have analogized the lawyer's role under the collaborative model to that of being a "friend" to the client, where the lawyer acts as a listener, sounding board, clarifier, evaluator, and caring advisor.[17] Through these attributes, the lawyer employs and imparts "practical wisdom" for his client and helps her to exercise "practical reason" in decision-making.[18] Of course, the collaborative model of counseling and the role of the lawyer as a professional "friend" require that the lawyer employ a high level of interpersonal skills. In general, in the view of the authors of this book, the collaborative model is descriptive of the most balanced decision-making approach in most cases.

[4] Using Different Decision-Making Models

It should be apparent from the foregoing discussion that to use any single counseling model in all situations would be inappropriate. There is simply no "one-size-fits-all" approach to legal counseling. Insofar as counseling is essentially a process of decision-making, the most appropriate model to employ in a particular situation will depend largely upon the type of decision to be made, taking into account (1) the particular needs and expectations of your client, (2) the particular subject matter of the representation, and (3) your particular role in

---

16. Robert F. Cochran, Jr., et al., *The Counselor-At-Law: A Collaborative Approach to Client Interviewing and Counseling* 6–7 (1999).

17. *See* Paul J. Zwier & Anthony J. Bocchino, *Fact Investigation: A Practical Guide to Interviewing, Counseling, and Case Theory Development* 145–152 (2000); Thomas L. Shaffer & Robert F. Cochran, Jr., *Lawyers, Clients, and Moral Responsibility* 40–54, 113–134 (1994); Anthony T. Kronman, *The Lost Lawyer: Finding Ideals of the Legal Profession* 131 (1993); Thomas D. Morgan, *Thinking About Lawyers as Counselors*, 42 Fla. L. Rev. 439, 453 (1990).

18. *See* Robert F. Cochran, Jr. et al., *The Counselor-At-Law: A Collaborative Approach to Client Interviewing and Counseling* 7, 176–182 (1999); Anthony T. Kronman, *The Lost Lawyer: Failing Ideals of the Legal Profession* 14–17 (1993).

the representation—whether as draftsman, advocate, litigator, agent, dealmaker, negotiator, spokesperson, or general advisor. Moreover, different models may be appropriate to employ at different stages of a particular representation because there will usually be different kinds of decisions to be made and different functions that you will have to perform during the representation.

For example, from the standpoint of *decision-making control*, the lawyer-centered approach may be appropriate when your client expressly requests that you take unilateral action in the representation, when an emergency arises that requires you to preserve your client's rights and there is no time for consultation, when your client is under a disability and it is necessary to take some action to protect her interests (*see also* §6.06), or when the decisions to be made are technical or tactical in nature, such as decisions relating to drafting, procedure, trial tactics or trial strategy. On the other hand, collaborative or client-centered counseling would be essential when making decisions such as whether to file a lawsuit, whether to accept a settlement offer or whether your client in a criminal case should plead guilty, waive her privilege against self-incrimination and testify at trial, or appeal a conviction. As a matter of ethics, your client is the only person who can make final decisions on these types of matters (*see* §6.03). A collaborative or client-centered approach may also be most appropriate when deciding what offers or counteroffers to make in negotiations, when you are called upon to serve as an intermediary between clients who consult you on a matter that affects both of them (*see also* §6.08), when deciding what claims or defenses to raise in a lawsuit, or when deciding how to structure a new business enterprise. In short, different counseling approaches are warranted in different situations.

§2.04 Counseling to Prevent Harm to the Client and Others

The preceding discussion has focused on how you strike the balance between your client's control over the representation and your control over it. Closely intertwined with this question is an even more controversial question: the extent to which you should assert power over your client to protect her from herself, or to protect others from her. For example, if your client insists on a course of action that you believe will seriously harm her personal or legal interests or will do serious injury to the legitimate rights of a third person, to what extent should you try to intervene and prevent the harm?

Guidance in answering this question is, in some circumstances, addressed by obligations imposed upon you by the Rules of Professional Conduct discussed in Chapter 6 of this book. For example, if your client insists on pursuing a course of action that would be unlawful or would cause you to violate a rule of professional conduct, you may have to withdraw from the representation (*see* § 6.11). If your client becomes afflicted by a disability such that you reasonably believe she cannot adequately act in her own interests, the ethical rules allow you to seek the appointment of a legal guardian or take other, unilateral protective action on behalf of your client (*see* § 6.06). Generally, however, these types of circumstances are rare.

The more common situation occurs when your client wants to pursue a course of action, which, though not unlawful or unethical, is contrary to your best judgment and is likely to pose grave consequences for her or otherwise cause serious harm to the legitimate rights or interests of others. For example, if you represent a mother in a custody case who, without *any* rational basis or arguable legal basis, is determined to deprive the father of all visitation rights with their young child, the mother's attitude and position are not only likely to undermine her chances of being awarded sole custody in the eyes of a judge, but may also cause serious harm to the child. In situations such as these, short of seeking your client's permission to withdraw from the representation, what should you do?

One scholar has posited three different roles that are worthy of consideration in this regard: the lawyer as "Guide," "Governor," or "Guardian":

> The guide's role is to take his client wherever the client wants to go. This role is not limited to that of a technician; it includes also those of explorer, strategist, and counselor. The guide maps out options and assists the client to clarify the client's thinking and feeling about the options. When asked, he gives advice as to which option he believes to be most consistent with the client's expressed objectives, simply clarified. The guide has no will apart from the client's will, except to serve the client's will.
>
> The governor's role is to limit where the client may go, in order to prevent the client from trespassing on the legitimate interests of others. The governor respects the client's wishes completely, unless and until they lead the client to choose a course of action that the governor believes will violate some standard of justice or fairness that is owing to third parties or to the body politic. Then the governor restrains the client from acting on the choice.
>
> The guardian's role is to promote the client's best interest. Unlike the governor, the guardian is unconcerned with protecting the interests of other people insofar as they conflict with the client's. Unlike the guide, the guardian exercises independent judgment in determining

what the client's interests are. He considers the client's choices as a relevant factor, but overrules them if he thinks that they are wrong.[19]

In situations where your client's decision to pursue a particular course of action would be injurious to her or cause unjust injury to others, the Guide-Governor-Guardian roles basically indicate two options. First, you could adopt the role of Guide, in which case you would support and advance your client's decision regardless of the injurious consequences. Second, you could adopt the role of Governor or Guardian, in which case, as Governor, you would overrule any decision that would unjustly injure the rights or interests of third persons, or, as Guardian, you would overrule any decision that would be injurious to your client's best interests.

The problem with the first option is that, by simply acquiescing to your client's undesirable decision, your representation may result in harming her rather than helping her, and you might compound the overall damage by senselessly harming others as well. The problem with the second option is that, by simply overruling your client's undesirable decision, you will effectively supplant your proper roles as representative and advisor to your client with the roles of master and dictator over her.

The obvious third option is that you could engage in collaborative counseling and seek to persuade your client not to pursue the injurious decision. In this situation, this is the most appropriate approach. It avoids dictatorial decision-making by you, preserves client dignity and client self-determination, and enhances the prospect that your client will recognize that your advice to pursue an alternative course of action is genuinely being given to advance her best interests based upon your objective professional judgment and expertise. As a practical matter, in the vast majority of situations, you will find that such efforts at persuasion will be successful, particularly if undertaken patiently and persistently.

In the end, if your efforts at persuasion are unsuccessful, you will have to decide whether to (1) nevertheless accede to your client's harmful course of action, or (2) withdraw from the representation under the Rules of Professional Conduct, which permit withdrawal if your client insists upon pursuing an objective that you consider "repugnant" or with which you have a "fundamental disagreement" (*see* §6.11). As between these choices, your decision will no doubt be largely governed by the severity of the harm you believe will occur if you proceed to advance your client's undesirable course of action. If the harm

---

19. Anthony G. Amsterdam, "Handling a Problem Situation," in Materials for NYU School of Law's Lawyering Course 26 (1988).

is likely to be substantial, withdrawal from the representation may be appropriate, so long as your withdrawal would not create an even greater harm to your client. After all, your fundamental role is to help your client, not to harm her. If your client is unwilling to benefit from your independent professional judgment, your ability to effectively represent her will become extremely difficult, if not impossible.

It is essential to emphasize, however, that withdrawal from representation is a drastic option that should only be considered in the most serious situations. From the standpoint of professional ethics, you are generally required to abide by your client's decisions concerning the objectives of the representation (*see* §6.03). While this obligation applies regardless of the subject matter of the representation, it is particularly acute in criminal cases where, for example, a lawyer may never overrule a criminal defendant's knowing, intelligent, and voluntary decisions about matters affecting "fundamental" constitutional rights such as whether to plead guilty, waive a trial by jury, testify at trial, or appeal a conviction (*see id.*). Thus, whenever your client decides upon a course of action that you believe will be substantially injurious, and you are unsuccessful in persuading her to adopt an alternative course of action, you generally should only seek to withdraw from the representation if doing so would not work a greater injury to her than would occur if you proceeded to implement her undesirable decision (*see also* §6.11).

§2.05 A Caring Perspective on Counseling

Caring about your clients can make you a better lawyer. Clients typically need your guidance and counsel on matters affecting critical rights and interests that have a significant impact on their personal well-being. A client who believes that her lawyer actually cares about what happens to her often feels more comfortable with and confident in her lawyer, and that comfort and confidence will help the lawyer and client work together more effectively. For all the celebration in the popular media of the lawyer as "hired gun," most clients would prefer to have their matters handled by someone who cares.

Adopting a caring perspective does not mean that you become enmeshed in all of a client's personal issues. You are not trained in psychotherapy, and you are not being paid for that service. By maintaining some distance from your client's emotional response to the legal issues, you can provide your client with a much-needed fresh perspective to the legal problem. A caring perspective does mean, however, that you see yourself as trying to help others, in part because you want to make their lives a little better. Such a perspective entails a degree of personal involvement. While not all lawyers can care about all clients in all contexts, the more you can care about your clients the more satisfied they are likely to be with your services. In addition, caring about your clients is likely to leave you more satisfied with yourself over the course of your career.

§2.06 Patience in Counseling

Finally, consistent with the interpersonal nature of the counseling process and the importance to your client of the decisions to be made and actions to be taken, you must be patient in your role as counselor. This means that you must not only take the time to be thorough in the counsel you give, but you must also take the time to be thorough in obtaining and considering all information that may be pertinent to your counsel. As proponents of the client-centered approach particularly emphasize, you should make a deliberate effort to understand your client's situation from her perspective, involve her in exploring potential solutions, and encourage her to appropriately participate in the decision-making process. After all, as between you and your client, your client is always the ultimate owner of her legal situation or problem. What you own is the unique professional capacity to help her deal with it, and this helping role can only be accomplished effectively if your client is integrally involved in the representation.

§2.07 The Role of Emotional Intelligence

We know that we relate best with one another if we understand and empathize with one another's feelings or emotions. When that occurs, we better communicate with each other and help each other. This understanding and empathy for another's feelings or emotions is commonly referred to in the psychological literature as "emotional intelligence" or "EI."

The importance of EI is not new because it is known to us from common experience. In psychology, the importance of EI was first raised in the mid-1960s[20] and was popularized in a 1995 book by science journalist, Daniel Gole-

---

20. *See* Michael Beldoch, "Sensitivity to Expression of Emotional Meaning in Three Modes of Communication," in J.R. Davitz, et al., *The Communication of Emotional Meaning* at 31–42 (McGraw-Hill 1964).

man, in *Emotional Intelligence—Why it can matter more than IQ*.[21] Since that time, psychologists have developed and debated different definitions of EI and have conducted numerous studies about its role in interpersonal relationships, including in business relationships and in the attorney-client relationship. The common theme of this academic research and discussion is that EI is an attribute and skill that each of us can use in improving our personal and professional relationships with others.

Although there are different formulations of EI, the concept is generally defined as the capacity to: (1) perceive the emotions or feelings of others (and in ourselves); and (2) harness or manage those emotions or feelings in our thinking, problem-solving, and interactions with others. A core aspect of these capacities is the ability to truly *empathize* with the person with whom we are interacting—effectively to "put ourselves in the shoes" of the other person without the interference of our own emotions or feelings that we must control or manage to treat other persons with real *empathy*.

For example, consider a prospective client who comes to you for advice about a divorce with issues including marital property distribution, child support, custody, and child visitation, or about compensation for a serious injury sustained in an automobile accident. Effective EI means that you must be acutely attuned to—and *empathize* with—the unique emotions or feelings of the client in these distressed circumstances. In the divorce case, this may involve the client's emotions and feelings about the breakdown of the marriage, the client's economic uncertainty for the future, the wrenching impact of a divorce on the children, feelings of anxiety, anger, betrayal, and perhaps revenge. In the personal injury case, the client's feelings and emotions may be affected by ongoing pain, inability to work, lack of self-worth, uncertainty about the future, the cost of necessary medical care, and the like.

Your understanding and empathy towards the client about these matters will not only affect *what* course of action you will recommend to your client, but also *how* you will advise your client about the recommended course of action. For instance, in the divorce case, if your client's feelings or emotions are dominated by anger and vindictiveness, your understanding and acknowledgement of these emotions will shape the *manner* in which you encourage your client to talk about the best interests of agreeing upon a property settlement and the long-term best interests of the children in terms of child support, custody, and visitation. So too, in the personal injury case, your empathy for your client's pain and anxieties will shape the *manner* in which you may encourage

---

21. Daniel Goleman, *Emotional Intelligence* (Banton Books 1995).

your client to pursue physical therapy as you arrange for medical-payments coverage under his/her own insurance and intercede with his/her employer about the temporary disability.

In both cases, as EI teaches, your effective counseling involves an acute, *empathetic* perception of the emotions and feelings of the client where your own emotions and feelings (or "ego") are harnessed or managed to counsel the client in a way that best treats the client as a "person" having unique and complex emotions and feelings. In this way, you are not authoritarian, dictatorial, overbearing, or self-serving. Instead, with appropriate EI, you will be a more effective communicator with the client, will be able to more effective in advising your client, and you will more effective in establishing a trusting attorney-client relationship.

Cultivating this type of EI in attorney-client counseling can be enhanced by a lawyer attentive to the following:

- What is the client's body language?
- What emotions or feelings lurk behind the client's story or words?
- What does the client say when asked, "why" he/she feels a certain way or says something in a certain way?
- What words of "personal" assurance can you provide to your client to alleviate his/her feelings or emotions?
- What legal advice should you give your client now, but defer for a later time?
- What assurances can you give your client that you will support and protect him/her and that you can and will shoulder his/her legal issues?
- What will you say to your client about always being available to him/her and how you are resolved to truly "care" for him/her?

§2.08 The Role of Values

The feelings or emotions underlying the understanding and empathy necessary for "emotional intelligence" (EI) are often, though not always, grounded in and driven by the client's "personal values." Personal values are often categorized in sociological, cultural, and political terms such as "left," "right," or "moderate." But these terms are not descriptive of the "personal values" that typically drive the feelings or emotions of a client who comes to you for legal advice. Instead, the personal values that typically drive a client consist of complex dispositions that involve values embodied by, for example: appreciation; autonomy; awareness; caring; compassion; cooperation; courtesy; creativity;

dependability; diligence; discipline; dignity; empathy; fairness; foresight; help-fulness; honesty; humility; imagination; independence; integrity; kindness; moderation; modesty; politeness; openness; optimism; patience; perseverance; respect; restraint; self-awareness; self-discipline; self-esteem; self-reliance; sensitivity; sharing; sincerity; sympathy; temperance; tolerance; trustworthiness; truthfulness, and other attributes or dispositions. These types of values, or notions of them, have an integral effect upon client behavior.

A lawyer's EI when counseling a client should be acutely attentive to these kinds of personal client values because that attentiveness will help you empathize with your client in a way that will help you decide *how* to effectively counsel your client and what values to probe with your client. For example, in the divorce case mentioned in §2.07 above, the client's receptiveness to, and decisions about, an amicable property settlement and resolving the issues of child custody and support are likely to be affected by the client's values involving cooperation, fairness, honesty, respect, restraint, sensitivity, tolerance, and trustworthiness with the client's spouse and for the wellbeing of the parties' children. Similarly, in the personal injury case mentioned above, the client's values of autonomy, fairness, independence, perseverance, self-esteem, and self-reliance may be integral to your plan for seeking compensation for the client, whether by an expedited settlement or otherwise. The overall point is that your understanding and empathy with your client's values will enhance your ability to effectively advise your client.

In addition to the foregoing types of personal values of the client that are important to counseling and the attorney-client relationship, some classical philosophical ethics are worthy of note. Generally, ethics philosophers identify the following considerations in a value-based or ethical decision:

> (1) The relative good or harm of the proposed decision for the greatest number of persons involved (Utilitarian theory);
> (2) The extent to which a "right" exists or a "duty" is owed in the proposed decision (Natural Rights theory);
> (3) The extent to which the decision should be governed by considerations of equity or fairness (John Rawls);
> (4) Whether the decision would be the best one that everyone in like circumstances would adopt (Kant's deontology);
> (5) Whether the decision would be considered consistent with "good character" (Virtue Ethics); and/or
> (6) Whether the decision would advance one's self-interest in the long run (Egoism).

These general theories of ethics are, of course, not litmus tests in counseling a client. But they exemplify typical value considerations that may affect the ultimate decision-making of a client and therefore inform your approach to counseling the client. For example, a client decision may be unwise if it may harm many others, or violate some legitimate "right" or "duty" owed to others, or be unfair, or be inconsistent with a decision that would be best for all persons in like circumstances, or be inconsistent with "good character;" or not be in the client's best interests in the long run. The overall point is that these types of considerations may be appropriate for you to explore with your client in connection with utilizing EI in attorney-client counseling.

Chapter Three

The Initial Client Meeting

SYNOPSIS

§3.01 Objectives of the Initial Client Meeting

For a new client, the initial client meeting marks the beginning of the attorney-client relationship. At this meeting, your objectives include:

(1) Putting the client at ease and developing rapport;
(2) Interviewing the client to get a basic factual picture of the client's situation;

(3) Explaining the attorney-client privilege, if appropriate;

(4) Obtaining a sense of the client's objectives;

(5) Determining whether representing the client would constitute a conflict of interest;

(6) Making a decision about representing the client and establishing the nature and scope of the representation;

(7) Giving the client appropriate preliminary advice;

(8) Establishing an initial course of action;

(9) Establishing attorney's fees and other financial obligations for the representation; and

(10) Making arrangements for follow-up conferences and communication with the client.

It is important to keep in mind that the first meeting with a new client is only an *initial* meeting that will be followed by further client conferences. You and the client may have to meet a number of times before a final decision can be made about whether you will represent him and what that representation will entail. Moreover, even if it is decided at the initial meeting that you will represent the client, it is not uncommon for the scope of the representation to be initially limited to obtaining additional information or conducting further investigation before you and the client will be in a position to fully analyze and decide upon a course of action. Final decisions about the ultimate nature and scope of the representation may not be made until the second or third meeting with the client. Thus, in most cases, the initial client meeting is only the starting point of your representation and role as counselor to the client.

This chapter provides an overview of how you go about accomplishing the principal objectives of the initial client meeting in the context of the counseling functions outlined in Section 2.02, in which you "Establish a Professional and Interpersonal Relationship with Your Client" and "Obtain Information Relevant to Your Client's Situation and Potential Courses of Action." Chapter 4 provides specific techniques for client interviewing, which is a major component of the initial meeting and subsequent client conferences, and concludes with an illustration of an attorney-client dialogue during an initial client meeting and interview. Chapter 5 discusses the three remaining functions of the overall counseling process outlined in Section 2.02 that call upon you to: "Analyze Potential Courses of Action;" "Advise Your Client about Potential Courses of Action;" and "Decide Upon the Course of Action to be Taken and Implement the Course of Action." Chapter 5 concludes with an illustration of an attorney-client dialogue during a decision-making meeting.

§ 3.02 Handling the Initial Phone Call from the Client

New clients, or existing clients who have a new legal matter, rarely walk into your law office to see you unannounced. Typically, the client will initially contact your office by telephone to make an appointment. Lawyers usually handle this initial contact in one of two ways.

First, some lawyers use their secretary or a paralegal to "screen" all incoming calls from prospective clients. The secretary or paralegal briefly talks with the client, determines the general nature of the client's situation or legal problem, and, if the particular matter falls within the lawyer's area of practice, advises the client about any consultation fee for the initial meeting and sets up an appointment for the client to see the lawyer.[1] One

---

1. Under Rule 5.3 of the Model Rules of Professional Conduct, you are obligated to ensure that the conduct of your receptionist/secretary, paralegal, or law student intern is compatible with your professional obligations as a lawyer. This means, among other things, that you are obligated to ensure that your non-legal assistants do not engage in the unauthorized practice of law by giving legal advice and that they do not reveal information protected by the attorney-client privilege (*see* §6.07). As a general guide, you should instruct your receptionist/secretary to do the following when receiving a "cold call" from a prospective client: (1) identify the general nature of the prospective client's situation (and whether it is an emergency) to determine if the particular mater is *clearly not* one handled by your law office, in which case the prospective client should be referred elsewhere; (2) if the prospective client's matter is ambiguous or even *remotely* related to your practice, the prospective client should be told that you (or another specifically-named lawyer in your office) will call the prospective client back and approximately when that return call will be made; and (3) if the prospective client asks about attorney fees, he or she should be told that such fees vary depending upon the circumstances and should be discussed with the attorney, except that standard fees for an initial office conference or for routine matters (*e.g.*, the preparation of a simple will, incorporation, or other routine transactional document) may be quoted. As these narrow instructions indicate, the fundamental objective of the receptionist/secretary is to (1) only screen out prospective client matters that are *clearly not* handled by your law office; and (2) otherwise provide an appropriate time frame when you or another lawyer in your office will return the prospective client's call. This will ensure that the evaluation of a prospective client's situation is conducted only by a lawyer and not by a non-legal assistant.

drawback to this approach is that there is no personal contact between the lawyer and the client before the initial meeting. Simply "signing up" the prospective client for an appointment is impersonal and affords no opportunity for the lawyer to get any sense of the client's particular situation. In addition, in the absence of having some conversation with the client before the initial meeting, the lawyer cannot determine whether there is some immediate action that must be taken to protect the client, or whether it would be useful for the client to take some interim action or obtain certain information before coming to the initial meeting.

Under the second approach, the lawyer will either personally "screen" all phone calls from prospective clients, or, if an appointment for the client has already been set up by a secretary or paralegal, the lawyer will phone the client in advance of the meeting to briefly discuss the client's situation. In this way, the lawyer can obtain a general understanding of the nature of the client's matter in advance of the initial meeting, determine if a statute of limitations is about to run, provide the client with any emergency advice if necessary, and instruct the client about any information that he should obtain in the interim and bring with him to the meeting.

Having a short phone conversation with the prospective client before the initial meeting will help you and the client be better prepared for it and help to ensure that the status quo is preserved until the two of you are able to meet. In light of what the client tells you over the phone, you might also be able to conduct some preliminary legal research or review certain documents that the client sends you in advance of the meeting. Most importantly, this personalized phone contact will go a long way in helping to build rapport with the client.

It is important to remember, however, that an initial phone conversation with the prospective client is not the time to hear his entire story or to decide whether you will represent him. Your goal is simply to find out just enough information to confirm your willingness to meet with him, and to determine whether he needs any immediate advice to protect his interests before you are able to meet. At times, you will discover in the initial phone conversation that, for one reason or another (including the existence of a conflict of interest), you will be unable to help the client with his particular situation. When that occurs, you can explain that you do not believe a meeting would be useful, and, if appropriate, refer him to another lawyer or some other person who might be able to help him. If you have determined that legal action on his behalf is time sensitive, explain to him the urgency of obtaining legal advice before the expiration of the relevant time period.

§3.03 Beginning the Meeting and Developing Rapport

In representing any client, it is important to develop a relationship that is marked by close rapport. You want the client to trust you, have confidence in you, and be comfortable with you. You want him to see you as being honest, straightforward, and dependable, as being competent and diligent in your legal services, and as being a person with whom he feels comfortable in interacting. Developing this rapport of trust, confidence, and comfort begins with the first impressions you create when you greet the client and sit down to begin the initial meeting.

In greeting a client, the most personable approach is to greet him in your law office's reception area and personally escort him to the office or conference room where you will hold the initial meeting. Introduce yourself by using your first name, shake hands, and address the client by first name if appropriate. Be on time for the appointment. Even if you are only a few minutes late, apologize for the delay.

If a friend or family member accompanies the client, remember that the attorney-client privilege generally does not extend to confidential communications between an attorney and client that are made in the presence of third persons. Therefore, exchange any pleasantries with the client's friend or family member in your reception area, but do not invite any third person to attend your private meeting with the client unless there is a special need for the third person's attendance.[2]

Every effort should be made to keep the meeting free from unnecessary interruptions or distractions. Accordingly, make sure your secretary holds all telephone calls, and do not permit other persons to enter the room during the meeting unless absolutely necessary. It is essential that the client have your undivided attention throughout the meeting.

At the outset of the meeting, it is sometimes appropriate to engage in some "small talk" to put the client at ease. Some clients will be anxious or nervous at the beginning of the meeting, and some friendly "chit chat" usually helps to start the meeting on easy ground. However, be careful not to get carried away with this type of "ice breaking." In most situations, after exchanging a few pleasantries, many clients are perfectly content to "get down to business."

---

2. Confidentiality under the attorney-client privilege is not waived when communications with the lawyer are made in the presence of family or friends who are reasonably necessary to provide support to the client or who are otherwise necessary to facilitate communication with the attorney. McCormick, *Evidence* §91 at 335 (4th ed. 1992).

If there is a particular time constraint on the meeting (e.g., the appointment is scheduled for only one hour), you might mention the time constraint at the outset so that the client is not caught by surprise when the allotted time draws to a close. Tell the client that your overall objective for the initial meeting is to get a basic understanding of his situation and to find out whether you might be able to help him.

§3.04 Interviewing the Client to Get a Basic Factual Picture of the Client's Situation

Once the client is at ease, you should open the meeting with a general question that invites the client to tell his story and explain why he has come to see you. For example you might ask:

- *How can I help you?*
- *What can I help you with?*
- *What can I do for you?*
- *So, what brings you here today?*

Asking this type of opening question marks the beginning of your interview with the client. The process and techniques for client interviewing are detailed in Chapter 4. For present purposes, it is important to keep in mind that at this stage of the meeting your primary goal is get a basic factual picture of the client's situation. You want to find out: Why has the client come to see me? What are the basic facts and circumstances of his situation? Is his situation or problem something that I can help him with?

You will enhance your ability to obtain the factual information pertinent to answering these questions if you keep three points in mind. First, avoid interrupting the client at this stage. Let him talk, and let him vent if necessary. Second, encourage him to share his underlying interests, needs, feelings, and concerns about his situation. That is, let him share his story, situation or problem in his own way, from his own perspective. And third, hear what the client has to say empathically and non-judgmentally. This is the time to patiently *listen* to the client, not to counsel him.

In addition, be sure to ask the client if he has brought any documents with him to the meeting. If so, you might briefly review them before your client talks about them. However, regardless of whether the client has brought with him a contract, a lawsuit, or an indictment, it is imperative that you take the time to listen to the client's situation in his own words. That is, resist any temptation to allow documents to inappropriately control the interview. At the outset, you want to know what your client has to say about the matter, not merely what some third person has written about it.

§3.05 Explaining the Duty of Confidentiality, If Appropriate

In obtaining a basic factual picture of the client's situation, you of course want the client to be honest with you and to confide in you. Frequently, as where the client has been sued or has been charged with a crime, his situation will be quite embarrassing and stressful. In these circumstances, it is sometimes useful to encourage the client to speak freely with you by reminding him that what he tells you is protected by the duty of confidentiality. In particular, most clients don't know that the duty applies even if you end up not representing the client (*see* §6.07).

In practice, some attorneys do not explain the duty in the initial client meeting. They think that their clients understand that speaking to an attorney is a confidential communication, or they fear that discussing the duty may signal that the lawyer believes that the client has done something wrong. Other lawyers feel that the nature of their legal services (e.g., drafting transactional documents) does not warrant any special discussion of the duty.

These views are understandable. Discussing the duty is sometimes unnecessary or doesn't make sense in terms of the case or the client. On the other hand, it is usually a good practice to include some statement about the duty at some point during the meeting. One never really knows what a client has to say, or has to hide, when he walks through the door. The failure to discuss the duty at all may even constitute malpractice in some situations. In any event, you don't want your client to unintentionally waive the duty by disclosing what happened at the meeting to others such that the waiver will come back to haunt you and your client.

When you mention the duty, be tactful. For example, at an appropriate time during the interview, you might simply allude to the duty in an offhand way: "Well, as you probably know, everything we speak about in this room is strictly confidential ..." Expressed in this way, the duty is mentioned in the context of general privacy concerns without implying that you feel the client is hiding information or is not being completely truthful with you.

§3.06 Obtaining a Sense of the Client's Objectives

When the client explains his situation, he will often indicate what objectives or goals he has in mind for dealing with his situation and how he thinks they may be accomplished. If he does not, probe his objectives or goals directly. This is important because obtaining a sense of the client's objectives will help you understand his initial expectations of you, and those expectations may be integral to deciding whether you will represent him, and, if so, what the nature and scope of your representation will be. In probing the client's objectives or goals you might ask:

- *What are your goals?*
- *What do you want to happen?*
- *What do you want to do?*
- *Which of the things you mentioned is more important to you?*
- *What is the most important thing?*
- *How would you rank your concerns in the order of their importance?*
- *Do you have any ideas about how the situation might be resolved?*

Of course, in many instances, the client will be unsure about his objectives and will have little or no understanding about how you might be able to help him. After all, the client's primary purpose in meeting with you will often be to find out what, if anything, you might be able to do for him. Nevertheless, to the extent you are able to obtain at least some perspective from the client about what he would like to accomplish, that information will be useful to you when you engage in the counseling functions of advising him about his options, helping him decide on an appropriate course of action, and when implementing the course of action (*see* Chapter 5).

In addition, having a sense of the client's objectives and his thoughts about how they might be accomplished will often alert you to the importance of his *non-legal* as well as legal concerns. In many cases, you will find that the client's primary goals, interests, or needs relate to matters that the law either cannot solve or can only partially solve. For example, a client who has been sued for breach of contract may be far less concerned about the merits of the suit than with the impact that the suit may have on his reputation and business relationships with other customers. A spouse faced with a demand for alimony may be far more concerned about vindicating himself from accusations of marital misconduct than with being able to pay for the amount of the post-separation support sought by his wife. A truck driver who has been given a speeding ticket may be far less concerned with the amount of the fine he would have to pay if convicted than with the effect that a conviction may have on his continued employment with his trucking company. In short, knowing about the client's non-legal as well as legal concerns is critical to understanding the exact nature of the client's situation, which, in turn, may have a critical effect on the objectives and means of your representation.

§3.07 Determining the Existence of a Conflict of Interest

After you have listened to the client's description of his situation and have some understanding of his objectives, you will usually have enough information to determine whether representing him would create a conflict of interest. The most common conflict-of-interest situations are discussed in Section 6.09.

If it becomes apparent that representing the client would be barred by an impermissible conflict of interest, you should cut the meeting short and explain to him the general nature of the conflict that disqualifies you from representing him. In explaining this conflict, you should, of course, be careful not to reveal any attorney-client privileged information that may form the basis for the conflict. You should also assure him that you will not disclose to others any information you learned from him up to this point. If your representation would not be automatically barred by a conflict of interest but would raise a potential conflict, the applicable ethical rules will only permit you to represent the client if you reasonably believe that your representation will not adversely affect your duties to another client or third person and if the new client consents to the representation after you have fully explained to him all pertinent implications of the potential conflict (*see* §6.09).

§3.08 Deciding Whether to Represent the Client and Establishing the Nature and Scope of the Representation

After conducting a preliminary interview with the client, a decision will have to be made whether you will represent him and what the nature and scope of that representation will be. Establishing a formal attorney-client relationship does not depend on any formality such as a written agreement, but arises upon the client's express or implied request that you act on his behalf and your express or implied agreement to do so (*see* §6.02). You and the client are generally free to limit the nature, scope, and objectives of the representation to certain legal services and not others. For example, you and the client may agree that you will represent him in the trial of the case but not on appeal, or that you will only represent him on a specific transaction but not on other transactions that may be related to the client's overall situation. Under the rules of professional ethics, whenever you establish the nature, scope, and objectives of the representation, you are required to consult with the client and obtain his consent (*see* §6.03). In short, you cannot act as the legal representative of a client without having his authority to do so.

In the context of the initial client meeting, when relatively routine legal services are involved (e.g., the preparation of a simple will or deed of trust, representation on a misdemeanor charge, or representation in an uncontested divorce case, etc.), the nature and scope of the representation will usually be easy to agree upon. On the other hand, in many situations, the information you obtain at the initial meeting will be insufficient to allow you and the client to decide upon the exact nature, scope, objectives, and means of the representation at that time. That is, the preliminary nature of the initial meeting often gives rise to the need to obtain additional information, conduct further investigation, and conduct legal research before you and the client can meaningfully discuss potential courses of action and decide upon a course of action that will define the ultimate nature and scope of the representation. For instance, before you agree to sue a doctor for medical malpractice on behalf of your client, you will need to examine your client's medical records and seek an expert medical opinion about the appropriateness of your client's course of treatment.

Consequently, at the time of the initial client meeting, you and the client may only be in the position to agree upon a limited form of representation, such as an agreement that you will research the applicable law, conduct further factual investigation, and perhaps take certain limited actions to protect or preserve the client's rights. After these tasks are performed, you will meet with the client again to counsel him about potential courses of action, collaborate with him in deciding upon a specific course of action, and begin to implement the course of action. Only then can the precise nature and scope of the representation be clearly established.

If you and the client decide you will represent him on a limited basis pending further client meetings, you should carefully define the scope of your representation by specifying the particular services you will render and confirm the scope of your representation in a follow-up letter. Similarly, if it is decided you will not represent the client at all, it is prudent for you to reiterate that decision in writing. Remember, any ambiguity as to either the existence or scope of the representation will often be resolved in the layperson's favor.

§3.09 Giving Preliminary Advice

If you represent your client on a limited basis to conduct further investigation or research, it would of course be inappropriate for you to give him final legal advice about his situation before you have conducted the investigation or research. Nevertheless, a client will often press you for preliminary advice or a tentative assessment or prediction about the outcome of his situation. Receiving at least *some* preliminary advice is an understandable and legitimate client expectation.

There are essentially three ways in which you can, and should, provide your client with preliminary advice without rendering premature or otherwise inappropriate legal opinions about his situation. First, it will often be appropriate to provide your client with certain kinds of "protective" advice, such as advising him not to talk with other persons about the case, instructing him to refer any inquiries he receives about the case from other persons directly to you, or advising him to refrain from taking certain actions pending your next meeting with him.

Second, it may be appropriate to give your client a general overview of some of the legal considerations or legal processes that may affect his situation. For example, in a potential negligence case, you might briefly describe the elements of proof: the existence of a duty of care, breach of that duty, proximate cause of damage, and the types of damages recoverable. If litigation might be involved or your client has been charged with a crime, it may be appropriate to briefly outline the pretrial process, what happens at trial, and the process of taking an appeal. Similarly, it may be appropriate to provide your client with basic legal information about matters that may have to be considered in his situation, such as the statute of limitations for a particular cause of action, statutory guidelines for determining child support, or the maximum sentence for a particular offense.

Third, to the extent the information you obtain during the initial meeting at least indicates the types of options or courses of action that may be pertinent to your client's situation, these can be outlined in a noncommittal way. For example, if your client is interested in starting a new business venture, it may be appropriate to generally discuss the different options of establishing a corporation, a professional association, or a partnership. If your client is a defendant in a civil suit, you might outline various affirmative defenses that may be applicable to his situation. In doing so, however, you should emphasize that your preliminary advice or assessment of the situation is only tentative and is entirely dependent upon the further research, investigation, or information gathering that you and your client have agreed should be undertaken before you will be able to provide him with definitive advice.

§3.10 Establishing an Initial Course of Action

If you have decided to represent the client, before concluding the initial meeting, you should explain (1) what you will do next and when it will be done, and (2) what your client should do next and by when that should be done. As mentioned above, when the ultimate nature and scope of your representation have not yet been established, your tasks might involve researching the law or conducting additional fact investigation. Your client's tasks might include locating certain documents, obtaining other specified information, or even preparing a written account of key events. Appropriately involving your client at the outset of the representation sets the right tone for the attorney-client relationship and marks the beginning of a collaborative approach to the representation.

§3.11 Establishing Attorney's Fees

Rule 1.5(b) of the ABA Model Rules of Professional Conduct mandates that, except when charging a regularly represented client on the same fee basis or at the same rate, "[t]he scope of [your] representation and the basis or rate of [your] fee and expenses for which [your] client will be responsible shall be communicated to [your] client, preferably in writing, before or within a reasonable time after commencing the representation." (*See also* §6.10). Your fee might:

(a) be fixed;
(b) be calculated on an hourly rate;
(c) include a retainer in the form of an advance fee payment, where the outstanding balance of the advance is reduced as you perform your services and earn the fee;
(d) include a nonrefundable retainer; or
(e) constitute a contingent fee that is calculated as a percentage of the total monetary amount or interest in property recovered for the client.

Regardless of the particular type of fee, you are obligated to inform your client about the rate of the fee or other basis on which it is calculated. With the exception of a contingent fee, which must be in writing, you may communicate the rate or basis of the fee orally or by furnishing your client with a simple memorandum or copy of your customary fee schedule.

Because misunderstandings about fees are a common source of client complaints about lawyers to disciplinary authorities, the best practice is to explain your fee to the client at the initial meeting and then put it in writing. Your explanation and written fee agreement should specify:

(1) the particular legal services you have agreed to provide your client;

(2) any limits on the scope of those services, such as whether your representation includes an appeal;

(3) how the fee will be computed and how your client will be billed;

(4) any anticipated change in the fee rate in the future, and what different rates will be charged for paralegals or other lawyers who work on the case; and

(5) what costs and expenses (e.g., for court filings, expert witnesses, investigators, stenographers, transcriptions, photocopying, travel, computer-assisted research, etc.) your client will be responsible for paying.

In addition, many clients will ask you at the initial meeting to estimate the total fees and costs you anticipate for the representation. Use your best judgment in providing an estimate, and perhaps provide your client with a range: "I would estimate that total fees and costs will be no less than $10,000 and may be as high as $20,000 depending upon how things go." Always emphasize to your client that your estimate is only a rough approximation that is subject to change depending on the circumstances.

§3.12 Making Arrangements for Follow-Up Conferences

Before adjourning the initial meeting, be sure that you have (1) obtained all necessary information about how to contact your client, (2) discussed what tasks you and your client will perform until you confer again (*see* §3.10), and (3) made at least tentative arrangements for the next conference with your client. In addition, explain to your client your office hours and how he can best contact you during the course of the representation (e.g., by phone or e-mail). This includes explaining the roles of your secretary, paralegal, and any associate attorneys who will be assisting you in handling the client's matter.

Emphasize, however, that even though other persons in your law office may be assisting you in the case, your client should not hesitate to contact you directly.

Most attorneys whose fees are based on an hourly rate charge their clients for phone conferences. If this is your practice, make sure your client understands it. At the same time, however, encourage your client to contact you whenever he feels it may be appropriate. Tell him that you are usually able to return your phone calls within 24 hours of receiving them, but that sometimes there may be an additional delay if you are involved in a protracted trial. *Keep your promise about promptly returning phone calls.* Failure to return client calls is one of the leading sources of complaints about lawyers to disciplinary authorities.

§3.13 Documenting the Initial Client Meeting

Your documentation of the initial client meeting should consist of (1) any pertinent documents you have obtained from your client, (2) your interview notes or post-interview memorandum to the client's file (*see* §4.09), and (3) basic information for contacting the client, including notes about the initial course of action to be taken and any arrangements that have been made for the next client conference. The latter matters might be documented on a form like the following:

New Client Information Form

Date: _____   File No. _____

Client name: _____

(Nickname): _____ Legal matter: _____

Home address: _____

Work/business address: _____

E-mail address: _____ Facsimile No.: _____

Preferred address for receiving correspondence:

☐ Home ☐ Work/business ☐ E-mail ☐ Facsimile

Home phone: _____ Work/business phone: _____

Cellular phone/pager: _____ Preferred phone number:

☐ Home ☐ Work/business ☐ Cellular phone/pager

Best time to reach client: _____

Client's legal situation & objectives:

_____

_____

Attorney tasks: _____

_____

Client tasks: _____

_____

Deadlines/important dates: _____

Other notes: _____

_____

Next appointment date/contact with client: _____

Chapter Four

Interviewing the Client

SYNOPSIS

§4.01 Introduction

Interviewing your client is, of course, a major component of the initial client meeting. As mentioned previously, at the initial meeting, your interview will often be limited to getting only a basic factual picture of your client's situation. Even if an attorney-client relationship is established at the initial meeting, the ultimate nature and scope of your representation may not be decided upon until you have met with your client again and conducted a more in depth interview that is followed by counseling your client about potential courses of action and deciding upon an appropriate course of action.

This chapter discusses the process and techniques for interviewing your client at the initial meeting and during any follow-up meetings. The chapter begins with a brief discussion of certain commonly recognized facilitators and inhibitors of communication that are useful to keep in mind throughout the interviewing process and later when you counsel your client. The chapter concludes with an illustration of an attorney-client dialogue during an initial client meeting and interview.

§4.02 Facilitators of Communication

Psychologists have identified a number of factors or motivational circumstances that facilitate interpersonal communication.[1] For purposes of legal in-

---

1. For more expansive discussions about facilitators and inhibitors of communication, *see* G. Goodman, *The Talk Book* (1988); Raymond L. Gorden, *Interviewing, Strategy, Techniques, and Tactics* (4th ed. 1987); David A. Binder, et al., *Lawyers as Counselors: A Client-Centered Approach*, Chapters 4–5 (1991); Robert M. Bastress & Joseph D. Harbaugh, *Interviewing, Counseling, and Negotiating*, Chapter 8 (1990); Gerard Egan, *You & Me: The Skills of Communicating and Relating to Others* (1977); Gerard Egan, *The Skilled Helper* (3d ed. 1986); Anthony G. Athos & John J. Gabarro, *Interpersonal Behavior: Communication and Understanding Relationships* (1978); Mathew McKay, et al., *Messages: The Communication Book* (1983); Aron W. Siegman & Stanley Feldstein eds., *Non-Verbal Behavior and Communication* (1987); John L. Barkai, *How to Develop the Skill of Active Listening*, 30 Prac. Law 73 (1984).

terviewing and counseling, the most important of these are (1) conveying empathetic understanding, (2) engaging in active listening, (3) encouraging communication through conveying expectations and recognition, and (4) keeping an open mind about what is relevant.

[1] Conveying Empathetic Understanding

"Empathy" means identifying with another person's experiences and feelings. It means putting yourself in another person's shoes. Conveying empathetic understanding for your client is important because her feelings about her situation are often just as important as, if not sometimes more important than, the facts of the events giving rise to her situation or legal problem. Regardless of whether your client expresses her feelings openly, subtly, or not at all, she will have feelings about matters such as how and why her situation occurred, about the people who are involved or affected by her situation, and about what may happen as a result of her situation or legal problem. Conveying empathy for your client will enhance communication because it tends to make her feel more open and comfortable in talking with you.

There is no single way to convey empathetic understanding. However, you can show empathy for your client's feelings, personal perspectives, and points of view by, for example:

- Allowing your client to talk without unnecessary interruption;
- Maintaining appropriate eye contact;
- Being closely attentive to what your client is saying;
- Being closely attentive to your client's non-verbal expressions (i.e., body language);
- Encouraging your client to express her feelings, thoughts, needs, interests, and concerns;
- Making responsive statements that acknowledge your client's feelings and concerns;
- Refraining from asking questions about sensitive matters until rapport has been established;
- Expressly stating a willingness to help your client in whatever way you can; and
- Engaging in "active listening."

[2] Engaging in Active Listening

Many lawyers like to talk more than they like to listen. This is a common and understandable shortcoming. As advisors, lawyers are accustomed to giving advice; and as advocates, they are accustomed to performing and making presentations. Even lawyers who make a conscious effort to listen, often listen only partially and become distracted by thinking about what they want to say or ask next. In addition, many lawyers listen only passively, rarely making any verbal or non-verbal responses to indicate that they have actually heard and understood what the client has said.

"Active listening" is an enhanced method of communication by which the listener (1) is highly attentive to the complete context, content, and feelings expressed by the speaker's verbal and non-verbal behavior, and (2) accepts and acknowledges, in a non-judgmental way, the content and feelings expressed by the speaker by making reflective responses which mirror or capsulize what the speaker is saying and feeling. Active listening is a method of explicitly demonstrating not only comprehension, but also empathy and understanding.

There are five principal ways in which you can enhance communication with your client through active listening:

(1) Allow your client to tell her story and avoid unnecessarily controlling the conversation.

(2) Be attentive to your client's non-verbal cues such as:
- Tone of voice
- Volume of voice
- Pace of speech (pauses, accelerations, varying rates of speed)
- Body posture
- Eye contact
- Gestures
- Facial expressions

(3) Be attentive to how your client structures her story by considering matters such as:
- Where did she begin her story? Where did she end it?
- What parts of the story did your client develop in detail? Which did she gloss over?
- Which parts of the story did she treat as background and which parts did she consider "the main event"?
- How did your client sequence her story? Was it chronological or in order of matters of importance? Which parts of the story seemed logically connected to one another?
- What parts of the story did she repeat? Which parts did she omit?

Being attentive to these types of matters may provide you with clues about those things that your client deems most important, those things that she might be reluctant to reveal, and how she thinks and feels about her overall situation.

> *(4) Acknowledge what your client is saying by occasionally using short prompts such as:*
> "Yes" (or nodding your head, "Yes")
> "Please, go on"
> "So, then what happened?"
> "That's interesting"
> "Can you tell me more about …?"
> "Uh-uh"; "Mm-hmm"; "I see"
> "Oh"; "Really"
>
> *(5) Mirror what your client is saying or feeling by occasionally paraphrasing the essence of her remarks in a non-judgmental way:*
> "It sounds like you feel …"
> "That must have been hard for you"
> "You must have been disappointed"
> "I imagine that you are relieved by that"
> "It seems like you're torn about what to do"
> "I can see how that might be troubling … I think I can help; but first, can you tell me more about …?"

In employing the techniques in *(4)* and *(5)* above, it is critical not to overuse them. A ritualistic singsong of "Mm-hmm," "I see," "That's interesting," "It sounds like you feel…," "I imagine you were upset…," etc., will come across as forced and fake. Focus on listening *intently*. If you do that, your active listening responses are more likely to be appropriately spontaneous and natural.

[3] Encouraging Communication through Conveying Expectations and Recognition

Most people tend to act in accordance with the perceived expectations of those with whom they interact. In addition, most people have a strong need for attention and recognition from others. These desires to satisfy expectations and receive attention and recognition are strong motivators that often affect how people communicate.

Accordingly, when interviewing your client, if you explain your expectations about the types of information that would be useful to you in evaluating her situation or legal problem, she may be more forthcoming in providing that information than she would be had you not expressed those expectations. For example, if your client is reluctant to talk about a particular subject, after gently reminding her about the attorney-client privilege (*see* § 3.05), you might explain why that subject is important to talk about in order to fully understand her situation. Moreover, if you give your client "recognition" for her forthrightness in sharing information (e.g., "I know this is difficult for you, but what you are saying is very helpful"), she is likely to continue to be responsive and cooperative in providing important information.

[4] Keeping an Open Mind about What Is Relevant

For reasons of efficiency and simplicity of legal analysis, lawyers often routinize certain legal services and reduce the facts relevant to them into standard patterns or categories that match familiar types of legal cases. One scholar describes this process as follows:

> [T]he [client] tells a story of felt or perceived wrong to a third party (a lawyer) and the lawyer transforms the dispute by imposing "categories" on "events and relationships" which redefine the subject matter of dispute in ways "which make it amenable to conventional management procedures." This process of "narrowing" disputes occurs at various stages in lawyer-client interactions.... First, the lawyer may begin to narrow the dispute in the initial client interview. By asking questions which derive from the lawyer's repertoire of what is likely to be legally relevant, the lawyer defines the situation from the very beginning. Rather than permitting the client to tell a story freely to define what the dispute consists of, the lawyer begins to categorize the case as a "tort," "contract," or "property" dispute so that questions may be asked for legal saliency.[2]

This tendency to reflexively and prematurely categorize the client's legal situation before obtaining all the facts surrounding her story often causes a lawyer to make erroneous assumptions and jump to conclusions about what information from the interview is relevant and what information is mere surplusage. As a result, the lawyer may end up "hearing" only select portions of the client's overall situation, which may inhibit complete communication by discouraging

---

2. Carrie Menkel-Meadow, *The Transformation of Disputes by Lawyers: What the Dispute Paradigm Does and Does Not Tell Us*, 1985 Mo. J. Disp. Res. 25, 31 (1985). *See also* Robert F. Cochran, Jr., et al., *The Counselor-At-Law: A Collaborative Approach to Client Interviewing and Counseling* 39 (1999) (also quoting Professor Menkel-Meadow and calling this process the "hardening of the categories.").

any discussion of facts that he perceives to be irrelevant. The danger is that the lawyer may end up largely misunderstanding the true nature of the client's legal and non-legal needs.

To guard against this danger, it is important to keep an open mind about what may or may not be relevant when interviewing your client. It is far better to hear out the client's entire story than to abbreviate the interview at the risk that essential information (and particularly information that your client deems important) will not be obtained. This open-mindedness will not only enhance communication, but also will build rapport and likely result in more effective representation.

§4.03 Inhibitors of Communication

Just as psychologists have identified various circumstances that facilitate communication, they have identified factors that tend to inhibit full and open communication. In lawyer-client interactions, the most important inhibitors are (1) fears of embarrassment or hurting the case, (2) anxiety, tension, or trauma, (3) etiquette barriers and prejudices, and (4) differing conceptions about relevant information.[3]

[1] Fears of Embarrassment or Hurting the Case

Clients often come to lawyers with situations or legal problems that are personally embarrassing or that sometimes cause strong feelings of guilt or shame. For example, a client may have committed a crime for which she has now been charged or neglected a business matter for which he has now been sued. In these types of situations, she may be understandably reluctant to provide complete information about what happened for fear that you will view her conduct as being disgraceful, or at least, foolish.

Similarly, regardless of whether the client's particular situation may produce feelings of embarrassment or shame, a client may be reluctant to disclose information that she perceives may somehow "hurt her case" in the sense of producing an adverse outcome. This reluctance to reveal damaging information may also be grounded in a fear that you will consider her case to be a "loser" and decide not to represent her.

---

3. *See also* David A. Binder, et al., *Lawyers as Counselors: A Client-Centered Approach* 35–40 (1991); Robert M. Bastress & Joseph D. Harbaugh, *Interviewing, Counseling, and Negotiating* 176–184 (1990).

Whether your client fears embarrassment or fears that she will hurt her case, complete disclosure of all pertinent facts is, of course, essential to effective representation. Knowing the full extent of your client's participation in the events giving rise to a criminal charge or lawsuit is critical in order to evaluate potential defenses. Information that may be damaging to your client's cause of action or assertion of some legal right is important in assessing the merits of her claims and in preparing to counter anticipated defenses or other legal efforts to defeat her plan of action. Neither you nor your client can run or hide from adverse facts. The sooner you know the bad facts, the sooner you can prepare to counter them.

Accordingly, when faced with these communication inhibitors, you should draw upon the communication facilitators of (1) conveying empathetic understanding for your client's difficult situation, (2) engaging in active listening by non-judgmentally accepting and acknowledging her uncomfortable feelings, and (3) encouraging her to communicate by explaining the need for full information and by expressing recognition for her forthright disclosures. In addition, in an appropriate situation, you might once again explain that her confidences are protected under the attorney-client privilege.

[2] Anxiety, Tension, or Trauma

For the same reasons discussed in the preceding subsection, a client's willingness to communicate may be inhibited due to anxiety or tension. Alternatively, a client may be reluctant to talk about a traumatic event, such as the death of a loved one, a debilitating injury, or the circumstances surrounding the break up of a marriage. Apart from fears of embarrassment or hurting the case, the client may be angry, depressed, or humiliated. Here again, communication is likely to be enhanced if you draw upon the facilitators of empathetic understanding, active listening, and encouraging communication through expectations and recognition.

[3] Etiquette Barriers and Prejudices

Sometimes a client will be uncomfortable in talking with her lawyer about certain matters due to "etiquette barriers"[4] grounded in social norms or conventions. For example, a client may have difficulty talking about intimate

---

4. *See* Raymond. L. Gorden, *Interviewing, Strategy, Techniques, and Tactics* 76–78 (1969).

matters (such as sex or intimate medical problems) with a lawyer who is of the opposite sex. Similarly, the age, social status, or economic status of a client may affect how comfortable she is in talking with a lawyer of a significantly different age or significantly different social or economic status. Depending on the extent of these differences, the client may feel inferior or subordinate to the lawyer or, alternatively, superior and dominant to the lawyer. In short, differences in gender, age, and socio-economic status may sometimes inhibit open communication between you and your client when talking about certain subjects.

In addition, various prejudices, biases, or cultural differences may impede communication. Unfortunately, racial or sexual stereotyping may cause a client to be uncomfortable in trusting and interacting with a lawyer who is of a different race or of the opposite sex. A bias against public defenders may cause an indigent criminal defendant to lack initial confidence in her court-appointed lawyer. Even religious, moral, or philosophical differences between client and lawyer may inhibit open communication.

To deal with an etiquette barrier or prejudice that is impeding communication, you can use sensitivity and explanation. Tactfully acknowledge the barrier or prejudice and, if necessary, openly discuss the differences between yourself and your client. If the barrier or prejudice relates to the subject matter of the representation, acknowledge the delicacy of the matter and explain to your client that you are accustomed to handling such matters with the confidentiality, respect, and sensitivity they require. If your client still remains uncomfortable talking about the matter, you might consider calling upon an associate lawyer who does not have the same identity differences to interview the client on the particular subject.

[4] Differing Conceptions about Relevant Information

Clients frequently approach lawyer interviews with preconceived notions about what information is legally relevant to their situations. Indeed, some clients even have strong preconceptions about the exact types of legal remedies or services that would be appropriate to resolve their problem. Consequently, it is not unusual for clients to have conceptions about relevant information that are markedly different from what their lawyers consider relevant. This may make it difficult for a client to see the connection between her lawyer's questions and the client's situation, and make it difficult for the lawyer to understand why the client persists in talking about certain matters that the lawyer thinks are essentially irrelevant to the problem at hand. Either way, communication is impeded.

In dealing with differing conceptions about what information is relevant, as discussed in Section 4.02[4], you should always guard against prematurely categorizing your client's legal situation and keep an open mind about the potential relevance of any information that your client wants to impart. At the same time, because the information you begin to obtain during the interview will inevitably alert you to particular legal considerations, you should not hesitate to ask about specific, potentially relevant information that your client does not otherwise gratuitously volunteer to you. If your client appears to be irritated at your seemingly irrelevant questions, simply provide her with a brief explanation of why the requested information may be important to fully understand her legal situation.

§ 4.04 Purposes of Interviewing

As mentioned in Section 3.04, your initial purpose in interviewing the client is to get a basic factual picture of his situation so that you can determine whether you can help him. In addition, you need to obtain a sense of his overall objectives—i.e., what he wants to accomplish (*see* § 3.06). If you determine that you may be able to help the client, the purposes of your interview become more expansive. Either at the initial meeting or at a subsequent meeting, you must obtain all information pertinent to his situation, objectives, and potential legal theories or courses of action that may be available to accomplish his objectives. Knowing how to ask different types of questions during the interview and how to use effective information-gathering techniques can significantly facilitate these purposes.

§ 4.05 Types of Questions

Knowing how to craft a question to obtain the desired information is one of the lawyer's most important tools. Young children learn the art of asking questions as soon as they learn to speak. With practice, they learn that certain forms of questions will give them more information and other forms will give them less information. As a lawyer, you will need to hone your questioning skills so that you can maximize information gathering.

Most questions can be categorized into five different types: (1) open questions, (2) follow-up questions, (3) closed questions, (4) leading questions, and (5) summation questions. In a client interview, you will usually use all five types of questions. Choosing when to use which type depends on the exact information you need and where you are in the information-gathering process. Regardless of the particular type of question you use in an interview, it is useful to always keep two rules in mind: first, make your questions as simple as possible; and second, ask only one question at a time.

[1] Open Questions

Open questions invite the client to answer with as much information as possible. When a lawyer first asks the client an open question such as "How can I help you?" she is inviting the client to explain in as much detail as possible why the client has sought help. An open question is a broad invitation to convey information. Open questions are not limited in scope or narrowly focused. Open questions are non-judgmental and do not suggest an answer. Instead, they permit the client to choose his own topic and his own way of responding to and structuring the information requested.

Journalists are taught to ask open questions by beginning most questions in the early stages of an interview with one of the following words: "Who?", "What?", "When?", "Where?", "Why?", and "How?". As lawyers, we can learn much from journalists. They are trained questioners who make a living by efficiently gathering as much information as possible from the people whom they interview. In addition to the journalists' "five W's and an H", as these words are nicknamed, you can add three other phrases to the group: "Please tell me about…," "Describe…," and "Explain.…"

In a client interview, the client is usually the one who possesses the most knowledge of the facts of the potential case. The most efficient way for you to learn the facts is to permit your client to convey them in his own way, unfettered by interfering questions. Open questions turn control of the release of information over to your client. By listening to your client's choice of words, characterization of the facts, the cadence of his responses, and the structure of his answers, you can maximize information gathering.

For example, assume a client has sought representation in a personal injury case involving a car accident. Contrast the amount of information the lawyer obtains by asking open questions that invite information as opposed to leading questions that suggest the answer:

- **Open Question:**

  Q: How can I help you?

  A: I was injured in a bad car accident. The other driver's insurance company has refused to pay my hospital bills even though the other driver was at fault. My friends suggested that a lawyer might be able to help me get the money I'm owed.

- **Leading Question:**

  Q: You were in an automobile accident?

  A: Yes.

The lawyer who asked the open question has learned that (1) the client was injured; (2) the client thinks the other driver was at fault; (3) the other driver was insured; (4) the client's injuries required medical treatment; and (5) the client has discussed his case with friends. The lawyer who has asked the leading question has learned only one fact: the client was in an automobile accident.

- **Open Question:**

  Q: What happened?

  A: Well, on December 28th I was driving from my home in North Carolina to visit my mother in Kentucky when a snowstorm came through the mountains of Western North Carolina. The road conditions were treacherous and I was driving really slow. There were all these ice patches on the road, and it was hard to stop without skidding. The car in front of me slowed to a crawl and I slowed down. The guy behind me was driving too fast and plowed into me. That set up a chain reaction. I hit the car in front of me and that car hit the one in front of him. My car was squashed like an accordion.

- **Leading Question:**

  Q: Your car was damaged in the accident?

  A: Yes.

Again, contrast the amount of information the open question elicited as opposed to the single fact the lawyer learned from the leading question. Note that the open question began with one of the journalist's recommended words (i.e., "what"), while the leading question was a sentence that suggested a specific answer. The open question resulted in a paragraph of information, while the leading question resulted in a monosyllabic response.

Open questions are particularly useful at the beginning of an interview because they encourage your client to talk. After you ask an open question, listen carefully to the response. Many clients have planned what they want to tell you about their case before coming to the interview. Through careful listening you can quickly learn which things are most important to your client.

By allowing your client to control the initial flow of information through his answers to open questions, you are permitting him to vent his feelings as well as the facts relevant to his situation. The rest of the interview will go more smoothly if he has permission to express his feelings early in the interview. If your client is focused on his anger or frustration at what has happened to him and does not have permission to express his feelings, he may not be able to listen to any advice you give later in the interview. If you encourage him to tell you about his case by using open questions, and demonstrate that you are listening carefully to his feelings as well as the facts, he will believe that he has finally been "heard." Once he realizes you are focused on his case and are empathetic to his feelings as well as the facts, he will usually be able to respond to more detailed questions and listen to your advice.

Because your client has permission to choose which information to share in response to an open question, open questions also provide him "recognition" (see § 4.02[3]). Your client quickly perceives that you have confidence in his ability to decide what is important and how to structure his story, and this often motivates him to answer more forthrightly and thoroughly.

When asking open questions, avoid using phrases that communicate any limitation on information you seek. If there are no restrictions on the information requested, your client will recount not only what is important to him, but he will also provide more detailed information. Many lawyers unconsciously include limiting phrases such as "a little about," "generally," or "briefly" in their questions. These phrases tend to limit information gathering. They discourage a full recital of events and feelings. Contrast the following open questions with the following limiting questions:

- **Open Question:**
  Q: Why were you traveling to Kentucky?
  A: My mother was having a difficult time. It was her first holiday after my Dad's death. I hoped my visit would cheer her up. Also, I needed to check on the administration of my Dad's estate before the end of the year.
- **Limiting question:**
  Q: Would you tell me a little about why you were traveling to Kentucky?
  A: To visit my mother.
- **Open Question:**
  Q: How long is the trip from Durham, NC to Louisville, KY?

*A: Well, it can take anywhere from ten to fourteen hours depending
on the weather and traffic. In the winter there's the risk of snow and
ice. In the summer, they're always tearing up the road somewhere,
funneling the traffic to one lane and holding everyone up.*

- **Limiting Question:**

  Q: Briefly, how long is the trip from Durham, NC to Louisville, KY?
  A: About twelve hours.

Although you may need to ask more pointed or narrow questions later in the
interview, at the open-question stage you want to avoid any limitations on obtaining information.

In addition to asking open questions, you should also use the active listening
techniques discussed in Section 4.02[2] to keep your client talking. Encourage
your client to expansively recount his story by occasionally using the short
prompts of "I see," "Mm-hmm," and "Can you tell me more about?" Avoid interrupting your client or seizing control of the interview when your client
pauses in his story. In most instances, the unrestricted client will convey information more quickly and in greater depth if he has control over the flow of
the story. Your silence at a pause in his story will encourage your client to keep
talking. (*See* §4.06[3]).

In addition to using open questions at the beginning of an interview, you
will find that they are useful at the beginning of a new topic. An open question
signals your client that you want to know everything about the topic and you
trust him to give you that information. For instance, in the car accident case
illustrated above, assume that you now want to change the subject from how
the accident occurred to the injuries the client suffered:

- **Open Question:**

  *Q: Now that we've covered how the accident happened, please tell me
  about your injuries.*
  *A: When the guy behind me hit my car, my head was thrown forward.
  And then when I hit the car in front, my head was thrown back. I've
  had to wear this collar since the accident. Also, my right leg was broken
  when my car hit the car in front.*

Although this question is technically not a "question," it acts as an open
question by inviting a broad response with the phrase, "please tell me about."
Similar phrases such as "please explain" and "please describe" make a sentence
into an open question and encourage your client to give you the details on a
new topic.

One danger of open questions is that they are not effective with a client who cannot focus on a coherent story but instead rambles through a maze of unconnected details. In that situation, you will get more information if you ask narrow questions to help your client focus on the subject of the interview. However, you need to guard against prematurely concluding that your client is rambling. Some lawyers who are anxious to "get to the bottom of the problem" assume the client is rambling and attempt to seize control by jumping to closed questions before giving the client a chance to fully respond to open questions. This causes the client to edit and limit the information he is sharing.

[2] Follow-Up Questions

Effective interviewers use pointed or directed follow-up questions to clarify a client's series of responses to open questions. These follow-up questions seek clarification of subjects raised in the client's initial story. They are more narrowly focused than open questions, but do not suggest an answer. They seek limited information and anticipate a short response. Such questions frequently incorporate phrases from the client's previous answer. For example, in the car accident case, the lawyer might ask a series of pointed or directed follow-up questions to clarify the information obtained in the client's answers to the open questions asked above:

- **Pointed or Directed Follow-Up Questions:**
  Q: What time of day did the accident happen?
  A: It was late in the afternoon, a little before dark.
  Q: What lane were you in just before the car following you "plowed" into the rear of your car?
  A: I was in the far right lane designated for trucks and slow-moving vehicles.
  Q: Exactly what did you mean when you said the road conditions were "treacherous"?
  A: Icy, slippery, low visibility.

Follow-up questions build rapport with your client because they indicate how closely you are listening. If you incorporate into your questions some of the phrases your client has used in his answers, you will communicate to your client that you are paying attention to his story and want to understand him completely. Such attention is comforting and flattering to your client.

The danger of follow-up questions is that the lawyer can move too early into the follow-up stage of questioning and thereby shut down the client's expansive answers to open questions. Once the lawyer interrupts the flow of the story with more directed follow-up questions, the client often has a tendency to assume that the information about which the lawyer is inquiring is the most important. He may then omit other details of the story and focus only on what the lawyer has asked about. Most effective interviewers stick with open questions until they have heard the basic story. Then they go back through the story with more pointed follow-up questions that seek clarification of important details.

[3] Closed Questions

The third type of question in the lawyer's repertoire is the closed question. These questions are very narrow and seek one or two-word answers. They do not suggest the answer, but they do convey an expectation of brevity to the client. These questions often begin with a verb. They are used to clarify minute details. Examples of closed questions from our car accident case might be:

- **Closed Questions:**
  Q: Were you wearing a seat belt at the time of the accident?
  A: Yes.
  Q: Were you alone in the car?
  A: No, my son was asleep in the back seat.
  Q: Was he injured?
  A: Not really. Just a few bruises.

Although closed questions are extremely important to clarify details, they will inhibit information gathering if they are overused or used too early in the interview. They can turn the interview from an in-depth story told by a client into a back-and-forth exchange of short questions from the lawyer followed by short answers from the client.

If you find that your interview has degenerated into labored questioning followed by monosyllabic responses from your client, pause and reflect on the types of questions you have been asking. If you want your client to do more of the talking, release control to him by starting your questions with the reporter words or phrases discussed in Section 4.05[1]. Once you craft open questions, your client will usually start talking in longer sentences and volunteer more information about his case.

[4] Leading Questions

Leading questions suggest an answer in the question. When a lawyer asks a leading question in an interview, she is expecting the shortest possible answer.

Leading questions are used to confirm facts that logically flow from the story the client has told. They are a short cut to gathering information. Examples of leading questions from our car accident case might be:

- **Leading Questions:**
  Q: *You were traveling at less than twenty-five miles per hour at the time of the accident weren't you?*
  A: *That's right.*
  Q: *The car in front of you was also traveling at less than twenty-five miles per hour, isn't that right?*
  A: *Yes.*
  …. …. …. ….
  Q: *Your son was the only passenger in your car?*
  A: *Yes.*
  Q: *It was snowing at the time of the accident?*
  A: *Yes.*

Leading questions can be constructed in two ways. In the first method, the lawyer who wants to confirm a fact makes a statement of the fact and adds a tag line that indicates the statement is a question. In the first two examples of leading questions above, the statements occur at the beginning of the questions, and the tag lines of "weren't you?" and "isn't that right?" at the end of the sentence signal the client that he is expected to confirm or deny the stated fact. In the second method of constructing leading questions, the lawyer makes a statement of fact, but uses her voice to indicate that the statement is actually a question that requires a response by the client. The third and fourth questions above show the lawyer making a statement, but raising her voice in a questioning manner as indicated by the question mark at the end of the statement.

Either method of asking leading questions will work if the question is confirming a single fact. If the lawyer includes two facts in her question, the client's answer will be confusing because it will be unclear which fact the client is confirming or denying. For example, if the lawyer asks, "Your son was the only passenger in the car, and it was snowing at the time of the accident?" the client's answer of "Yes" might be to the first fact, the second fact, or both facts. When asking leading questions, it is essential to limit the inquiry to one fact per question in order to obtain accurate answers.

Occasionally, the lawyer will ask a leading question to which she thinks she already knows the answer and she receives an unexpected response. If the answer to the leading question is unexpected, the lawyer will then need to pursue the topic with more open questions to understand the details and clarify the facts. For example, if the lawyer asks the leading question, "You had your high beam headlights on didn't you?" and the client says, "No", the lawyer who was expecting a "Yes" answer should then pursue the topic with a more open question such as, "Why not?" or "How did you make sure other drivers could see you in the snow?" The client can then elaborate on his earlier response by explaining, "The visibility was so bad that I found my high beams reflected off the snow as it fell. I turned on my hazard lights so the guy behind me could see me, but I left my headlights on low beam to minimize the reflection." By asking an open question after the unexpected response to the leading question, the lawyer has learned clarifying details.

Skilled lawyers can also use leading questions to give a client permission to admit a fact that he may be embarrassed to disclose. For instance, a lawyer might recognize that a client does not want to admit that he had been drinking before driving home from a party. The lawyer might ask, "Since it was New Year's Eve, I assume you might have had something to drink at the party?" The lawyer's leading question has given the client an acceptable way to disclose a difficult fact.

In summary, leading questions are useful in an interview for two purposes. First, they are useful to confirm information. Second, they can be used to facilitate a client's admission of an embarrassing or difficult fact. If they are overused or used too early in the interview they may inhibit the free flow of information from your client. If you ask leading questions in a cold or hostile tone, they can also impair the rapport you are trying to establish with your client. Because leading questions are often considered the province of trial attorneys as they conduct a harsh cross-examination, they should be used sparingly and gently in an interview. Your client will not take kindly to being cross-examined in an interview.

[5] Summary Questions

Summary questions list the facts and feelings the lawyer has learned in the interview. Summary questions are useful to make sure that the lawyer has heard everything the client has shared. They invite the client to elaborate or explain anything the lawyer may have misunderstood or omitted. A lawyer uses summary questions at the end of a topic and at the end of an interview to verify that she has learned the important facts and feelings from the client. For instance, in our car accident case, a lawyer might ask the following summary questions:

- **Summary Questions:**

    Q: Now I want to make sure that I have all the facts that show the other driver was at fault. The road conditions were treacherous. You were in the far right lane traveling slowly behind a line of cars that were moving at less than twenty-five miles per hour. You were using your hazard lights and your low beam headlights so that you were visible to cars behind you. There were icy patches on the road that made driving any faster dangerous. The car that hit you was traveling at a much higher rate of speed when it plowed into you. Have I omitted anything?

    A: The only thing you didn't say is that it was snowing at the time of the accident.

    Q: Is there anything else I have left out?

    A: No, I think you got everything.

    …. …. …. ….

    Q: Let's go over how you felt when the other driver's insurance company denied coverage for the injuries you suffered. Initially you were angry. Then you felt that they didn't understand what had happened. When you tried to explain how fast their driver was going on the icy road, you felt they weren't listening to you. Have I understood what you said?

    A: Yes, I think that about covers it.

Generally, summary questions should only be used for the more important topics in the interview. They should not be a verbatim playback, but a paraphrase of the client's story. They act as a probe of the client's memory to verify that he has completely and accurately recounted the important facts for each topic. If summary questions are overused, they can unnecessarily prolong the interview with boring recapitulations of every detail the client has shared.

§4.06 Information-Gathering Techniques

There are a number of special techniques that can facilitate efficient and comprehensive information gathering in an interview. Lawyers have come to rely on five particularly helpful techniques: (1) the funnel, (2) the time line, (3) the strategic use of silence, (4) the use of probes to rouse failed memories, and (5) the use of writings or demonstrations to recreate events. The funnel and the time line incorporate the five types of questions discussed in the preceding Section into a framework that maximizes the retrieval of information. The strategic use of silence often helps to facilitate the disclosure of delicate information from the client to the lawyer, particularly when combined with empathetic understanding, active listening, and recognition. The fourth technique, the use of probes to rouse failed memories, helps the client remember events he has temporarily forgotten or suppressed. The last technique, the use of writings or demonstrations to recreate events, may be helpful to understand matters that may be difficult to picture from purely verbal descriptions.

[1] The Funnel Technique

Gathering valuable information in an interview may be likened to searching for valuable items in a dark room. Suppose you enter a dark room with three things to help you find your way: a floodlight, a regular flashlight, and a penlight. Naturally, you would first orient yourself to the entire room by using the floodlight. As you identified particular areas where valuables might be stored, you would explore with your flashlight. When searching the smallest crevices or spaces, you would use your penlight. Similarly, in interviewing, skilled lawyers will seek out valuable information by beginning with open questions (like a floodlight) to illuminate the client's overall story. They then will use follow-up and closed questions (like the flashlight) to explore and understand particular parts of the story. And finally, they will use leading questions (the penlight) to pinpoint and clarify the finest details of the story. In interviewing, this method of obtaining valuable information is illustrated by a different metaphor, commonly referred to as the "funnel" technique.

When utilizing the funnel approach, a lawyer visualizes a common funnel as the structure of the questions she will ask on a particular topic. Each question corresponds to a place along the length of the funnel. The open questions, discussed in Section 4.05[1], correspond to the open mouth of the funnel. The follow-up questions, discussed in Section 4.05[2], that pursue clarification of the answers given in response to the open questions, fit just below the mouth of the funnel. The narrower closed questions, discussed in Section 4.05[3], correspond to a place one-half to two-thirds of the way further down the funnel. Leading questions, discussed in Section 4.05[4], are toward the bottom of the funnel. Finally, summary questions that are asked at the end of a topic to make sure that the lawyer has understood all the information, see Section 4.05[5], fit at the bottom of the funnel. The summary questions correspond to a filter that strains and tests the information that has been winnowed down through the funnel. The diagram below shows how these different types of questions fit along the length of the funnel.

The Funnel

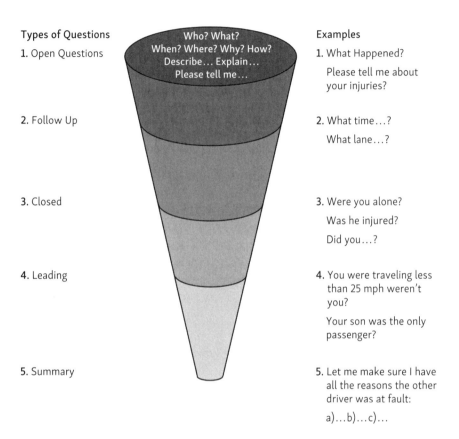

Types of Questions

1. Open Questions

2. Follow Up

3. Closed

4. Leading

5. Summary

Who? What? When? Where? Why? How? Describe... Explain... Please tell me...

Examples

1. What Happened?

   Please tell me about your injuries?

2. What time...?

   What lane...?

3. Were you alone?

   Was he injured?

   Did you...?

4. You were traveling less than 25 mph weren't you?

   Your son was the only passenger?

5. Let me make sure I have all the reasons the other driver was at fault:

   a)...b)...c)...

As shown in the diagram, a lawyer will start with an open question to elicit a broad response. As the lawyer learns more about the client's situation, the lawyer will move from open questions to follow-up and then closed questions. When the lawyer thinks she has obtained a fairly clear picture of the situation, she then begins to ask a few leading questions to confirm that she has learned the necessary details. Finally, after she has a complete picture of the client's situation, she then asks some summary questions to verify that she does in fact have the complete picture and has not misunderstood or forgotten any of the important facts. By asking these five types of questions in an orderly pattern, the lawyer has "funneled" the information and ensured that she has gotten all the important details as well as the entire picture.

Each major topic of your client's situation may be "funneled." For example, if your client tells you that he wants to discuss how he can recover for the personal injuries he suffered in the car accident as well as for the damages to his vehicle, he has presented two topics that should be funneled separately. Although many of the facts obtained by funneling the two topics will overlap because the personal injuries and the damages to the vehicle occurred in the same accident, each topic includes separate facts. Accordingly, you will need to conduct at least two separate funnels to exhaust the information your client has on these separate topics.

Many lawyers think of the first few open questions in the interview as a way to "get the list" of topics that the lawyer will funnel throughout the interview. Because you cannot effectively funnel two topics at the same time, it is usually a good idea to jot a note to yourself to return to the second topic after you have completed the first funnel.

The advantage of the funnel technique is that it presents an orderly framework for comprehensive information gathering. The disadvantage of the technique is that it is helpful only to the extent that the topic or topics you choose to funnel merit the time spent in inquiry. Therefore, efficient use of the technique requires that you choose the important topics that merit the time spent in funneling.

[2] The Time Line

Another technique for enhancing information gathering is to construct a time line of the client's situation. A client will often feel comfortable describing his situation with an opening sentence that begins with the phrase, "Well, the whole problem began with…." The lawyer can then encourage her client to recount his story in chronological order by asking open questions that focus on what happened next.

When using the timeline technique, most lawyers attempt to get an overview of the client's story by asking open questions that reveal the beginning, middle, and end of the situation. They then go back to fill in the details with follow-up and closed questions. After they have a fairly good picture of the situation, they then ask a few leading questions to verify information that appears to logically follow from the sequence of events. Finally, they ask summary questions to make sure there are no gaps in the timeline picture they have obtained.

When you use the timeline technique, make sure you understand where the story appropriately begins and ends. Too often clients and lawyers start the time line too late or end it too early. They tend to think the time line should start with a legally significant event, instead of with a factually significant event. For instance, in a personal injury case, the car accident that resulted in the injuries to your client is not the beginning event of the time line. Instead, you will want to inquire about the road conditions before impact, the condition of the cars before impact, and the physical condition of the drivers before impact. Likewise, the time line should include not only the present medical condition of your client, but also his future treatment needs.

The advantages of using a time line are that gaps or omissions in the story are easy to spot, and the time line is easy to follow for both lawyer and client. The disadvantages are that some topics do not flow sequentially and therefore may be omitted, and some clients think more topically than chronologically. For instance, in a contract dispute, the events leading up to the signing of the contract and the subsequent breach may flow chronologically and be easy for the client to recount in a time line. However, the fact that the other party to the contract became insolvent may not occur to the client as part of the chronology of the overall story. Instead, that fact is more likely to be revealed in response to a topical question about the financial condition of the other party.

The timeline method works particularly well when your client is trying to recall a specific sequence of events or when it would be useful to slow down what happened into a slow-motion description, as in a slow-motion movie. The time line can also aid a client who is reconstructing the important events in written form. If your client is having difficulty focusing on the time line during the interview, or if the interview time has drawn to a close before the client has finished recounting all of the key events to his story, you can ask your client to write out a time line at home. Most clients find the time line method easy to use on their own.

[3] The Strategic Use of Silence

As mentioned previously, lawyers often talk too much. They are accustomed to oral presentations. Words are their stock and trade. They forget that others are not as accustomed to verbalizing facts and feelings. Consequently, lawyers sometimes forget that a client may need time to think through an event in order to organize and formulate the words to completely describe it. To be an effective interviewer, you must be a patient listener; and one technique of patient listening involves the strategic use of silence.

Novices in the use of open questions sometimes mistake silence on the part of the client as a misunderstanding of the question. They then ask a second narrower question to clarify the first open question. The client then answers the second question. The broad initial question that invited expansive information remains unanswered.

In contrast, effective interviewers resist the temptation to prematurely ask a second narrower question. They patiently wait in silence while the client organizes his thoughts to answer the broad question. They do not attempt to fill the silence. As a result, they are often rewarded with a well-reasoned and detailed answer to the broad question.

In addition to using silence to permit your client to organize his thoughts to respond to a question, you may also use silence as a probe when no question is pending. Psychologists and psychiatrists have learned that people will often volunteer important information to fill an uncomfortable silence. This information might otherwise be withheld due to embarrassment or fear. Accordingly, just as a therapist uses silence to encourage her patient to reveal information, you can strategically use silence to encourage your client to reveal additional information.

[4] Failed Memory Probes

At times, a client may "shut down" during the interview. The client may say, "I don't remember" in response to a question; he may switch to another subject without finishing the particular story he was relating; or he may just sit back in uncomfortable silence. Before the interview can continue, you must diagnose what has caused this momentary interference or interruption in the dialogue. Clients usually shut down due to memory lapse, discomfort with the topic, or exhaustion.

If you conclude that your client has merely forgotten details that he once knew, you can use either a time line or visualization to rouse his memory. For instance, if your client says he can't remember whether he was wearing a seatbelt at the time of the collision, you might try the timeline technique to jog his memory:

- **Time Line Probes:**
  Q: Where was the last rest stop you took before the collision?
  A: We stopped for gas and a snack in Hickory, NC.
  Q: Describe each thing you did right before you got back onto the highway.
  A: Well, first I unlocked the car. Then, I opened the door and got into the driver's seat. I was carrying a cup of coffee that I placed in the drink holder between the two front seats.
  Q: What happened next?
  A: I guess, I put on my seatbelt and started the car, but I don't really remember.

Q: Where was your son when you started the car?
A: He was in the backseat. Oh, I remember now. He wanted me to put his half-finished can of Coke in the drink holder between the front seats because he wanted to take a nap. I had to unbuckle my seatbelt to reach the can. I took the can, placed it in the drink holder and buckled the seat belt back. I remember because we joked that he always waited until I had already buckled my seat belt before he asked me to take something from the backseat. That's the conversation we had as I was buckling my seatbelt for the second time.

With some clients you can also try to use visualization to probe failed memory. When using this technique, you ask the client to visualize a certain event and describe the details as if he were experiencing the event in the present. For instance, if your client says he can't remember if he was wearing his seat belt at the time of the collision, you might try the following:

- **Visualization Probes:**

  Q: Imagine yourself immediately after the collision. Visualize that time if you can. The guy behind you has just plowed into the rear of your car. I know this may be difficult for you, but try to go back in your mind to that time and tell me exactly how you feel.
  A: I'm stunned. Then the pain hits. I can't move. My right leg is bleeding and the pain seems unbearable. The entire weight of the front of the car seems to be on my leg.
  Q: What else do you feel?
  A: Well, I'm panicked about my son. I call out his name. He answers. He says he's scared. He wants to know what happened. Then he starts crying when he sees the blood on my leg. He gets real upset when he realizes I can't move.
  Q: Is he hurt?
  A: He says his knee hurts, but he'll be okay. He's scared about me.
  Q: What else do you feel?
  A: My head and neck hurt from being thrown forward and then backward. My chest also hurts.
  Q: Why does your chest hurt?
  A: I don't know. I guess from hitting the steering wheel. No, wait a minute. I know why it hurts. It's from the seat belt. I remember now. I did have on my seat belt because the next day I had a big bruise across my chest where the seat belt was.

Sometimes when your client shuts down, it is not the result of a loss of memory, but from a feeling of awkwardness about the topic. Use your active listening skills to diagnose if the reason for the sudden change of topic or claimed lack of memory is truly from a memory lapse or from your client's discomfort with the topic. If you sense that your client is attempting to avoid the topic, you can either come back to it after you have established greater rapport with him, or you can pursue the topic by acknowledging the difficulty in discussing the issue. For instance, if your client seems uncomfortable discussing what happened to his son after the accident, you might empathetically acknowledge the difficulty of the matter as follows:

- **Acknowledging the Difficulty of the Topic:**
  Q: It must have been hard to care for your son when you were in such pain. What happened to your son when the ambulance arrived?
  A: It was terrible. I didn't know what to do. They let him go with me to the hospital, but I was really in too much pain to think much about his needs.
  Q: Earlier, you said you were divorced. It must have been hard to call your ex-wife after the accident happened.
  A: You're not kidding. She was fit to be tied. She hadn't wanted me to take him on the visit to Kentucky. She had been worried about the weather conditions. I called her just before I went into surgery. She was furious. I felt terrible because our son had to stay with a social worker until his mother could get to the hospital to pick him up the next day. My ex blamed me for putting our son at risk.

Finally, a client may shut down during an interview from exhaustion. If your client has been recounting the facts of his case for a period of time, he may lose his focus and need a break. Suggest a break, or offer him a cup of coffee or drink of water. If your client still has trouble focusing on your questions after the break, you need to schedule a follow-up interview at a later time.

[5] Using Writings or Demonstrations to Recreate Events

Some events are difficult to understand from purely verbal descriptions. For example, in an automobile accident case, a diagram of the accident scene and the positions of the vehicles will often provide the best picture of what happened. When there are numerous heirs to a will, a diagram of a family tree may be helpful in understanding potential beneficiaries. A written time line of the phases of a construction project may be helpful in drafting a contract governing the parties' obligations in developing a residential subdivision. A physical demonstration may help explain a key event, such as how a person was injured or how a person acted. Accordingly, when appropriate, you should not hesitate to have your client recreate an event on paper, whether a drawing, chart, or written summary. Similarly, having your client physically demonstrate an event will often help you better understand what happened.

§4.07 Exploring the Client's Objectives

When a client first enters your office, he has at least one objective or goal in mind. He is seeking legal representation for a reason. Often he comes to the initial interview with several objectives. He may be able to articulate one or more of his objectives, but others may not yet be fully formed in his mind. As mentioned previously, one purpose of the initial interview is to begin the process of identifying your client's objectives. A second purpose is to begin the process of translating your client's objectives into a concrete plan of action.

A client will often indicate his objective in the first few sentences of the initial interview. The client may say, "I need a will," or "I have been sued," or "I want help in recovering for my injuries." Each sentence articulates a reason why the client scheduled the initial meeting with the lawyer. However, many times the reason initially expressed for seeking legal representation will only be the beginning of the process of identifying the client's objectives. For instance, when a client says that he has been sued, the lawyer will realize that she has to analyze the lawsuit, explore possible defenses, investigate potential counterclaims, and discuss settlement prospects. In other words, the client's initial expression of his objective is only the first step in a lengthier process of clarifying objectives and arriving at potential solutions.

A good starting point for identifying your client's objectives is to focus on his actual needs. By using open questions to explore your client's feelings and concerns about his situation, you can begin to discern a picture of his overall needs. As you learn more about those needs, you can employ either the funnel method to explore specific topics or the timeline method to establish a framework for understanding important events. Once the factual picture becomes clearer, you can then ask more direct questions to find out what your client wants to accomplish.

It is also helpful to encourage your client to express his objectives in terms of factual results instead of legal remedies. For instance, if your client says that he wants to declare bankruptcy, you should ask him to articulate his objective factually. What, exactly, does he want to protect? If he says he wants to protect his home from creditors, then protection of his home, not bankruptcy, is his factual objective.

By encouraging your client to define his objectives factually, you may be able to broaden the legal remedies that may be available to accomplish those objectives. For instance, you and your client may be able to explore several methods of protecting your client's home and not be limited to the single remedy of bankruptcy. For example, it may be possible for you to draft a notice that the client claims his homestead exemption as a means of protecting his home, or you may be able to negotiate a debt repayment plan with your client's creditors that will extinguish the need for bankruptcy. In sum, exploring your client's objectives in terms of his needs and what factual results he wants to obtain will help clarify his objectives and the most appropriate means that may be available for achieving them.

§ 4.08 Exploring Legal Theories

After you have a basic understanding of your client's overall objectives, you should begin exploring legal theories that may be relevant to accomplishing those objectives. As a result of your legal training, it is inevitable that even during the initial stages of the interview you will have already begun to spot potential legal issues and remedies in the case. In exploring legal theories, however, it is essential not to prematurely diagnose your client's legal situation. As the interview progresses, you may find it helpful to jot simple legal terms on a sheet of paper as you listen to your client's description of the situation. After you have a complete factual picture of the situation, you can refer back to your list to see if any of the legal theories you initially identified are applicable and should be more fully explored in connection with your client's factual objectives.

It will often be appropriate to ask closed questions when obtaining information relevant to potential legal theories because their viability depends upon specific factual showings. For example, a claim for intentional infliction of emotional distress typically requires a showing that the client's distress was severe or disabling in nature; a temporary restraining order requires a showing of irreparable harm; waiver may be a defense to conversion if the owner of the property accepted it back from the converter along with a sum of money for use of the chattel; a contract may not generally be rescinded based on unilateral mistake, but it may be avoided based on mutual mistake. Thus, to identify legal theories, you will have to ask specific questions that focus on the particular elements of potential claims, defenses, and legal remedies that may be applicable to your client's situation.

§4.09 Taking Notes During the Interview

During the interview, it is very difficult to convey empathetic understanding and engage in active listening if you are preoccupied with note taking. To maximize information gathering and build rapport with your client, you should avoid doing anything that will distract him from telling his story and distract you from understanding it. On the other hand, you must have a method for remembering what you are told during the interview and documenting the matters decided at the meeting.

Lawyers usually use one of four methods to document the substance of the interview: (1) tape-record it, (2) have a paralegal or secretary sit in on the interview and take notes, (3) personally take detailed notes, or (4) personally take brief notes and write out or dictate a memorandum to the file shortly after the interview is over. No single method is best in all circumstances, and in some situations a lawyer may use more than one of these methods at the same time.

Generally, recording the interview or having a third person take notes may inhibit or distract the client from sharing information. Many people feel more self-conscious when they are being recorded, and many feel somewhat less relaxed when they are speaking to an audience of two people instead of one. However, these inhibitions are unlikely to exist if you are meeting with clients who are members of the board of directors of a corporation or city council. In these types of situations, using a tape recorder or using another person to take notes during the interview will be neither inhibiting nor distracting.

Many lawyers find that the handwritten notes they take during an interview are sufficient to adequately document it. This is particularly true when relatively simple or standard legal services are involved. Many other lawyers prefer to take only abbreviated notes during an interview; and, shortly after it is over, they use those notes to dictate or type a more detailed summary of what transpired in a memorandum to the file. As between these choices, most lawyers use the one that best fits their personal style and the relative complexity of the client's situation. You can employ either method effectively so long as your note taking does not become a distraction to your client or impede you from engaging in active listening. Finally, basic information about how to contact your client and short notes about preliminary objectives and initial tasks that will be undertaken in the representation might be documented on a simple form like the "New Client Information Form" shown at the end of Section 3.13.

§4.10 Illustration of Initial Client Meeting and Interview[5]

Larry Odden is a partner in a general-practice law firm of eight lawyers. He received a phone call from a prospective client, Clara Miles, who told him she had been injured in a car accident approximately one year ago and wanted to talk with him about it. (The statute of limitations in a personal injury action is three years.) During the phone conversation, Clara said that a pickup truck ran a red light, broadsided her car, and that she sustained whiplash-type injuries to her neck and back. She said that her own insurance company paid the property damage to her car. She said she had a copy of her current medical bills and a copy of the accident report taken by the police officer who investigated the accident. She has not been contacted by anyone else about the accident, and she has not consulted with another lawyer.

Larry scheduled an appointment to meet with Clara at his office during her lunch break from her employment at a nearby clothing store. It was agreed the initial meeting would be limited to about an hour, and a follow-up appointment would be scheduled if necessary. Larry told her there would be no charge for the initial conference, and he asked her to bring the medical bills and accident report to the meeting.

At the time scheduled for the meeting, Larry greeted Clara in the firm's reception area and escorted her to a small conference room. After exchanging some pleasantries and small talk, the meeting proceeded as shown in the transcript below. (The footnotes in the transcript point out Larry's use of various techniques discussed in the preceding sections of this Chapter.)

1. L: Well, Clara, tell me how this accident happened.[6]
2. C: Let's see, where to begin ... (pause).[7] Last February, Saturday the 8th, my husband Dan and I, and our son Tommy, were driving up Franklin Street here in town. We were going to find a place to get

---

5. This illustration is intended to show how a skilled attorney might handle an initial client meeting and interview. Of course, however, you might conduct the interview quite differently and may even disagree with some of the approaches taken by the lawyer. Bear in mind that the lawyer's approach is, in significant respects, affected by his personal style and interviewing philosophy. In addition, the lawyer's interaction with the client is significantly affected by the client's personality, demeanor, and body language—all of which are not readily apparent from a mere transcript.

6. This is an open question to elicit the basic story.

7. Larry does not interrupt. He lets Clara decide where she wants to start her story.

some lunch and then go to the Carolina basketball game. Carolina was playing N.C. State that day. Anyway, as we were going through the intersection of Franklin and Estes Drive, a pickup truck ran a red light on Estes and hit our car from the right. That's basically how it happened.

3. L: What happened after the collision?

4. C: Well, I was really shaken up. It was a huge bang. After it happened, I remember turning around in my seat to see if Tommy was all right. He was in the back seat, had his seatbelt on thank God, and he was okay. My husband, Dan, he was driving; he seemed okay too. Our car was in the middle of the intersection, smashed in on my side, the passenger side, toward the front of the car. God, it was awful.

5. L: I can imagine.... ... (pause and silence). You say you were shaken up. Were you hurt?[8]

6. C: Yes. Well, I went dizzy for a moment, didn't black out or anything, but was like in shock for a moment. When the truck hit us, like I said, it hit us on the passenger side toward the front of the car, not the passenger door itself. I was sitting in the front seat, had my seatbelt on, but was jerked left. And my head hit the side of the headrest of the driver's seat. I didn't have a concussion or anything. Then I felt myself thrown back into my own seat. Then, after a couple of seconds, that's when I looked to see if Tommy and my husband were all right.

7. L: I see. What happened after you checked to see whether Tommy and your husband were okay?

8. C: Dan got out of the car, and then I got out and got Tommy out. Dan told us to go over to the sidewalk to wait. The traffic was beginning to back up by now with our car and the pickup blocking the intersection. It was a mess.

9. L: I know what you mean. Game day traffic is always bad. Was Tommy okay after you got him out of the car?

10. C: Yeah, like I said, he was all right. Maybe he was shaken up a bit, but he didn't have any injuries. He didn't complain about being hurt in any way.

11. L: How old is Tommy?

12. C: He's seven now; so, he was six at the time.

---

8. Larry conveys empathetic understanding here ("I can imagine"). He then pauses and is silent to invite Clara to resume her story as she wishes. When she does not, he chooses (again, empathetically) to focus on injuries for the time-being, deferring further questions about how the accident happened until later.

13. L: Since the accident, has this affected him in any way?[9]

14. C: No, not really. I know he was frightened right when it all happened, but he got over it real quickly. He's had no nightmares or fears about riding in the car, which I was worried about at first. In fact, now and then, he still jokes about it all.

15. L: I'm glad to hear that. These kids really have a way of bouncing back, don't they? I have a son myself. He's a year older than Tommy.[10]

16. C: Oh really?

17. L: Yes, and an eleven-year-old daughter too. They keep my wife and me quite busy.

18. C: You're telling me … (chuckling).

19. L: Do you and Dan have any other children?

20. C: No, just Tommy.

21. L: So, tell me what was going on while you and Tommy were waiting at the sidewalk.[11]

22. C: We just stood there, and it wasn't long before two, maybe three police cars showed up. I remember there were two officers starting to direct traffic, and the third officer started talking with Dan and the driver of the pickup truck. By the way, I brought the accident report you asked for.

23. L: Oh good; thanks. We can look at that in a minute. Were you involved in the conversation with the officer?[12]

24. C: Not at that time. It was so cold outside that Tommy and I went into the Food Mart at the corner of the intersection to keep warm. I think we got hot chocolate or something. And I just watched what was going on outside from the window in the Food Mart. The officer was talking with my husband and the driver across the street. I never met the driver.

---

9. This question explores whether there is any potential claim that may be brought on Tommy's behalf.

10. Larry's personal comment here and the colloquy through line 20 help to develop rapport with Clara.

11. This open question refocuses Clara back to the chronology of events.

12. Larry resists discussing the accident report at this time, preferring instead to concentrate on what Clara knows about what the officer said. (He will use the accident report later to confirm and elicit additional details from Clara about the accident, *see* line 52). At line 23 through 50, Larry uses the Funnel Technique to find out everything about Clara's conversation with the officer. Note the combination of open, follow-up, and closed questions at lines 25, 29, 33, 35, 39, 41, and 49; and note the leading and summary questions at lines 31, 43, 45, and 47.

25. L: Did the officer ever talk with you?

26. C: At one point, it was later on, he came into the Food Mart, and he asked me what happened. I told him that we had a green light, that the light turned yellow when we were going through the intersection, and then the truck came out of nowhere and hit us.

27. L: You don't mind if I take a few notes, do you?[13]

28. C: Oh, no, that's fine.

29. L: What did he say?

30. C: He said that's what my husband said, but that the other driver said he had the green light and was making a right-hand turn from Estes onto Franklin.

31. L: I see. So the driver of the pickup was not going through the intersection on Estes but was making a right-hand turn from Estes onto Franklin?

32. C: Yeah, apparently. But I didn't know that. All I knew was that he hit us. It happened so fast.

33. L: On Franklin Street, what lane were you traveling in?

34. C: We were in the far right lane, going straight on Franklin.

35. L: Did you have any further conversation with the officer?

36. C: No, not really.

37. L: Did he give a citation to anyone?

38. C: He told me he wasn't going to give anyone a ticket because he couldn't tell who was at fault. So nobody got a ticket.

39. L: Did he say anything else to you?

40. C: No, that's it. He was real nice.

41. L: Have you or Dan spoken to him since that day?

42. C: No.

43. L: Mm-hmm. So, the officer asked you what happened; you said your husband had the green light; that the light turned yellow when you got to the intersection; and then the truck came out of nowhere and hit your car.

44. C: Yes.

45. L: And the officer said that your husband basically said the same thing, but that the driver of the pickup said he had a green light.

---

13. Larry chooses to take notes at this point because of the particular importance of the conversation with the officer: what Clara told the officer and what the officer said to Clara will likely be admissible if both testify at trial. In addition, the officer's accident report may not recount the conversation, and Larry will otherwise need his notes about what was said during the conversation when he interviews the officer.

46. C: Yeah.

47. L: And then the officer said he wasn't going to charge anyone because he didn't know who was at fault.

48. C: Right.

49. L: Did I leave anything out?

50. C: No, that's it. But sometime later, before everyone left, he gave my husband a sheet of paper with the other driver's insurance information; and I've brought that with me also.

51. L: Oh, thank you. Let me take a look at that for a moment, along with the accident report.

52. [Larry briefly reads the insurance information form and the accident report. He then goes over the accident report with Clara and verifies various details in the report, such as the date and time of the accident, the make and model of the vehicles, the name of the driver of the pickup truck (Ronald S. Smith), the description of the damage to each vehicle, the speed limit on Franklin Street and Estes Drive (25 mph for each), the accuracy of the officer's diagram of the accident scene and positions of the vehicles after impact, the fact that there were no independent eyewitnesses to the accident, the fact that no ambulance was called and no-one reported being injured, and the fact that the officer didn't charge either of the drivers.][14]

53. L: Clara, this accident report is signed by Officer Boles. I know him. Do you remember if that's the name of the officer who spoke with you?

54. C: Yes, that's him. I didn't talk with any other officer.

55. L: The report notes that the "road conditions were icy." Do you remember that?

56. C: Yes. There were small patches of snow and a bit of ice on the roads. We got a dusting of snow the night before and, like I said, it was very cold. But the roads weren't really covered with snow or ice, or anything like that.

57. L: There were just patches of snow and ice here and there?

58. C: Yes.

59. L: Do you remember if your car skidded at all when it was going through the intersection?

60. C: I don't believe so; I don't remember that.

---

14. From line 52 through 76, Larry uses the accident report and insurance form to confirm, elicit, and recreate various details in connection with the accident.

61. L: How about the pickup truck—did it skid at all?

62. C: I can't remember that either. It all happened so fast.

63. L: Was Dan driving a bit slower that day because of the road conditions?

64. C: I would have to say that everyone was driving perhaps a little slower, but not much. It was a little slippery I guess, but it was no big deal.

65. L: The report also notes that your car was not drivable and was towed from the scene.

66. C: Yeah, they had to call a wrecker.

67. L: Did you tell me over the phone that your insurance company paid for the property damage to your car?

68. C: Yes, they did.

69. L: How did that come about?

70. C: Well, Dan handled all of that. First, I think he called Mr. Smith's insurance company, All-Good Insurance, but they said they wouldn't pay because they thought my husband was at fault. So our insurance company ended up paying to fix our car.

71. L: Do you know if your insurance company paid for the damage to the pickup truck?

72. C: I don't know.

73. L: Do you know the name of the adjuster for your insurance company whom your husband spoke with?

74. C: No, not off hand. But I can get that information for you.

75. L: Okay. Let's see, the report also says that there was a passenger, a Jane Smith, in the pickup truck. Do you remember seeing her?

76. C: No, I really don't. I saw the driver because he was talking with the officer and Dan across the street. But I don't remember a passenger.

77. L: Okay. Clara, let's back up and talk more about how the accident happened. What I'd like to do is start about a minute or so just before the accident, and like a slow-motion movie, frame by frame, get a picture in my mind about what happened. Can you help me with that?[15]

78. C: I'll try. But I'm not really sure where to start.

---

15. At lines 66 through 112, Larry uses the Funnel Technique with a combination of Time Line Probes and Visualization Probes to obtain as much information as possible about how the accident actually occurred.

79. L: That's all right. Let me try to help. Let's see, you were driving down Franklin, toward town; you were in the front seat, passenger side; Dan was driving; Tommy was in the back seat. You were in the right-hand lane, approaching the intersection at Estes Drive. Do you remember seeing the Hotel Sienna on the right-hand side of the road just before the intersection?

80. C: Yes.

81. L: Okay, tell me what happened from that point, in slow motion if you can.

82. C: Well, okay, let's see … (pause). We're driving down Franklin; I did see the hotel … (pause).

83. L: What's the very next thing you saw?

84. C: I think there were two cars ahead of us … (pause). I'm having trouble remembering.

85. L: You're doing just fine. There were two cars ahead of you—

86. C: Yes, and we were one or two car lengths behind, going fairly slowly … (pause). I remember the light was green at that point. Then the phone rang. I reached for it on the dash near the radio. Dan said something like, "I got it," and he picked up the phone. I looked up; the light was yellow. I then looked at Dan for a split second. Then we must have been in the intersection. And then, wham; we got hit … (pause).

87. L: Anything else?

88. C: No, I think that's all. That's the best I can remember.

89. L: Okay, that's very helpful. Let me just rewind the tape back, so to speak, for a few seconds. You were one or two car lengths behind the car in front of you, and you saw the light was green at that point—

90. C: Yes.

91. L: Were any of the cars in front of you already in the intersection at that point?

92. C: No. They were just about to go into the intersection. Just about to enter into it.

93. L: All right. And your car was about one or two car lengths behind?

94. C: Right.

95. L: And then the phone rang and you looked down and reached for it?

96. C: Yes. It was next to the radio on the dash, toward the driver's side.

97. L: And then?

98. C: Dan said, "I'll get it" and he reached over and picked up the phone from the dash.

99. L: And did you see the traffic light at that point?

100. C: I leaned back in my seat when he picked up the phone, and then I glanced up and saw the light was yellow.

101. L: At this point, were you in the intersection?

102. C: I'm not sure. After I glanced at the light, I turned and glanced at Dan who was holding the phone to his ear, and he answered it, "Hello," or something like that.

103. L: And then?

104. C: It happened so fast. All I remember then was that we got hit.

105. L: Do you remember at what point you were actually in the intersection?

106. C: I'm not sure. We were probably just entering it or into it when I looked at Dan when he was holding the phone.

107. L: Did you ever see the light turn from yellow to red?

108. C: No. I only saw it green and then yellow. I'm sure the light was yellow when we went into the intersection.

109. L: Okay. That's helpful. Is there anything else you can remember in this slow motion sequence?

110. C: No. That's the best I can remember.

111. L: Did you ever find out who had been calling on the car phone?

112. C: No, we never found out. I guess the phone went dead when the accident happened. Dan is self-employed as a plumber, so maybe some customer called. But we never did find out who called.

113. L: Okay. Let's talk about the rest of that day. I believe you said that a wrecker came to tow your car—[16]

114. C: Yes. And there was another wrecker that came and towed away the pickup truck. Tommy and I just waited in the Food Mart the whole time.

115. L: What happened after that?

116. C: Well, not too long after officer Boles talked with me, he left and my husband came into the Food Mart. We called his brother who lives in town, and he picked us up and drove us home. We missed the game, of course; but we still saw most of it on TV.

117. L: What happened during the rest of the day?

---

16. Larry uses a headline ("Let's talk about the rest of that day") to resume the story from the time that the wrecker came to tow away the car. Note the open questions at lines 115 and 117.

118. C: That afternoon we just lounged around the house. My husband was okay; and like I said, Tommy was okay. But I was still feeling shaken up, and I was beginning to feel sore in my neck and a little in my lower back.

119. L: Mm-hmm.[17]

120. C: And toward evening it was starting to ache pretty badly, and Dan wanted me to call our doctor, I mean, Tommy's pediatrician. I don't really have a regular doctor, but Dr. Maria Partin is Tommy's doctor. Dan wanted me to call her. Anyway, I didn't at that time. But then I had a rough night. By morning, I could hardly get out of bed. I could hardly turn my head and my back was real stiff … (pause).

121. L: Please go on.…[18]

122. C: So, the next morning I called Dr. Partin, and she gave me the name of a doctor to call, but I've forgotten his name now. I ended up not calling him. Instead, the following day, Monday, I called Dr. Sally Byler, a chiropractor in town, whom my sister recommended and had once seen when she had a back problem. And then I saw Dr. Byler for about four months.

123. L: Uh-uh. Did you see any other doctors for your injuries?

124. C: No, just Dr. Byler.

125. L: What was Dr. Byler's course of treatment?

126. C: She gave me therapy, three times a week at first, and then two times a week. I had electrical muscle stimulation to my neck, shoulders and back; manipulation; and ultrasound therapy. I brought the bills for you. [Clara hands the bills to Larry].

127. L: Thanks.[19] The last entry on these bills is for a visit on April 14. Have you seen Dr. Byler since then?

128. C: No. The treatments helped me a lot at first, but then they were getting too expensive. Dan's insurance wouldn't cover the treatments, and we've had hard times money-wise over the past year with Dan's new plumbing business. He used to have a partner in the business, but they broke up. So Dan was starting his own business, sort of starting all over again building up new customers. It's been hard making

---

17. This is an example of Engaging in Active Listening through "acknowledgement."

18. Notice how Larry does not interrupt Clara but encourages her.

19. Note that Larry chooses not to ask any follow-up questions about Dr. Byler's "course of treatment." Larry's purpose here is merely to get a general description about the course of treatment, which will otherwise be detailed in the medical records.

ends meet, so I stopped going to her. Anyway, my condition just sort of leveled off, not getting any worse, but not getting any better.

129. L: I see. Tell me more about your injuries, Clara. You've talked about the night right after the accident. Can you give me a description of your injuries from that time up until now?[20]

130. C: Yeah. When I first started seeing Dr. Byler, I could hardly turn my head and I had difficulty walking and bending because of pain and spasms in my lower back. The mornings were the worst times. For the first two months, that would have been mid January to early March or so, the treatments helped me a lot and I did home exercises. Then, my neck and back sort of leveled off … (pause). I gained fifteen pounds, and I've still not lost that extra weight. I just can't make myself exercise. I used to walk every day, but I haven't since the accident. The constant pain saps my energy. My neck is still stiff in the mornings, but that usually goes away during the day. Like, I don't feel any neck pain right now. But my back, it aches, like a dull ache, almost all of the time, and mostly when I stand and sit for long periods of time. It's been an awful year, the stress and all—but I guess I'll just have to learn to live with it.

131. L: This must be hard for you, day in and day out.[21]

132. C: Yes. [Clara becomes somewhat tearful].

133. L: (Pause) … Did Dr. Byler recommend any medications?

134. C: No. I guess I could take aspirin or something like that, but I've never really believed in taking a lot of medicines. I tried Tylenol for a while, but it didn't seem to do much good.

135. L: It's been about eight months now since you last saw Dr. Byler. Have you thought about going back to see her or consulting with another doctor?[22]

136. C: No, not really. Our money situation is still real tight and, like I said before, I guess I've just resigned myself to having to learn to live with this and just make the best of things.

---

20. Larry wants to focus on Clara's injuries from *her* perspective because her description of how they have affected her are unlikely to be fully reported in the medical records.

21. This is an example of encouraging communication by giving Clara "recognition."

22. Larry is obviously concerned about the eight-month gap in treatment in light of Clara's ongoing back pain. In lieu of suggesting to Clara at this point that she might want to consider obtaining further medical treatment, Larry chooses for now to tactfully find out why Clara has not sought further treatment. (Larry will revisit this issue in a later decision-making conference with Clara, *see* § 5.10 at lines 74 through 96).

137. L: Were you employed at the time of the accident?[23]

138. C: No. I first started working at Belk's as a sales clerk two weeks ago. I work five days a week, nine to three o'clock; with a lunch break in between. It's helping make ends meet, but it's hard on my back.

139. L: I admire you for taking on work with all that you're going through. Do you think you can continue working those hours with your back as it is now?

140. C: I think I can manage. I guess I'll just have to.

141. L: I understand. When you mentioned your lunch break, Clara, that reminded me—when do you have to be back at Belk's?

142. C: Oh, [looking at her watch], I still have some time. My supervisor said I could extend this lunch break a bit longer if I had to. But I'll have to get back after a while.

143. L: All right. Let me ask you this, Clara: what are the things that concern you most about your situation—about all that you've been through?[24]

144. C: I'm worried about being a good mother and wife. I'm not my old self. I'm cranky when I'm aching all the time. It's been very stressful—our financial situation and all. It's been hard for me, very hard emotionally. Dan works all the time he can, trying to reestablish his business, and I need to help make ends meet. But it's so hard to work and then take care of Tommy, rushing back after work to meet him at the bus stop after school, etc. And it's hard for me with the housework, with Dan doing more than his fair share. In fact, Dan did all the household chores for about three months. I could hardly do anything. For almost four months we couldn't even have intimate relations, if you know what I mean. It was awful. I just want my old self again, and I'm worried about my back in the long term—it's been nearly a year now.

145. L: Again, I admire all you're doing.[25]

146. C: Thanks, that's nice of you to say. Do you think I have a good case? I mean, I'm not the kind of person who wants to take advantage, but my sister once made a claim in an accident case and received some compensation for all she went through. That's why I called your office

---

23. This is a legal theory-testing question to explore whether Clara may have a claim for lost wages.

24. This question is designed to explore Clara's "objectives."

25. This is another example of giving Clara "acknowledgement" and "recognition."

to begin with. I know that All-Good, Mr. Smith's insurance company, thinks Dan was at fault; but that's not true. And my family and I have been through a lot.

147. L: Yes, I think I can help you, Clara. If Mr. Smith made his turn against the red light, he would be considered "negligent." In other words, he would be considered at fault. And that would give you what's called a personal injury claim against him that should be paid by All-Good. Dan would also have a claim for what is called loss of consortium—the loss of your services to the family and loss of intimate relations for three or four months.[26]

148. C: How much do you think I could get?

149. L: That's something I can't answer right now. There's some information that we will still need to get. As you know, there are two sides to this story. It's not unusual for there to be a dispute about the facts in a case—

150. C: (Interposing), Will you represent me? And would you also represent Dan in his claim if he wanted you to?

151. L: As I say, I think I can help you. But let me clear up an important but somewhat technical point first.[27]

152. C: Okay.

153. L: I know that the facts, according to you and Dan, were that Mr. Smith ran the red light. On the other hand, if in fact the light had changed to green before Mr. Smith made his turn, then Dan may have been negligent and you may have a legal claim against him, which would be covered by the insurance company for your car under the law of our state. In saying this, please understand that I'm merely saying that it would be a conflict of interest for me to represent you and Dan in a claim against Mr. Smith, and at the same time represent you in any claim against your husband. The advice I give you and the dis-

---

26. At lines 147 through 151, Larry's guarded responses to Clara's questions, "Do you think I have a good case?" and How much do you think I can get?," appropriately avoid a premature evaluation of Clara's case. Larry has not yet interviewed Dan, other possible witnesses to the accident, or the officer; he has not reviewed the medical records and bills; and Clara is apparently in need of further treatment in light of her continuing back problems. Under these circumstances, it would be irresponsible at this time for Larry to render any firm opinion about the merits of the case.

27. At lines 151 through 155, Larry explains a potential conflict of interest if he represented Dan (*see also* §6.09), and he otherwise takes the opportunity to explain the attorney-client privilege.

cussions between us are protected by the attorney-client privilege. The same privilege exists for Dan if I represent him. But, if I represent you and Dan when you might pursue a claim against him, I would be put in a position that would violate those privileges.

154. C: I see. But I would never make a claim against my husband or our insurance company because Dan did nothing wrong.

155. L: Yes, and I understand. I know that what I just said was awkward, but I wanted you to know about this technical matter because, as you know, there are two sides to the story about exactly what happened, even though your version and Dan's version are the same. And, as for representing Dan, I could only consider that if he decided he wanted to meet with me and after he and I had an opportunity to talk like we are doing here.

156. C: Thanks. I know what you mean. Like I say, I would only want to be compensated by Mr. Smith's insurance company. I think they are responsible because he was at fault. I know Dan is being supportive of me in all of this, and I'll leave it up to Dan whether he wants to meet with you about any claim. How would I pay you for representing me?

157. L: Our firm's fee in this kind of case is called a contingent fee. The fee is a one-third percentage of the gross amount we are able to recover for you, either from a settlement of the case or from a trial. If we have to file a lawsuit against Mr. Smith, you will have to pay for certain costs such as filing fees to the court, and certain other expenses incurred in preparing for trial. Those costs would be your responsibility regardless of the outcome of the case.

158. C: What if you are unable to recover any money for me?

159. L: Then there is no fee, because a third of zero is zero.

160. C: And these costs if a suit is filed—how much can they run?

161. L: Well, of course, it varies from case to case. But my best estimate is that, in a case such as yours, total costs would be $3,000 to $5,000 if there were a trial. [Larry briefly provides a further explanation of costs, such as deposition costs and fees charged by doctors for time spent while testifying].

162. C: Could I pay that over time, in installments to your firm?

163. L: Yes; we can make arrangements for that.

164. C: Do you think we will have to file a suit?

165. L: I really can't answer that right now, Clara. It's one of several options, which we need to discuss at some length. Because our time

is getting short right now, I suggest we talk about that at our next meeting.[28]

166. C: Okay. When should we meet again?

167. L: I think we should schedule our next appointment in about three weeks. That seems like a long time, but there are a number of things I need to look into in the meantime, and there are a few things I need you to get for me. Then we can meet again and discuss different options and decide on a game plan. Is that all right?[29]

168. C: Sure. What do you need from me?

169. L: Do you have any photos of the damage to your car?

170. C: No, but I think the insurance adjuster for our insurance company had some photos taken.

171. L: You mentioned you could find out the name and phone number for that adjuster. Could you check on that for me and call me about it in a few days?

172. C: Sure.

173. [Larry then explains the procedure for obtaining Clara's medical records and has her sign a medical release form authorizing Dr. Byler to release a copy of Clara's medical records to the law firm. He also reviews with her a copy of the firm's standard contingent fee contract (*see* §6.15), and tells her he will send an original contract to her in the mail for her signature. He also makes a copy of the accident report, insurance information sheet showing Mr. Smith's insurance information, and the medical bills from Dr. Byler to keep in the file. Finally, he obtains from Clara pertinent contact information to fill out a "New Client Information Form" like that shown in Section 3.13].[30]

174. L: All right, Clara, this is what I will do before our next meeting. As I mentioned, I'm going to get your medical records from Dr. Byler. After you get me the name and phone number of the adjuster for your insurance company, I will try to get from him or her a copy of the photos of your car and find out if the adjuster has any more information about the accident. Third, I'll also talk with Officer Boles to find out if he can tell me anything more about what Mr. and Ms. Smith

---

28. For the same reasons given in note 26 above, Larry defers for now any discussion about Clara's options.

29. From line 167 through 174, Larry establishes an initial course of action (*see* §3.10).

30. In this way, Larry has formally entered into an attorney-client relationship with Clara.

said about the accident. At some point, I would also like to talk with your husband so I can hear his description of the accident first hand, but I think we can wait on that for now. Once I've done these things, and I think it will take about two weeks to get the medical records, I'll have my secretary call you so we can set up another appointment. Is that all right with you?

175. C: Yes. I understand.

176. L: Okay then. Finally, Clara, please do not hesitate to call me at any time. Our office hours are 8:30 a.m. to 5:00 p.m., Monday through Friday. If you have any concerns or some situation comes up that you need to call me about, please do. I'd rather know about it earlier than later. If I'm not in the office or available when you call, I'll be sure to call you back. I usually can do that the same day you call or the day after. But I will get back with you, okay?[31]

177. C: Yes.

178. L: Also, Clara, if anyone from either insurance company calls you about the accident, tell them you can't talk with them, and just tell them to call me. Okay?[32]

179. C: Yes. Thank you so much. I enjoyed meeting you. And I'll call you in a day or so about the name and phone number of the adjuster for our insurance company. And if Dan wants to talk about making a claim also, I'll have him call you.

180. L: Thank you, Clara. And I enjoyed meeting you too.

---

31. Notice how Larry expressly opens a channel of ongoing communication for Clara.

32. This is an example of providing protective advice to the client.

Chapter Five

Decision-Making and Implementing the Decision

SYNOPSIS

§5.01 Introduction

After you have thoroughly interviewed your client and obtained all factual and legal information pertinent to his situation, you must analyze potential courses of action, advise him about potential courses of action, collaborate with him in deciding upon the best course of action, and implement the course of action. This chapter discusses the process and techniques associated with these remaining functions of the overall counseling process.

§5.02 The Process of Legal Decision-Making

When counseling your client in decision-making, you and your client must address six largely interrelated questions:

1. *What is your client's factual and legal situation?*
2. *What are your client's objectives or goals?*
3. *What legal and non-legal options are available to your client for achieving his objectives?*
4. *What are the pros and cons and likely outcomes of each option?*
5. *Which option should your client choose? And,*
6. *How will the option chosen be implemented?*

Usually you and your client will have answered the first two questions in the initial interview. Often the answers to questions 3 through 6 will be developed during a series of meetings with your client. You will learn some answers through independent research and investigation, and you will develop other answers during conferences throughout the course of the representation.

In the actual counseling session, addressing these questions involves six corresponding tasks:

1. *Summarizing your client's factual and legal situation;*
2. *Refining and clarifying your client's objectives;*
3. *Identifying potential options for achieving your client's objectives;*
4. *Discussing the pros and cons of each option;*
5. *Helping your client decide which option to choose; and*
6. *Implementing your client's decision.*

As indicated above, these fundamental questions and tasks are largely interrelated. Although they may serve as a step-by-step agenda for the counseling session (which is the way they are treated in this chapter for instructive purposes), they are often addressed in a more loosely structured, free-flowing discussion between you and your client. During this discussion, there will be times when you will be advising your client, asking questions of him, and listening to him. Although most of the discussion should be "collaborative" in nature, there may be times when it will be appropriate for the discussion to be more "lawyer-centered" or "client-centered" (*see* §2.03[4]).

In addition, you must keep in mind throughout this decision-making process that the Rules of Professional Conduct specifically require you to do three things: (1) abide by your client's decisions concerning the objectives of the representation and consult with him as to the means by which they are to be pursued (*see* §6.03); (2) explain matters to your client to the extent reasonably necessary to permit him to make informed decisions regarding the representation (*see* §6.04); and (3) exercise independent professional judgment and render candid advice (*see* §6.05).

§5.03 Summarizing Your Client's Factual and Legal Situation

Usually, a good starting point at a decision-making conference is to summarize your client's factual and legal situation. This helps to set the stage for clarifying your client's objectives. You have to completely understand your client's objectives before you and your client can meaningfully consider potential options for achieving those objectives.

In summarizing your client's factual situation, be brief and focus on the key facts. There is no need to rehash his entire story. The summary should be objective and balanced in the sense that you should include unfavorable as well as favorable facts when applicable, and not skew the facts either for or against your client. If your client has strong feelings about his situation, include your understanding of them in the summary. The primary purposes of the summary are to (1) confirm your understanding of your client's overall situation, and (2) set the stage for putting his situation into its applicable legal context. At the end of the factual summary you might ask your client, "Is what I've described a fair summary of your situation?"

In addition, and just as briefly, describe how your client's factual situation fits into the law or applicable legal process. This is important so that your client can get a general understanding for how the law may enable or constrain his objectives. At this stage, it will often be sufficient to identify the legal context in very general terms (e.g., "In breach of contract cases, the law basically aims to put you in the same monetary position you would have been in had no breach occurred;" or "The lawsuit against you asks for money damages for the fair market value of the truck and physical and emotional injuries caused by the accident."). Remember that your main purpose at this point is to merely give your client a sense of the general area of the law or legal process that governs his situation. A more detailed explanation of the law may be appropriate when you and your client discuss the pros and cons of potential options for dealing with his situation.

§5.04 Refining and Clarifying Your Client's Objectives

After briefly summarizing your client's factual and legal situation, clarify your understanding of his overall objectives or goals. The question is, what does he want to accomplish? Although your client is likely to have given you at least a general sense of his objectives at the initial client meeting (*see* §3.06) or during a more in-depth interview, he may have changed his objectives or refined them since you last saw him. Moreover, in the interim, additional events may have occurred to cause him to revise his objectives. In most cases, you will be able to confirm what you learned from him in the earlier interview (e.g., "So, as I understand it, you would like to work out an agreement with your wife about child support—as in a 'separation agreement' that I just mentioned.").

The specificity of your client's objectives will, of course, depend upon the particular subject matter of the representation, the applicable law, and the number and types of decisions that need to be made. For example, while it is important to know that your client has the overall objective of working out an amicable agreement with his wife about child support, it will ultimately be necessary to be more specific about his objective in terms of the amount of child support he is willing to pay. The applicable law may largely shape this subsidiary objective (e.g., state-mandated child support guidelines). Similarly, if your client has the overall objective of entering into a new business relationship with a supplier of goods, he will need to clarify his objectives about the basic elements of a deal—e.g., quantity, price, and the time and method of delivery.

Thus, depending upon the particular nature of your client's situation and the decisions to be made, he may have multiple general objectives, and he may be unable to formulate more specific objectives until he has a greater understanding of the applicable law and his options. Accordingly, it will be necessary for you to help your client refine and clarify his objectives throughout the decision-making process.

§5.05 Identifying Potential Options for Achieving Your Client's Objectives

After your client's basic objectives have been confirmed or clarified, the next logical question is, what options are available to him for achieving these objectives? At this stage, the task is to identify all reasonably viable options that are (1) at least minimally consistent with your client's objectives, (2) personally acceptable to your client in the sense that he has not already ruled them out of bounds, and (3) not barred by law.[1] There is no reason to identify options that are merely "theoretically" possible but which are unrealistic under the circumstances. On the other hand, no realistic option should be overlooked, and it is important to identify all viable *non-legal* as well as legal options.

Unless your client has already listed potential options he has in mind (as might occur during the discussion about his objectives), you should take the lead in outlining the legal and non-legal options you believe may be viable. You should state these options briefly and in neutral terms. That is, reserve any discussion about the details of the options, their pros and cons, and their non-legal and legal ramifications until all options have first been identified. In listing the options that have occurred to you, you might simply say, "As I see it, you have three options: first, you can …; second, you could …; and third, you might be able to …" After providing your list, particularly if your client's situation might be addressed by non-legal solutions, you might ask him, "Have any other options occurred to you?"

§5.06 Discussing the Pros and Cons and Likely Outcomes of Each Option

Once your client's options have been identified, you and your client should discuss the pros and cons of each option and the likely outcomes of each. "Pros" and "cons" are essentially consequences that are considered either "good" or "bad," or desirable or undesirable. These consequences may be tangible or intangible, and they may affect the client or other persons. Of course, the relative weight to be accorded to any consequence will depend upon the likelihood that the consequence will occur. Thus, discussing the pros and cons of different options often involves considering a wide variety of tangible and intangible consequences affecting your client and others under circumstances where making predictions about the likelihood of those consequences may be quite difficult.

---

1. *See* Robert F. Cochran, Jr. et al., *The Counselor-At-Law: A Collaborative Approach to Client Interviewing and Counseling* 137–138 (1999) (referring to these factors as "minimal acceptance criteria").

In the overall process of discussing pros and cons, it is useful to keep four things in mind. First, you can focus the discussion by going over only one option at a time. In deciding which option to discuss first, you might choose one that your client came up with or one in which he has expressed particular interest. Otherwise, you might simply start with the first option you listed. In any event, try to discuss the various options separately rather than collectively.

Second, before getting into the pros and cons of an option, make sure that your client first has an adequate understanding of what the option entails. For example, you will usually have to provide a more detailed explanation of a legal option than a non-legal one. If the option involves the filing of a lawsuit, you will need to explain matters such as the legal claims that would be raised, the remedies that would be sought, and an overview of the pretrial process. If your client is charged with a crime and the option under discussion is a potential plea bargain, you will need to explain matters such as the charges against your client, the prosecution's burden of proof, your client's right to a jury trial, the process of entering into a guilty plea, and the specific elements of a possible bargain. In short, there can be no meaningful discussion about the pros and cons of an option unless the client understands what it involves.

Third, once you move to a discussion of the pros and cons of each option, don't hesitate to directly ask your client what "upsides" or "downsides," or "advantages" or "disadvantages" he sees about each option. In addition, in a highly complex case, it may sometimes be useful to ask your client to prepare a written list of pros and cons about various options in advance of your meeting,[2] or you might construct such a list with your client as you discuss each option at the meeting. However, the utility of this exercise will depend upon whether your client is intellectually inclined to think about pros and cons in a balance-sheet type of format. For many clients, this approach is artificial and unnecessarily time consuming.

Fourth, just as your client's situation and objectives may present non-legal as well as legal options, there may be non-legal as well as legal pros and cons to those options. In general, non-legal pros and cons affect your client in a variety of personal ways outside of the law, whereas legal pros and cons relate to the potential outcomes of your client's legal rights or remedies. The dis-

---

2. See David A. Binder, et al., *Lawyers As Counselors: A Client Centered Approach* 307–308 (1991); Robert F. Cochran, Jr., et al., *The Counselor-At-Law: A Collaborative Approach to Client Interviewing and Counseling* 146–147, 163–164 (1999).

tinction is important because your discussion of these different types of pros and cons involves somewhat different approaches.

[1] Discussing Non-Legal Pros and Cons

"Non-legal" pros and cons are consequences that tangibly or intangibly affect your client or others psychologically, socially, economically, and morally or ideologically. These consequences are usually highly personal and subjective, and they are frequently integral to a client's ultimate decision about which option to choose. For example, for various psychological, social, or moral reasons, a client charged with a serious crime may choose the option of going to trial rather than pleading guilty to a lesser charge under a plea bargain, even though the most likely outcome of the trial option is that he will be convicted on overwhelming evidence. Similarly, a client who has a strong case to recover substantial damages may choose to settle it for a much smaller sum rather than go to trial because of certain non-legal consequences of taking the case to trial.

In discussing non-legal pros and cons, you and your client should consider, as appropriate, how each option may affect his:

(1) Psychological interests:
- Level of anxiety or stress
- Self-esteem, self-respect, and self-image
- Need for recognition, status, power or authority
- Sense of personal satisfaction or well-being
- Willingness to take risks

(2) Social interests:
- Family, friends, co-workers, and other third persons
- Personal reputation
- Good will
- Past, present, and future interpersonal relationships

(3) Economic interests:
- Financial obligations for attorney's fees and litigation costs
- Financial security or credit rating
- Short-term or long-term profits
- Business or institutional efficiency
- Past, present, or future business relationships
- Loss of time at work

(4) Moral or ideological interests:
- Moral or philosophical principles
- Religious or political beliefs

- Sense of fairness or integrity
- Desire to promote or avoid precedent

Whether the effects of a particular option on any of these matters constitute a "pro" or a "con" is, of course, for your client to decide. In addition, he will often be in a better position than you to foresee the non-legal pros and cons that are likely to result from a particular option. Nevertheless, you can help your client identify these pros and cons by raising the ones that occur to you and by encouraging him to consider how each option may affect him in terms of the types of interests listed above.

[2] Discussing Legal Pros and Cons

"Legal" pros and cons are the most likely legal consequences of a particular option that affect your client or others. Generally speaking, a legal consequence that advances your client's objectives will fall within the "pro" column, and a legal consequence that undermines your client's objectives will fall within the "con" column. Here, unlike non-legal pros and cons, you are in a better position than your client to forecast the legal outcomes of an option and determine whether they will advance or undermine your client's objectives. After all, predicting legal consequences is a major part of giving "legal advice."

As mentioned previously, when a legal option is involved, you must first explain the legal process or legal principles pertinent to the option (e.g., the general process of asserting a claim, defending a lawsuit, or incorporating a business; or the legal principles underlying a particular cause of action, defense, or provision in a contract, etc.). When discussing the legal pros and cons of an option, whether a legal option or a non-legal one, you must also explain (1) the legal ramifications of the option in terms of its legal advantages and disadvantages, and (2) your best prediction about the legal outcome of the option.

When discussing a legal option, these explanations will often involve providing your client with an analysis of the overall merits of his case—i.e., how a jury, judge, administrative body, board or commission, or licensing agency is most likely to view the evidence and what the outcome of the particular legal proceeding or process is most likely to be. When a non-legal option is being discussed, pertinent legal consequences should be pointed out as well. For example if your client has been sued, the option of doing nothing in response to the suit (assuming that option might be viable under the circumstances) is likely to be that your client will incur a judgment by default, and if the judgment is not paid, your client's property may be at risk and credit rating may be impaired. Remember that regardless of whether you are discussing the legal pros and cons of a legal or non-legal option, you must explain the law in *plain English.*

When predicting the legal consequences of an option, you should never overstate or understate, or overestimate or underestimate, your prediction. Reasonably accurate predictions about legal outcomes, though often difficult to make, are critical to comparing options and arriving at a decision about the best option. Sometimes, a useful way to couch a prediction for your client, whether in litigation or transactional matters, is to state it in terms of a specific percentage (or range of percentages) of likelihood, rather than in vague terminology.

For example, if you couch your client's chances about a particular outcome as being "very good," "quite good," "pretty good," "either way," "not so good," "not very good," or "not good," your client may not understand what you really mean or may entirely misunderstand your assessment. On the other hand, some clients may have a better understanding of what you mean if you speak in terms of chances like "80%," "70%," "60%," "50–50," "40%," "30%," or "20%."

Along with expressing the likelihood of success in percentage terms, it may be useful to discuss a range of potential outcomes,[3] such as:

- *best possible*
- *best likely*
- *most likely*
- *worst likely*
- *worst possible*

For example, in a personal injury case, you might predict that the "most likely" outcome for your client at trial would be a verdict of approximately $100,000, that the "best likely" result would be twice that amount, and that the "worst likely" result would be $10,525.32 (representing the undisputed amount of his doctors' bills). Assuming that the case presents at least *plausible* "best possible" and "worst possible" outcomes, these might be mentioned as well; but there would be no need to mention them if those possibilities were purely theoretical. In predicting "best"-case or "worst"-case scenarios, these should also be described in percentage terms (e.g., "I think the best we could hope for is a verdict of about $200,000, but I would put only a one-in-four chance on that happening; on the other hand, I would say that the chances of recovering only your doctors' bills are even smaller, less than 10%."). The

---

3. *See also* David A. Binder, et al., *Lawyers as Counselors: A Client-Centered Approach* 339–340 (1991).

same technique may be used when making predictions about non-litigation matters (e.g., "I would say that the best likely result is that the City will just go ahead and grant your request to rezone to an R-1 district, but I would place only a 25% chance on that; the worst likely scenario is that the Council will prohibit your building altogether, but that's very unlikely—perhaps a 5% chance at most; and the most likely result is that they will allow you to build the building with a conditional use permit, which I would put at a 70% chance of happening.").

The legal outcomes of options are often difficult to predict because your bottom-line assessment depends upon making certain sub-predictions. For example, whether a jury is most likely to award $100,000 or $200,000 may largely depend upon whether the trial judge will admit or exclude certain evidence, or how the judge will rule on an unsettled question of law pertaining to damages. Similarly, whether a City will allow your client to build a day-care center in a particular zoning district may depend upon whether the State will first grant him a license to operate the proposed center. In these situations, you should *briefly* outline for your client the various factors and sub-predictions that relate to your overall assessment about the outcome of the option. After doing so, the best you might be able to say about the value of the case is that it is worth somewhere between $100,000 and $200,000, or that the chances of your client being able to build his day care center are a "toss up." In sum, when it is difficult for you to make a prediction about a legal consequence or outcome, you should not be afraid to explain why the prediction is difficult in light of the different factors, assumptions, and sub-predictions you have had to consider. Give your client the benefit of your best judgment, but, when applicable, don't hesitate to emphasize, "It all depends."

§5.07 Helping Your Client Decide Which Option to Choose

After you and your client have discussed the non-legal and legal pros and cons of each option, the question is, which option should your client choose? In theory, the best option is the one that is most likely to advance the greatest number of your client's objectives under circumstances where the non-legal and legal "pros" of the option outweigh the "cons." However, it is a mistake to suppose that choosing the best option is simply a process of tallying up the pros and cons of each option to identify the one that has the greatest number of advantages and least number of disadvantages. Different clients value and weigh pros and cons differently. Although most clients will consider the pros and cons of various options holistically and decide upon a best option in light of all the circumstances, some clients will choose one option over another solely because of some special value they place on one or more consequences of an option. Assuming your client fully understands his options and their pros and cons, you should respect the value preferences underlying his choice of a particular option.

On the other hand, if you believe your client is making a bad decision that is inconsistent with *his* values or objectives, don't hesitate to advise him against the decision and explain why. In this regard, it is entirely proper for you to discuss moral, economic, social and political considerations, as well as the law (*see* §6.05). Your client's decision about his options must be knowing, intelligent, and voluntary; and, as mentioned previously, you have an ethical obligation to "exercise independent professional judgment and render candid advice" (*see also* §6.05). Accordingly, if you believe your client is making a bad decision, you might go over his options and their pros and cons again to ensure that his decision is fully informed. In addition, if time is not of the essence, you might encourage your client to take some additional time to think through his options and meet with you again at a later time to make a final decision.

If your client is undecided about which option to choose, encourage him to "talk through" his options. Consider asking him questions such as:

- *Which option do you think will satisfy most of your objectives?*
- *Are there any particular upsides or downsides that you see about a particular option?*
- *All things considered, which option makes the most sense to you?*
- *Which option appears to be fairest to you?*
- *Which option do you think would be best for you in the short run, or in the long run?*
- *Is there anything about a particular option that concerns you most?*
- *Which option would most satisfy you personally?*
- *Is there any further information you would like to have before making a decision?*
- *Would you like to "sleep on the matter" for a while?*
- *Is there anyone else you would like to talk to before making a decision?*
- *Is there anything further that I can do to help you make your decision?*

The last of these questions will often prompt your client to ask, "If you were me, what would you do?" Indeed, clients ask this question without any prompting at all. How you handle it will largely depend on the particular decision to be made and whether you believe it calls for a more lawyer-centered, client-centered, or collaborative approach to counseling.

For example, as discussed in Section 2.03[4], if the decision relates to technical legal matters such as drafting, legal procedure, trial tactics or trial strategy, you might take a more lawyer-centered approach over the decision-making process and not hesitate to render an opinion about the best decision to make. On the other hand, if the decision involves matters such as whether to file a lawsuit, whether to accept a settlement offer, or whether your client should waive one or more of his "fundamental" rights in a criminal case, your response would have to be collaborative or client-centered in the sense that only your client can make the final decision on these matters. For example, if your client asks you what you would do when faced with the choice of pleading guilty or taking the case to trial, after fully discussing and advising him about the non-legal and legal pros and cons of the choices at hand, you might say:

> I understand why you are asking me what I would do if I were in your shoes. But this is a decision that affects your fundamental legal rights, and therefore only you can make it. I can help you think through this important decision by going over again its upsides and downsides and the various options available to you. But I hope you will understand that it would be unfair to you for me to try to speculate on what decision I would make when I will not be personally affected by it. Only you have the right to make this decision.

Then you might proceed by reviewing the pros and cons of the decision again or asking your client one or more of the questions listed above.

Lastly, if the decision relates to matters such as what offers or counteroffers to make in negotiations, what claims or defenses to raise in a lawsuit, or how to structure a transaction or new business enterprise, you might take a more middle-ground approach when responding to your client's question about what decision you would make. Here, you might strike a balance between making a directive and nondirective response by explaining which option you think would best satisfy your client's objectives and values, but at the same time pointing out that the final decision is for your client to make.

§5.08 Implementing Your Client's Decision

After your client has decided upon a course of action, you must continue to counsel him during the implementation of the decision. The Rules of Professional Conduct specifically require that you (1) "consult with [your] client as to the means by which [the objectives of the representation] are to be pursued" (*see* §6.03), and (2) "keep [your] client reasonably informed about the status of a matter [and] promptly comply with reasonable requests for information" (*see* §6.04).

For example, after your client has decided upon the substantive aspects of a will, contract, or other transactional matter, you will need to review with him all documents prepared in connection with the matter. If the representation involves litigation, you will need to counsel him throughout the discovery process, during settlement negotiations, when preparing for trial, throughout any trial of the case, and in connection with any appeal. In short, you have an obligation to keep your client reasonably informed about the status of the representation and appropriately counsel him about other decisions that need to be made in light of changed circumstances or new developments.

§5.09 Crisis Counseling

A prospective or existing client will sometimes call you in a situation that he perceives to be a crisis. For example, the client may have just been arrested and put in jail, served with a lawsuit, lost his job, been seriously injured, or separated from his wife. Events like these often constitute "crises" for clients because the immediate situation overwhelms them with such a degree of anxiety, fear, or anger that they become panic stricken or rendered virtually dysfunctional. When counseling a client in these circumstances, it is useful to keep three things in mind.

First, after your client has told you the nature of the crisis, you should calmly and confidently assure him that you will help him get through the crisis. Along with this reassurance, give him any necessary immediate advice to preserve the status quo and arrange to meet with him as soon as possible. For example, if your client has been arrested and is phoning you from jail, you might say:

> *… Okay, John, I understand what's happened. We can deal with this, but I need you to be patient for a little bit. I will come see you at the jail at 4:00 o'clock this afternoon, and we will be able to talk then about what we need to do to get you released. Don't worry if I'm not there exactly at 4:00; the jail has only three meeting rooms and there is sometimes a delay in getting an available room. In the meantime, don't talk with anyone about this matter, and don't call your sister about the bond. She won't know what to do at this point, and I can call her later to explain everything after you and I have met. Are you clear about the present plan?…. Okay, just hang in there, and I'll see you this afternoon.*

Second, when you meet with your client, you must be especially calm, patient, and understanding about his situation. This is a critical time to convey empathetic understanding (*see* § 4.02[1]). Let your client vent his emotions, if necessary; and keep in mind that the stress of the situation may make it very difficult for him to rationally explain and understand what has happened. Along with reassuring your client about your ability to help him, it is usually best to set out a specific course of action about what you and your client will do to protect his rights in the short run. For example, at the conclusion of the meeting with your client at the jail, you might say:

> *... So here's the plan, John. First, I will call your sister tonight to explain the situation and find out what she can do about helping with the bond. Second, I will call the U.S. Attorney tomorrow morning to discuss the bond situation and see if we can get your case before the magistrate first thing Monday morning. Third, I'll come see you again sometime tomorrow afternoon after I've talked with the U.S. Attorney. Finally, like I said before, I don't want you talking with anyone about this matter, and that includes talking about our plans for making bond. As for your sister, don't worry about her; I know what to say to her, and I think I will be able to calm her down before you see her. Do we have an agreement about the plan?*

Finally, in some crisis situations, your client's intellectual and emotional state may be impaired to the point that you believe he should be referred to a mental health professional or some other support agency or program. If this is the case, explain that his emotional affliction is not abnormal and that many people benefit from specialized counseling or support. If your client is amenable to a referral, advise him about a specific person or agency that he can call. Ideally, if your client consents, you should call the mental health professional or support agency yourself to make an appointment for your client. Often clients who are suffering from an emotional problem cannot find their way through a bureaucratic maze to schedule an appointment. Your help can facilitate the scheduling process.

§5.10 Illustration of Decision-Making Conference[4]

As shown in Section 4.10, Larry Odden held an initial meeting and interview with Clara Miles and agreed to represent her in a personal injury case.

---

4. This illustration is intended to show how a skilled attorney might handle a decision-making conference. Of course, however, you might conduct the conference quite differently

The day after the meeting, Clara called Larry and told him that John Jones was the name of the adjuster for her insurance company that paid for the property damage to her car. Larry obtained photos of the property damage to Clara's car from Jones and spoke with him about the company's investigation of the accident. Jones said that Ronald Smith, the driver of the pickup, called Jones a few weeks after the accident to say that he (Smith) had seen a doctor for neck strain following the accident. However, Jones said he has not heard anything further from Smith about his alleged injuries. Larry also met with Officer Boles and learned that Jane Smith, the passenger in the pickup truck, was Ronald Smith's wife, and that she corroborated Mr. Smith's story that he had a green light when he made his right-hand turn from Estes Drive onto Franklin Street. In addition, Larry has received a copy of Clara's chiropractic records from Dr. Byler.

Larry's secretary scheduled a follow-up appointment for Clara to meet with Larry. That office conference, after an exchange of greetings, proceeded as shown in the transcript below. (The footnotes in the transcript point out Larry's use of various techniques discussed in the preceding sections of this Chapter.)

1. L: Clara, I have obtained a copy of your medical records from Dr. Byler; and I've spoken with Officer Boles and Mr. Jones, the adjuster for your insurance company.

2. C: Okay.

3. L: I learned from Officer Boles that there were no independent eyewitnesses to the accident. But, he said that Jane Smith, the passenger in the pickup truck, is Mr. Smith's wife; and she, like her husband, says that Mr. Smith had a green light when he was turning from Estes onto Franklin.[5]

4. C: She's just saying that because her husband is saying that. But that's not what happened.

5. L: It just goes to show, once again, that there are two different stories about what happened.

---

and may even disagree with some of the approaches taken by the lawyer. Bear in mind that the lawyer's approach is, in significant respects, affected by his personal style and counseling philosophy. In addition, the lawyer's interaction with the client is significantly affected by the client's personality, demeanor, and body language—all of which are not readily apparent from a mere transcript.

5. From line 3 through 15, Larry summarizes and discusses Clara's factual situation (and how it points to a theory of negligence) based on additional information he has received from the officer.

6. C: Will this hurt my case? Before, it was Dan's word and my word against Mr. Smith; now it's two against two, our word against theirs. Does this mean I don't have a case?

7. L : No, it doesn't mean that. What Ms. Smith says really doesn't change matters much. From the beginning, there have been two versions about what happened—yours and Dan's on the one hand, and Mr. Smith's on the other. Mr. Smith either had a green light or he didn't. In any event, I'm beginning to develop a theory that Mr. Smith was at fault for the accident even if the light had just turned green before he started his turn.

8. C: Oh, what's that?

9. L: Well, I met with Officer Boles out at the accident scene. He showed me more exactly where each vehicle was positioned after the accident. What he told me was a little bit different from what was shown on his diagram in the accident report. So I took a photo of the intersection, and I had Officer Boles draw on it to show the positions of the vehicles as he saw them right after the accident. [Larry hands Clara the photo].

10. C: [Looking at the photo], What does this mean?

11. L: I'll explain; but first, what do you think about how he has drawn in the positions of the vehicles on the photo? Does that look right to you?

12. C: It looks right. But everything happened so fast that I didn't pay much attention to exactly where our car and the pickup were located in the road when the accident happened. Maybe Dan will know better.

13. L: Yes, I should talk with Dan at some point. But this is what Officer Boles would testify to [pointing to photo]. As you can see from his drawing on the photo, your car has basically cleared the intersection; it is actually through the intersection. If that's right, it means that even if the light on Franklin had turned from yellow to red at this point [indicating on photo], your car was almost completely through the intersection when the light was still yellow. It means that if your car were almost through the intersection when the light turned red on Franklin and green on Estes, Mr. Smith should have looked to see that he could make his turn safely and that your car had cleared the intersection. Do you see what I mean?

14. C: I think so … (pause).

15. L: Officer Boles also pointed out to me that, unlike many other traffic lights in town, when the light for traffic on Franklin turns to

red, the light for traffic on Estes turns to green after a one- or two-second delay. The bottom line is that, if your car was almost all the way through the intersection when your light turned red, Mr. Smith should not have started his right-hand turn until one or two seconds after the Franklin Street light turned red. At least, that's a good argument for us to a jury. Does that make sense?

16. C: Yes, now I see what you're saying. But, if what you are saying is right, why would we have to go to a jury?

17. L: Well, we may not have to. Having a jury decide the case will be necessary if the case can't be resolved by agreement, by a settlement that is satisfactory to you. In other words, if Mr. Smith's insurance company, All-Good Insurance, says they are unwilling to settle, or they make a final offer that you are unwilling to accept, then a jury will have to decide the case.

18. C: I really don't think I want to go through a trial, if at all possible.

19. L: Trial is certainly a last resort. It's very time consuming, and the costs can be expensive like I mentioned last time. It can also be stressful, and it can be risky ... (pause). I do want to talk with you today about your various options so we can decide where to go from here. But, perhaps as a starting point, can we talk a bit more about some of the concerns you talked about last time?[6]

20. C: Okay.

21. L: You mentioned last time that you want your life back, that all of this has been hard on you emotionally and financially, and that you're worried about your back in the long term. Is that a fair summary?

22. C: Yes, it is. I guess, also, I would like to resolve all of this quickly. It's been such a financial strain on us. And I think I've gone through a lot emotionally as well as physically, and I feel I should be compensated for all the stress. As for my back now, well, I don't think it's going to get any better. I guess I'll just have to manage to live with it. Do you think we might have a chance of settling this case quickly?

23. L: If All-Good Insurance is willing to discuss settlement right now—and that's an "if"—I think they would settle the case quickly only if they could settle it very cheaply.

---

6. Before discussing potential options, Larry seeks to clarify Clara's "objectives" and concerns, particularly as they relate to the emotional and financial impact of the accident and her concerns about her back in the long run (*see* line 21).

24. C: Why is that?

25. L: If you settle the case, you will have to sign a document called a release, which is a promise that you will not sue Mr. Smith and make any further claim for your injuries. Once you sign a release, that's good for Mr. Smith's insurance company because then they won't have to pay for any future treatment for your back or future pain and suffering that you may incur after the release is signed. Dr. Byler's last medical report says you have chronic pain in your back, and the report recommends that you see an orthopedic surgeon for an evaluation of possible permanent injury. She goes on to say in her report that she "suspects permanent injury." When All-Good sees that report, the company might want to settle cheaply because they know that, once you sign a release, they will be off the hook for paying greater damages for possible permanent injury and future pain and suffering.

26. C: Why don't we just tell them that I will have future pain and probably have permanent injury? Can't we ask for that too?

27. L: Not unless a physician makes a formal diagnosis that you, in fact, have a permanent injury and that you will likely have future pain and suffering.

28. C: Why is that?

29. L: In your case, Clara, there are three types of damages that the law allows. First, you are entitled to the reasonable medical expenses you have incurred, which, according to Dr. Byler's bills are now $2,500. Second, you are also entitled to reasonable compensation for past and present pain and suffering. There's no formula for that; it's thought of as an amount that a jury would reasonably award based on all of the circumstances. Finally, if you have a permanent injury, you are entitled to additional compensation for that permanency—depending upon the extent of the permanency—along with compensation for future pain and suffering and perhaps future medical expenses. But, the law says that all of these future damages cannot be speculative. There must be evidence, such as a formal diagnosis and prognosis from a doctor, that permanent injury exists and that you are most likely to incur future pain and suffering. Then, the future damages are not considered speculative and a person may be compensated for them.[7]

---

7. From line 29 through 37, Larry explains the law of damages as it relates to her injuries.

30. C: I don't know if I have permanent injury, but I do know that I still have a lot of pain in my back; and it's there almost all the time. Do you think it would help my case if I went to an orthopedic doctor?

31. L: Well, if a doctor says you have permanent injury, then you would be entitled to compensation for that permanency. But, whether you go to another doctor, Clara, is a decision that I believe you should make based solely on your personal feelings about your health. I always tell my clients that this type of decision is so highly personal that it's not something that should be decided based on any legal case. If you have permanent injury, as Dr. Byler is worried about, that is something you will have to live with long after this case is over, regardless of whether you receive any compensation for future damages.

32. C: Yeah, I recognize it's a personal decision. I'm very worried about my back. But I'm not sure what to do (pause ...). When you were talking about damages, can I get damages for all the stress I've been through? There have been a lot of times over the past year when I have been very depressed.

33. L: That depends. Has your depression been chronic or disabling?

34. C: No. I just get depressed now and then about not being a good enough mother and wife when my back is hurting real bad. I've just been generally stressed out, you know, by the whole situation.

35. L: Yes. I know it's been hard on you. And then you have the added stress of trying to work—

36. C: Yeah, this first month of working has been rough.

37. L: I can imagine ... (pause). Going back to your question about compensation for stress, the law in our State only allows compensation for emotional distress, as a separate type of damage, if the distress is very severe, such as chronic depression or a disabling emotional condition which may be generally diagnosed by a mental-health professional. So, I'm not really sure that what you've described to me fits into this rather narrow category of what our courts refer to as severe and disabling emotional distress. At the same time, however, all that you have gone through, not just the actual physical pain in your neck and back, generally falls within the overall category of pain and suffering, and I would want the other side to know about it.

38. C: Right. Well, what are my options at this point?

39. L: Well, as I see it, there are basically three options to consider. Without stating them in any particular order of preference, one option is to go ahead now and file a lawsuit to encourage settlement and get

the ball rolling if the case can't be settled. A second option is not to file a lawsuit now, but instead start negotiations with All-Good. A third option is to hold off on doing anything for now, to allow you some time to think about whether you want to see another doctor and to see whether your back condition changes over the next few months or so. There are certain pros and cons to each option.[8]

40. C: I'd really rather not sue and go to trial. Do we really have to do that?

41. L: No, that's just one option to think about. And I'm just referring to filing a suit, not going to trial anytime soon. There are certain advantages to filing now, but there are disadvantages as well. What concerns you most about this option?[9]

42. C: Well, wouldn't filing a suit make them angry so they might not want to settle? And then, if we sued, my husband would be dragged into all of this. I don't want him to have to deal with all of this if we can avoid it. He's told me he'll be supportive of me, but he doesn't really want to be involved or make a claim for himself like we talked about last time.

43. L: I really don't think that filing suit would hurt our chances of settling the case, and it might well encourage settlement by showing that we mean business. But, let's talk first about your concerns regarding Dan. How does he feel about you making a claim?

44. C: As I say, he's supportive of me, but ... (long pause). When he broke up with his former partner in the plumbing business, this former partner, Al, accused Dan of having stolen some money from the business, which isn't true. But I'm afraid the other side might find out about that and try to dig up dirt on Dan, to say he's just a thief and a bad person and that no one should believe him about how the accident happened.

45. L: How long ago was this accusation made?

46. C: About a year and a half ago.

47. L: Did this partner, Al, take any legal action or seek any criminal charges against Dan?

48. C: No. The whole thing has just fizzled away. Nothing has happened. But I wouldn't want to stir it all up again.

---

8. From line 39 through 95, Larry discusses various options for Clara and the relative pros and cons of these options.

9. Notice how Larry expressly asks Clara about her concerns regarding the lawsuit option.

49. L: I can understand that. If you filed a lawsuit, I think it is unlikely the other side would find out about this accusation by Al or care much about it unless Dan has some conviction for stealing money or some other conviction—

50. C: Dan has no criminal record. And the accusation is just hogwash.

51. L: Yes. Partnership breakups can sometimes be like marriage breakups—

52. C: Yeah, it was ugly.

53. L: Well, even though I don't think that any accusation by Dan's former partner would come up in your case, there is an important way in which Dan could become directly involved in your suit if we filed right away. If we filed suit, it's quite possible that Mr. Smith would immediately file a counter suit against your husband. When I spoke with Mr. Jones, he said Mr. Smith called him a few weeks after the accident because Smith had apparently gone to a doctor for treatment of strain in his neck. On the other hand, Jones says he has not heard anything further from Mr. Smith since that time. Even so, I think there is a good possibility that if we filed a suit, Mr. Smith would bring your husband into the case and make a cross claim against him for any injuries Smith sustained. Of course, even if we didn't file a lawsuit, Mr. Smith might still bring a suit against Dan at some point, although that suit, like any we file, would have to be filed within three years of the date of the accident.

54. C: If Dan were countersued, who would represent him?

55. L: Your insurance company would hire a lawyer to defend Dan and would pay for that defense.

56. C: Would they hire you?

57. L: No, they would get another lawyer.

58. C: I don't really see any advantages to filing a lawsuit right away.

59. L: The main advantage is that it would show All-Good from the get-go that we are very serious about your claim. If I merely contact All-Good and start negotiations, the adjuster for All-Good may well say that he or she is not interested in talking because Mr. Smith insists he had the green light and was not negligent. On the other hand, if we file a lawsuit, All-Good would know that we mean business and would have to hire a lawyer to defend Mr. Smith. After some initial discovery in the case—some initial sharing of information between both sides—All-Good might then become more interested in talking about a possible settlement before spending a whole lot of money in defending the suit at a trial ...

60. C: (Interrupting), What if we first tried to negotiate with All-Good; and then, if they said they were not interested in talking, we go ahead and file a suit?

61. L: That's another option. It's the usual approach taken in a personal injury case, particularly when there is no dispute about who was at fault in the accident. I would prepare a document called a settlement brochure to send to All-Good. The brochure summarizes the facts of the case and your damages, such as your course of medical treatment, your pain and suffering, and any permanent injury and future pain and suffering. The brochure attaches a copy of the accident report along with your medical records and bills, and concludes with a demand—a specific request for money—to settle the case. After the adjuster reviews the brochure, he or she will make a counteroffer. And then further offers and counteroffers are made until one side makes a final offer. When a final offer is on the table, the case is either settled or it's not. And if it's not, your option is to file a lawsuit to ask a jury to decide the case.

62. C: Why don't we just do a settlement brochure?

63. L: We could. But if we do that at this time, we would not be able to make a solid claim for any permanent injury because we don't yet know whether a doctor would diagnose you as having a permanent injury. If, after settlement negotiations are underway, we found out that you in fact have permanent injury, it would be difficult for us to say to All-Good, "Look, we misjudged our initial demand, and we are now making a new demand that is greater than our first one." In other words, good-faith negotiations on our part will require some compromise by gradually reducing our initial demand, not by increasing it. If we lose credibility with All-Good, they are likely to cut off negotiations altogether.

64. C: So, why would filing a lawsuit right now be better?

65. L: It might be better, but that depends on how you weigh its upsides and downsides. The downside, from what we've been talking about, is that it may well bring Dan into the lawsuit as a defendant, rather than as just a witness to the accident. The upside is that All-Good would know that we are very serious in taking this case to trial if necessary. In recent years, All-Good has tended to take a "low-ball" approach to settlement negotiations in non-catastrophic personal injury cases. They know that most claimants don't have much money to pay for the costs of a trial, and that most people would rather get a smaller sum of money in their pockets than go through all the time,

stress, and expense of getting a larger sum at trial. So, All-Good's perception about how serious we are about going to trial is critical to their decisions about how much to offer in settlement.

66. C: I see. But if we file a lawsuit right now, we still wouldn't know if I have any permanent injury. Could we still ask for that in a suit?

67. L: Yes; we could. We could allege in a suit that we believe you may have permanent injury in light of Dr. Byler's latest report, which raises that issue. But what she has said isn't, by itself, sufficient proof of permanent injury because no definitive diagnosis of permanency has been made. You see, if we file a lawsuit right away, I don't expect settlement discussions to start right away. Instead, over the next five months or so, the other side would want to take your deposition, your husband's deposition, and officer Boles's deposition. There would also be time for you to see a doctor about any permanent injury or need for further treatment, if you chose to do that. And if that doctor said you had permanent injury, he or she would be deposed as well—

68. C: What's a deposition?

69. L: A deposition is a way of finding out the testimony of a witness. For example, if they wanted to take Officer Boles's deposition, I and the lawyer for Mr. Smith would arrange a time when Boles would come to this office so that Smith's lawyer could ask him questions about his investigation of the accident. A stenographer would be present who would transcribe all of the questions and answers given in the deposition. That way, the other side will know what Boles's testimony will be.

70. C: And, when would we start negotiations?

71. L: Negotiations might start during the deposition phase, but most likely they would take place in earnest during mediation. Our courts require that all cases of this type go through non-binding mediation well before trial. Once the lawyers believe they have enough information to evaluate the case, a mediator is selected, and a time is arranged for the parties and their lawyers to meet to seriously discuss settlement. The mediator tries to bring the parties together. It's a required process, but it's informal and takes place in a conference room like this. If the case doesn't settle, it proceeds to trial.

72. C: Do you think we would have good chance of settling this case at mediation?

73. L: Statistically speaking, I would say yes, because the majority of lawsuits do settle that way. From what we know about your case now, Officer Boles's testimony about the position of the vehicles is

important on the negligence question; and by the time of mediation, the other side would know his testimony from having taken his deposition. On the question of damages, once again, the issue of whether you have any permanent injury is quite important. This brings me to our third option—

74. C: You mean seeing another doctor before we do anything—

75. L: Yes. How do you feel about that?

76. C: I don't know. I was hoping we could settle the case pretty quickly, which would help out Dan and me financially. And I don't know how I would pay to see another doctor … (pause).

77. L: I thought you had some health insurance through Dan's plumbing business.

78. C: We did. But we couldn't afford to keep up the payments on it, so we dropped it sometime last April. It wasn't any good anyway for my injury because it wouldn't cover the chiropractic bills. We still keep insurance for Tommy, but Dan and I don't have any health insurance at this time.

79. L: I see … (pause). I am very sympathetic to your financial situation, Clara, but I don't think you can count on any guaranteed settlement of this case to help you out financially. It's a close case; and, at least at the beginning, there's a real chance that All-Good will decline to make any settlement offer at all for the simple reason that their insured, Mr. Smith, insists he had a green light. All-Good also knows, and it is important for you and me to keep in mind, that we are in a contributory negligence state. Under our law, that means that even if a jury were to believe that Mr. Smith was mostly at fault for the accident, if the jury also believes that Dan was somehow at fault, even in the slightest way, you would not be entitled to recover any damages at all from Mr. Smith. Most states don't have this harsh law, but we do.

80. C: It sounds bad for us, doesn't it—

81. L: Well, I don't want to create false hopes for you; and, at the same time I don't want to sound overly pessimistic. All I am saying is that, from what I know now, the case could go either way. We would have to prove by the greater weight of the evidence that Mr. Smith was negligent, and he would have to prove that Dan was contributorily negligent. Both sides would be taking a risk in front of a jury. And when there are risks for both sides, those risks tend to encourage compromise and settlement. I believe in your case, and I'll stand by you. Although there are no guarantees, my best judgment is that this

case can be settled in the end, although it may take some time to get to that point.

82. C: Do you think you might be able to get All-Good to make the payments for me to see another doctor?

83. L: I'm quite sure they won't do that in your case. But if you decide to consult another doctor—and, again, this is a decision that I think you should make solely on a personal level—I can get you up to $1,500 to use for paying another doctor.

84. C: How's that?

85. L: When I talked with Mr. Jones, I asked him whether you had a medical payments provision on your automobile insurance policy, and it turns out that you do. It has a limit of $2,000, which is available to you for medical bills for treatment of injuries in an auto accident regardless of how the accident happened. Dr. Byler's bills show that your unpaid balance to her is $500. So, you could use $500 of the $2,000 to pay off Dr. Byler, and that would leave you up to $1,500 to pay another doctor.

86. C: Oh, I didn't know that! But wouldn't your firm take a one-third fee out of the $2,000?

87. L: No, we wouldn't do that. This money is automatically available to you if you incur medical bills for an auto accident. Like a lot of other people, you just didn't know you had this benefit. So, no, we wouldn't take any fee out of the $2,000.

88. C: I see. Thank you. But what doctor should I see?

89. L: I don't think it would be appropriate for me to recommend a particular doctor, because I'm not one. But, it seems to me that if you make a personal decision to see another doctor, perhaps you could call Tommy's pediatrician, Dr. Partin, and ask her whom she might recommend. Didn't she recommend someone before?

90. C: Yes, and I had forgotten the name of the person she had recommended. I do remember, though, that the doctor she mentioned was an orthopedic specialist.

91. L: Well, that's the kind of doctor that Dr. Byler recommends in her last medical report. She's another person you could ask for a possible referral.

92. C: Yeah, that's a good idea. And how would I arrange to have my new doctor's bills paid out of my medical payments policy?

93. L: You could have the doctor's office just send the bills to my office and I'll pass them on to Mr. Jones. Or you could do that yourself. Jones will then write a check directly to the doctor's office. And if you

want to pay off Dr. Byler's remaining bill now, I can send the bill to Mr. Jones and he'll send her a check for the $500.

94. C: Would you do that?

95. L: Consider it done.

96. C: Larry, I'm basically feeling better about all of this. And I now think it makes sense for me to see if another doctor can help me. At least I will have some money to pay for that. But, can you tell me what you think I might be able to settle this case for, looking down the road?[10]

97. L: Do you mean, as things stand right now?

98. C: Yes, not taking into account what another doctor would say, because we don't know anything about that now—

99. L: Well, as we sit here today, if there were no dispute about negligence, I would estimate the value of the case to be in the $12,000 to $15,000 range in terms of what a jury would award. But, because it's a close case on negligence and contributory negligence, I think it's basically a toss-up about how a jury would decide who was at fault. In other words, there's a 50% chance you would get between $12,000 and $15,000, and a 50% chance you would get nothing. So I would discount the settlement value of the case by 50%, and that makes a settlement value of approximately $7,000. And that figure assumes you have not incurred any litigation costs.

100. C: Even $15,000 sounds somewhat low for what I've been through.

101. L: It is. But, generally, these cases don't result in high damage awards. Juries usually have difficulty sympathizing with neck and back pain unless it is very debilitating or the collision was very severe. It's hard for juries to put a value on an injury they can't see. It's hard for them to understand that, although you look healthy, you are in constant pain. Also, many juries are skeptical about medical treatment from chiropractors. On the other hand, I think a jury would like you, and they would listen carefully to all you've gone through. You must remember that my current evaluation of your case is based on only what I know now. There are many other factors.

102. C: It still doesn't seem like much money. But, you said it might be different if my back turns out to be a long-term problem—

---

10. At lines 96 through 103, Larry provides Clara with his best assessment of the case based on what he knows now, which does not include any information about possible permanent injury (*see also* line 107).

103. L: Yes. That can be a significant factor depending upon what a doctor says, particularly an orthopedic surgeon … (pause). You know, Clara, I've had many clients tell me that, in the end, they basically wouldn't trade any amount of money for what they've gone through. That's hard for people to believe who haven't suffered through an injury, but it's what many clients say.

104. C: Yeah, I sort of feel that way too.

105. L: Well … (pause), do you think you might want to consult with another doctor?

106. C: Yes; I'm pretty definite about that now. Do you think we should just wait on the results of that before we do anything else?

107. L: Yes, that's my best judgment. After we know more about your back situation, we will be in a better position to factor that into your overall case. And, perhaps another doctor will be able to provide you with some further treatment to help you.

108. C: After I see another doctor, what should we do?

109. L: That will depend, of course, on what your doctor says. If your doctor recommends further treatment—physical therapy, for example—you will have to decide whether you want to go through that. If your doctor says that there's really nothing more he or she can do and makes a final diagnosis, then there's no reason to delay proceeding with your case. At that point, a decision would have to be made about whether it would be best to file a lawsuit right away or start negotiations by making a demand through a settlement brochure. Fortunately, from the standpoint of protecting your legal rights, we are not faced with any deadline on your case at this time. The latest we would have to file a lawsuit to preserve your claim would be three years from the date of the accident. That would be February 8, two years from now.

110. C: If I end up having to go to physical therapy or get some other treatment, what about my time off from work?

111. L: As part of personal injury damages, the law entitles you to be compensated for your gross wages lost during the times you have to take off from work to undergo treatment. This applies regardless of whether you use paid sick leave or vacation time from your work. Gross wages consist of your gross hourly pay rate, before taxes and other deductions. It's another element of damages, like expenses for medical treatment.

112. C: I really don't want all of this to drag on too long. And I'm still sort of scared about filing a lawsuit, at least right away, because of how it might drag Dan into the suit … (pause).

113. L: How we proceed and when we proceed is ultimately your decision, Clara. Your desire to move this case along and not drag Dan into it are completely legitimate concerns. I can try to help you by giving you the best advice I can about your options and their pros and cons. And I want you to know that I will support you in any decision you make. There is no right or wrong to these decisions.[11]

114. C: I know now that I want to call Dr. Partin to get a referral to another doctor. I'm going to do that. But, after that, I'm really not sure about what route to take.

115. L: Perhaps this will help: I suggest that we don't have to decide that right now. If you call Dr. Partin and see another doctor, we will know more about your situation in the next two or three weeks. Then we can see where we are, discuss matters again, and plan a next step. At some point I will still need to talk with Dan about the details of the accident. And, if you want, I can also talk with him a bit about his concerns about Al and any consequences about your filing a lawsuit if we end up taking that route later on. How does that sound?[12]

116. C: I'm comfortable with that. I think that's a good plan for now.

117. L: Okay. So, why don't you give me a call after you've talked with Dr. Partin and decided on seeing another doctor. We can just keep in touch by phone for now. And, of course, please feel free to call me at any time if you have a question or want to discuss anything further in the meantime. Is that okay?

118. C: Yes, that's a good plan. Thank you, Larry. I'll call you after I talk with Dr. Partin.

119. L: You're welcome. It was nice to see you again. I'll look forward to hearing from you.

---

11. Notice how Larry expressly acknowledges that whether and how to proceed with the case (*i.e.*, the objectives of the representation, *see* §6.03) are ultimately for Clara to decide.

12. Notice how a concrete plan is formulated at the conclusion of the conference.

Chapter Six

Ethical Considerations in Counseling

SYNOPSIS

§6.01 Introduction

In 1983, the House of Delegates of the American Bar Association adopted the Model Rules of Professional Conduct (Model Rules) to replace the Model

Code of Professional Responsibility that had been adopted by the ABA in 1969. Most jurisdictions have adopted the Model Rules, in whole or in part, as the professional standards for lawyers. The Rules are "partly obligatory and disciplinary and partly constructive and descriptive in that they define a lawyer's professional role."[1] If a lawyer fails to comply with an obligation or prohibition imposed by the Rules, he may be subject to discipline. In addition, even though a violation of the Rules does not, by itself, establish a cause of action for malpractice,[2] noncompliance with the Rules may well give rise to such a claim.[3]

As part of your professional role as an attorney, there are a number of Rules that are particularly pertinent to the overall attorney-client relationship and counseling functions discussed in the preceding chapters. The Preamble to the Rules provides:

> As a representative of clients, a lawyer performs various functions. As advisor, a lawyer provides a client with an informed understanding of the client's legal rights and obligations and explains their practical implications. As advocate, a lawyer zealously asserts the client's position under the rules of the adversary system. As negotiator, a lawyer seeks a result advantageous to the client but consistent with requirements of honest dealings with others. As an evaluator, a lawyer acts by examining a client's legal affairs and reporting about them to the client or to others.

This Chapter discusses the most important Model Rules pertaining to your counseling role in establishing the attorney-client relationship, advising the client, representing clients who are under a disability, and serving as an intermediary between clients. Also discussed are other Rules that address some of the most common issues about client representation such as preserving confidential information, determining conflicts of interest, setting attorney's fees,

---

1. Model Rules at *Scope*.

2. *Astarte, Inc. v. Pacific Indus. Systems, Inc.*, 865 F. Supp. 693 (D. Colo. 1994); *Nagy v. Beckley*, 578 N.E.2d 1134, *appeal denied*, 584 N.E.2d 131 (Ill. 1991); *Lazy Seven Coal Sales, Inc. v. Stone & Hinds, P.C.*, 813 S.W.2d 400 (Tenn. 1991); *McNair v. Rainsford*, 499 S.E.2d 448 (S.C. App. 1998).

3. *See generally*, Munneke & Davis, *The Standard of Care in Legal Malpractice: Do the Model Rules of Professional Conduct Define It?*, 22 J. Legal. Prof. 233 (1998); Note, The Evidentiary Use of the Ethics Codes in Legal Malpractice: Erasing a Double Standard, 109 Harv. L. Rev. 1102 (1996); *Restatement (Third) of the Law Governing Lawyers* § 52(2) and cmt. f (2000).

declining or terminating representation, and dealing with persons other than your client.[4]

§6.02 Establishing the Attorney-Client Relationship

Because a lawyer not only represents clients but also is "an officer of the legal system and a public citizen having special responsibility for the quality of justice,"[5] many of the prescriptions and proscriptions contained in the Model Rules relate to a lawyer's responsibilities beyond the mere context of the attorney-client relationship.[6] Most of the ethical rules relating to counseling, however, presuppose the existence of an attorney-client relationship. Even so, it is essential to remember that your ethical responsibilities and fiduciary duties under the Rules will be triggered once a person consults you about a legal matter even if no employment relationship later arises. For example, if you give wholly gratuitous legal advice to another person, you will be held to the same standard of care as if you were formally employed.[7] In addition, your duty to preserve confidential communications (*see* §6.07) extends to any initial consultation between you and a prospective client even if you do not end up representing the client.[8]

The existence and establishment of the attorney-client relationship is a question of fact that is primarily governed by principles of contract and agency law. Usually, the relationship arises upon the client's request that you act on his behalf and your agreement to do so.[9] That is, the relationship typically arises

---

4. The Model Rules contain numerous other ethical prescriptions and proscriptions regarding the lawyer's professional role that are beyond the scope of this book. For example, Rules 3.1–3.9 address the lawyer's role as "Advocate;" Rules 5.1–5.7 set out the responsibilities of "Law Firms and Associations;" Rules 6.1–6.5 address the lawyer's "Public Service" role; Rules 7.1–7.6 address "Information about Legal Services;" and Rules 8.1–8.5 deal with "Maintaining the Integrity of the Profession."

5. Model Rules at *Preamble [1]*.

6. *See, e.g.*, Rules 4.1–4.4 (Transactions with Persons Other Than Clients); Rules 6.1–6.5 (Public Service); Rules 7.1–7.6 (Information about Legal Services); Rules 8.1–8.5 (Maintaining the Integrity of the Profession).

7. *See* Franko v. Mitchell, 762 P.2d 1345 (Ariz. App. 1988).

8. Model Rule 1.18; ABA Comm. On Ethics and Professional Responsibility, Formal Opinion 90-358 (1990); Nolan v. Foreman, 65 F.2d 738, *reh'g denied*, 671 F.2d 1380 (5th Cir. 1982); Westinghouse Electric Corp. v. Kerr-McGee Corp., 580 F.2d 1311 (7th Cir. 1978).

9. Anderson v. Pryor, 537 F. Supp. 890 (W.D. Mo. 1982); Committee on Professional Ethics and Grievances v. Johnson, 447 F.2d 169 (3d Cir. 1971).

when you expressly agree to take the case or agree to advise the client.[10] However, the existence of the relationship does not depend upon any formality such as a written agreement or the payment of a retainer.[11] The relationship may otherwise be established based on conduct from which an agreement to represent may be reasonably inferred or implied, including consideration of all of the facts and circumstances bearing on the reasonableness of the client's subjective belief that the relationship was established.[12]

Given that the attorney-client relationship might be implied from the surrounding circumstances in the absence of an express agreement, lawyers have been particularly cautioned about rendering legal advice in informal settings. For example, it has been said that because "[i]t is quite possible that courts may predicate an attorney-client relationship on casually rendered advice, [a]ttorneys would therefore be wise to avoid giving advice at cocktail parties, in building corridors, over the backyard fence, and at civic organization meetings."[13] The establishment of an attorney-client relationship by implication may also arise when a prospective client meets with you at your office for an initial consultation or you give legal advice over the telephone. In these situations, if you perceive there may be any misunderstanding about your decision not to represent the prospective client, confirm your non-representation in a letter by registered or certified mail.[14] Even if you send a letter confirming your non-representation, information revealed to you in earlier conversations and the advice you gave still remain protected by the attorney-client relationship and may *not* be disclosed by you to anyone without the prospective client's permission.

---

10. *See* Hunt v. Disciplinary Board, 381 So.2d 52 (Ala. 1980).

11. *See* Hashemi v. Shack, 609 F. Supp. 391 (S.D. N.Y. 1984); United States v. Constanzo, 625 F.2d 465 (3d Cir. 1980); Guillebeau v. Jenkins, 355 S.E.2d 453 (Ga. App. 1987).

12. *See In re* McGlothlen, 63 P.2d 1330 (Wash. 1983); United States v. Constanzo, 625 F.2d 465 (3d Cir. 1980); *In re* Petrie, 742 P.2d 796 (Ariz. 1987); Hashemi v. Shack, 609 F. Supp. 391 (S.D. N.Y. 1984); Kurtenbach v. Tekippe, 260 N.W.2d 53 (Iowa 1977). On the other hand, some courts insist that the attorney-client relationship does not exist in the absence of an express contract. *See, e.g.,* Pontiff v. Behrens, 518 So.2d 23 (La. App. 1987); Holland v. Lawless, 623 P.2d 1004 (N.M. App. 1981).

13. Friedman, *The Creation of the Attorney-Client Relationship: An Emerging View*, 22 Cal. W.L. Rev. 209, 220 (1986).

14. *See* Mayo v. Engel, 733 F.2d 807 (11th Cir. 1984).

§6.03 Establishing the Scope of the Representation

Model Rule 1.2 addresses your counseling responsibilities in conferring with your client about matters affecting the representation. In addition, the Rule speaks to your counseling responsibilities when your client is engaging in, or proposes to engage in, conduct that you know is criminal or fraudulent, or your client calls upon you to act in a way that would violate the Rules of Professional Conduct.

Rule 1.2 provides:

(a) Subject to paragraphs (c) and (d), a lawyer shall abide by a client's decisions concerning the objectives of representation and, as required by Rule 1.4, shall consult with the client as to the means by which they are to be pursued. A lawyer may take such action on behalf of the client as is impliedly authorized to carry out the representation. A lawyer shall abide by a client's decision whether to settle a matter. In a criminal case, the lawyer shall abide by the client's decision, after consultation with the lawyer, as to a plea to be entered, whether to waive jury trial and whether the client will testify.

(b) A lawyer's representation of a client, including representation by appointment, does not constitute an endorsement of the client's political, economic, social or moral views or activities.

(c) A lawyer may limit the scope of the representation if the limitation is reasonable under the circumstances and the client gives informed consent.

(d) A lawyer shall not counsel a client to engage, or assist a client, in conduct that the lawyer knows is criminal or fraudulent, but a lawyer may discuss the legal consequences of any proposed course of conduct with a client and may counsel or assist a client to make a good faith effort to determine the validity, scope, meaning or application of the law.

The relevant portions of the Comment to these provisions provides:

[1] Paragraph (a) confers upon the client the ultimate authority to determine the purposes to be served by legal representation, within the limits imposed by law and the lawyer's professional obligations. The decisions specified in paragraph (a), such as whether to settle a civil matter, must also be made by the client. See Rule 1.4(a)(1) for

the lawyer's duty to communicate with the client about such decisions. With respect to the means by which the client's objectives are to be pursued, the lawyer shall consult with the client as required by Rule 1.4(a)(2) and may take such action as is impliedly authorized to carry out the representation.

[2] On occasion, however, a lawyer and a client may disagree about the means to be used to accomplish the client's objectives. Clients normally defer to the special knowledge and skill of their lawyer with respect to the means to be used to accomplish their objectives, particularly with respect to technical, legal and tactical matters. Conversely, lawyers usually defer to the client regarding such questions as the expense to be incurred and concern for third persons who might be adversely affected. Because of the varied nature of the matters about which a lawyer and client might disagree and because the actions in question may implicate the interests of a tribunal or other persons, this Rule does not prescribe how such disagreements are to be resolved. Other law, however, may be applicable and should be consulted by the lawyer. The lawyer should also consult with the client and seek a mutually acceptable resolution of the disagreement. If such efforts are unavailing and the lawyer has a fundamental disagreement with the client, the lawyer may withdraw from the representation. See Rule 1.16(b)(4). Conversely, the client may resolve the disagreement by discharging the lawyer. See Rule 1.16(a)(3).

[3] At the outset of a representation, the client may authorize the lawyer to take specific action on the client's behalf without further consultation. Absent a material change in circumstances and subject to Rule 1.4, a lawyer may rely on such an advance authorization. The client may, however, revoke such authority at any time.

[4] In a case in which the client appears to be suffering diminished capacity, the lawyer's duty to abide by the client's decisions is to be guided by reference to Rule 1.14....

[6] The scope of services to be provided by a lawyer may be limited by agreement with the client or by the terms under which the lawyer's services are made available to the client. When a lawyer has been retained by an insurer to represent an insured, for example, the representation may be limited to matters related to the insurance coverage. A limited representation may be appropriate because the client has limited objectives for the representation. In addition, the terms upon which representation is undertaken may exclude specific means that might otherwise be used to accomplish the client's objectives. Such

limitations may exclude actions that the client thinks are too costly or that the lawyer regards as repugnant or imprudent.

[7] Although this Rule affords the lawyer and client substantial latitude to limit the representation, the limitation must be reasonable under the circumstances. If, for example, a client's objective is limited to securing general information about the law the client needs in order to handle a common and typically uncomplicated legal problem, the lawyer and client may agree that the lawyer's services will be limited to a brief telephone consultation. Such a limitation, however, would not be reasonable if the time allotted was not sufficient to yield advice upon which the client could rely. Although an agreement for a limited representation does not exempt a lawyer from the duty to provide competent representation, the limitation is a factor to be considered when determining the legal knowledge, skill, thoroughness and preparation reasonably necessary for the representation. See Rule 1.1....

[9] Paragraph (d) prohibits a lawyer from knowingly counseling or assisting a client to commit a crime or fraud. This prohibition, however, does not preclude the lawyer from giving an honest opinion about the actual consequences that appear likely to result from a client's conduct. Nor does the fact that a client uses advice in a course of action that is criminal or fraudulent of itself make a lawyer a party to the course of action. There is a critical distinction between presenting an analysis of legal aspects of questionable conduct and recommending the means by which a crime or fraud might be committed with impunity.

[10] When the client's course of action has already begun and is continuing, the lawyer's responsibility is especially delicate. The lawyer is required to avoid assisting the client, for example, by drafting or delivering documents that the lawyer knows are fraudulent or by suggesting how the wrongdoing might be concealed. A lawyer may not continue assisting a client in conduct that the lawyer originally supposed was legally proper but then discovers is criminal or fraudulent. The lawyer must, therefore, withdraw from the representation of the client in the matter. See Rule 1.16(a). In some cases, withdrawal alone might be insufficient. It may be necessary for the lawyer to give notice of the fact of withdrawal and to disaffirm any opinion, document, affirmation or the like. See Rule 4.1....

[12] Paragraph (d) applies whether or not the defrauded party is a party to the transaction. Hence, a lawyer must not participate in a

transaction to effectuate criminal or fraudulent avoidance of tax liability. Paragraph (d) does not preclude undertaking a criminal defense incident to a general retainer for legal services to a lawful enterprise. The last clause of paragraph (d) recognizes that determining the validity or interpretation of a statute or regulation may require a course of action involving disobedience of the statute or regulation or of the interpretation placed upon it by governmental authorities.

[13] If a lawyer comes to know or reasonably should know that a client expects assistance not permitted by the Rules of Professional Conduct or other law or if the lawyer intends to act contrary to the client's instructions, the lawyer must consult with the client regarding the limitations on the lawyer's conduct. See Rule 1.4(a)(5).

The mandate of Rule 1.2(a) that you must "abide" by your client's decisions concerning the objectives of the representation but only "consult" with him about the means by which they are to be pursued reflects a distinction between ends and means, whereby decisions about the ends are to be controlled by the client but decisions about the means may generally be controlled by you.[15] That is, decisions about the objectives of the representation, the ultimate resolution of the case, or matters affecting "substantive" or "fundamental" rights of the client are to be made by the client and pursued by you unless those objectives (1) fall outside the scope of the representation agreed upon between you and your client, (2) involve criminal or fraudulent conduct, or (3) call upon you to violate a rule of professional conduct. Consultation with your client is, of course, required to identify his objectives;[16] and you are also usually required to take all necessary actions consistent with those objectives even if not specifically requested by your client.[17] This obligation to abide by your client's objectives extends to adhering to his decision to cease pursuing a previously sought objective.[18]

---

15. *See* Blanton v. Womancare Clinic Inc., 696 P.2d 645 (Cal. 1985); Graves v. Taggares Co., 616 P.2d 1223 (Wash. 1980); Stricklan v. Koella, 546 S.W.2d 810 (Tenn. App. 1976).

16. *See, e.g., In re* Comstock, 664 N.E.2d 1165 (Ind. 1996) (failure to oppose motions to dismiss without consulting client).

17. *See, e.g., In re* Moore, 494 S.E.2d 804 (S.C. 1997) (duty to protect client's interests even though client did not specifically instruct lawyer to do so).

18. *See, e.g.,* Red Dog v. State, 625 A.2d 245 (Del. 1993) (lawyer must respect client's decision to forego further appeals and accept death penalty); Burton v. Mottolese, 835 A.2d 998 (Conn. 2003) (lawyer cannot continue to litigate case after clients instructed her to stop).

The client's right to control decisions directly affecting his "substantive" or "fundamental" rights is particularly important in criminal cases due to constitutional prescriptions under the fifth and sixth amendments to the United States Constitution. For example, the defendant has the right to decide whether to plead guilty, waive trial by jury, testify on his own behalf, represent himself, assert a particular defense, or appeal a conviction.[19] Your duty is to fully advise the defendant of all pertinent legal and practical ramifications affecting his decisions about these matters.[20]

On the other hand, in contrast to decisions about the objectives of the representation or matters affecting constitutional rights of the client, you generally have the right to control the means of the representation such as tactics, trial strategy, and the procedural aspects of the case.[21] Nevertheless, under Rule 1.2(a) and Rule 1.4(a)(2), you still have a mandatory duty to consult with your client about these matters. In situations where you and your client disagree about the means for achieving the client's objectives, most courts will uphold your authority to make unilateral decisions about tactical or procedural matters even in the face of your client's objections[22] so long as those decisions do not affect a substantial right or interest of the client. For example, you generally may decide which witnesses to call at trial, which motions to file, how to cross-examine, and how to select the jury.[23] On the other hand, your client's consent is usually necessary when stipulating to facts that will foreclose an essential

---

19. Jones v. Barnes, 463 U.S. 745 (1983); United States v. Boyd, 86 F.3d 719 (7th Cir. 1996); State v. Debler, 856 S.W.2d 641 (Mo. 1993); People v. Colon, 600 N.Y.S.2d 377 (N.Y. App. Div. 1997). *But see* People v. Williams, 72 Cal. Rptr. 58, 62 (Cal. 1998) ("Except for a handful of express constitutional rights that are deemed particularly 'fundamental' and personal, defense counsel is fully authorized to waive rights of constitutional dimension, directly by express waiver or indirectly by not raising an objection or making a particular motion.").

20. *See* Strickland v. Washington, 46 U.S. 688 (1984); United States v. Teague, 953 F.2d 1525 (11th Cir. 1992); United States v. Goodwin, 531 F.2d 347 (6th Cir. 1976); Herring v. Estelle, 491 F.2d 125 (5th Cir. 1974); Caruso v. Zelinski, 689 F.2d 438 (3d Cir. 1982).

21. Blanton v. Womancare Clinic Inc., 696 P.2d 645 (Cal. 1985); United States v. Boyd, 86 F.3d 719 (7th Cir. 1996); State v. Davis, 506 A.2d 86 (Conn. 1986).

22. *See, e.g.,* Nahhas v. Pacific Greyhound Lines, 13 Cal. Rptr. 299 (Cal. App. 1961); United States v. Clayborne, 509 F.2d 473 (D.C. Cir. 1974); People v. Schultheis, 638 P.2d 8 (Colo 1981); *In re* King, 336 A.2d 195 (Vt. 1975). *But see* State v. Ali, 407 S.E.2d 183 (N.C. 1991) (in the event of a disagreement about a tactical decision, the client's wishes must control in accordance with the principal-agent nature of the relationship).

23. *See* Graves v. McKenzie, 68 P.2d 769 (Cal. 1983); State v. Davis, 506 A.2d 86 (Conn. 1986); *In re* King, 336 A.2d 195 (Vt. 1975).

claim or defense,[24] when deciding what claims or defenses to assert,[25] and when deciding whether to appeal and the scope of the appeal.[26]

Rule 1.2(c) allows you to limit the scope of your representation to certain matters and exclude others. For example, you and your client might agree that you will handle the trial of the case but not the appeal,[27] or that you will represent him on a specific transaction, but not assume any duties beyond determining the legal sufficiency of documents involved in that transaction.[28] However, when limiting the scope of your representation, you are obligated to consult with and obtain the consent of your client; and your representation cannot be limited in a way that would materially impair the client's rights or diminish your professional obligations, such as your duty to advise your client of important legal rights ancillary to the overall subject matter of the representation.[29]

You may violate the prohibition in Rule 1.2(d) against counseling the client to engage, or assisting the client, in conduct that you know is criminal or fraudulent if you fail to inquire into your client's objectives when it would be reasonable to do so.[30] That is, you will not be excused from assisting your client's unlawful or fraudulent conduct if you acted without appropriately investigating whether your advice or actions might aid him in perpetrating a fraud or in otherwise committing a crime.[31] If, after reasonable inquiry, you believe that your client expects assistance not permitted by the Rules of Professional Conduct, Rule 1.4(a)(5) requires you to advise your client regarding the relevant ethical limitations on your conduct so that he can make an informed decision

---

24. *See* Linsk v. Linsk, 449 P.2d 760 (Cal. 1969).

25. *See* Boyd v. Brett-Major, 499 So.2d 952 (Fla. App. 1984); Orr v. Knowles, 337 N.W.2d 699 (Neb. 1983).

26. *See* Hawkeye-Security Insurance Co. v. Indemnity Insurance Co., 260 F.2d 361 (10th Cir. 1958); State v. Pence, 488 P.2d 1177 (Hawaii 1971); *In re* Grubbs, 403 P.2d 260 (Okla. Crim. App. 1965).

27. *See, e.g.,* Florida Bar v. Dingle, 220 So.2d 9 (Fla. 1969); Young v. Bridwell, 437 P.2d 686 (Utah 1968).

28. *See, e.g.,* Grand Isle Campsites, Inc. v. Cheek, 249 So.2d 268 (La. App. 1971), *modified*, 262 So.2d 350 (La. 1972).

29. *See, e.g.,* Greenwich v. Markhoff, 650 N.Y.S.2d 704 (App. Div. 1996) (even though retainer agreement purported to limit scope of representation to workers' compensation claim, lawyer had duty to advise client of potential personal injury action).

30. *See, e.g.,* Harrell v. Crystal, 611 N.E.2d 908 (Ohio App. 1992) (lawyer failed to properly investigate clients' investments and individuals involved when advising clients on tax shelters); People v. Zelinger, 504 P.2d 68 (Colo. 1972) (lawyer failed to inquire whether car given to lawyer for fee was stolen).

31. *See* ABA Com. on Ethics and Professional Responsibility, Informal Op. 1470 (1981).

about how to lawfully pursue his objectives.[32] If your client then continues to insist on pursuing an unlawful objective or a lawful objective by unlawful means, you should withdraw from the representation (*see* §6.11).

Rule 1.2(d), however, expressly allows you to "counsel or assist a client to make a good faith effort to determine the validity, scope, meaning or application of the law." This means that you will not violate the prohibition against assisting your client in unlawful conduct by giving advice on a doubtful question concerning conduct later found to be criminal or fraudulent. It is not unethical to advise a client about a legal position that you believe can be supported by a good-faith argument for an extension, modification, or reversal of existing law, so long as there is at least some realistic possibility that the position will be successful.[33] For example, if your client seeks legal representation after having been told that a city ordinance prohibits certain parades or demonstrations on public property and your investigation and legal research show that there is a good faith argument that the ordinance is unconstitutional, you should first explain the prohibitions of the ordinance to your client, and then advise him why you believe the ordinance is unconstitutional and the chances of a successful challenge to the ordinance.

§6.04 The Duties of Competence, Diligence, and Communication

It should be obvious that in representing a client you must act competently and diligently, and adequately communicate with your client. These quintessential requirements of proper client representation are set out separately in the Model Rules. The Comments to these Rules aptly summarize their meaning and scope.

[1] Competence

Model Rule 1.1 provides: "A lawyer shall provide competent representation to a client. Competent representation requires the legal knowledge, skill, thoroughness and preparation reasonably necessary for the representation."

The Comment to this Rule explains:

---

32. *See* People v. Doherty, 945 P.2d 1380 (Colo. 1997).

33. *See* ABA Comm. On Ethics and Professional Responsibility, Formal Op. 85-352 (1985).

[1] In determining whether a lawyer employs the requisite knowledge and skill in a particular matter, relevant factors include the relative complexity and specialized nature of the matter, the lawyer's general experience, the lawyer's training and experience in the field in question, the preparation and study the lawyer is able to give the matter and whether it is feasible to refer the matter to, or associate or consult with, a lawyer of established competence in the field in question. In many instances, the required proficiency is that of a general practitioner. Expertise in a particular field of law may be required in some circumstances.

[2] A lawyer need not necessarily have special training or prior experience to handle legal problems of a type with which the lawyer is unfamiliar. A newly admitted lawyer can be as competent as a practitioner with long experience. Some important legal skills, such as the analysis of precedent, the evaluation of evidence and legal drafting, are required in all legal problems. Perhaps the most fundamental legal skill consists of determining what kind of legal problems a situation may involve, a skill that necessarily transcends any particular specialized knowledge. A lawyer can provide adequate representation in a wholly novel field through necessary study. Competent representation can also be provided through the association of a lawyer of established competence in the field in question.

[3] In an emergency a lawyer may give advice or assistance in a matter in which the lawyer does not have the skill ordinarily required where referral to or consultation or association with another lawyer would be impractical. Even in an emergency, however, assistance should be limited to that reasonably necessary in the circumstances, for ill-considered action under emergency conditions can jeopardize the client's interest.

[4] A lawyer may accept representation where the requisite level of competence can be achieved by reasonable preparation. This applies as well to a lawyer who is appointed as counsel for an unrepresented person ...

[5] Competent handling of a particular matter includes inquiry into and analysis of the factual and legal elements of the problem, and use of methods and procedures meeting the standards of competent practitioners. It also includes adequate preparation. The required attention and preparation are determined in part by what is at stake; major litigation and complex transactions ordinarily require more extensive treatment than matters of lesser complexity and consequence ...

[2] Diligence

Model Rule 1.3 provides that "[a] lawyer shall act with reasonable diligence and promptness in representing a client." The Comment to the Rules provides in part:

[1] A lawyer should pursue a matter on behalf of a client despite opposition, obstruction or personal inconvenience to the lawyer, and take whatever lawful and ethical measures are required to vindicate a client's cause or endeavor. A lawyer must also act with commitment and dedication to the interests of the client and with zeal in advocacy upon the client's behalf. A lawyer is not bound, however, to press for every advantage that might be realized for a client. For example, a lawyer may have authority to exercise professional discretion in determining the means by which a matter should be pursued. See Rule 1.2. The lawyer's duty to act with reasonable diligence does not require the use of offensive tactics or preclude the treating of all persons involved in the legal process with courtesy and respect.

[2] A lawyer's work load must be controlled so that each matter can be handled competently.

[3] Perhaps no professional shortcoming is more widely resented than procrastination. A client's interests often can be adversely affected by the passage of time or the change of conditions; in extreme instances, as when a lawyer overlooks a statute of limitations, the client's legal position may be destroyed. Even when the client's interests are not affected in substance, however, unreasonable delay can cause a client needless anxiety and undermine confidence in the lawyer's trustworthiness. A lawyer's duty to act with reasonable promptness, however, does not preclude the lawyer from agreeing to a reasonable request for a postponement that will not prejudice the lawyer's client.

[4] Unless the relationship is terminated as provided in Rule 1.16, a lawyer should carry through to conclusion all matters undertaken for a client. If a lawyer's employment is limited to a specific matter, the relationship terminates when the matter has been resolved. If a lawyer has served a client over a substantial period in a variety of matters, the client sometimes may assume that the lawyer will continue to serve on a continuing basis unless the lawyer gives notice of withdrawal. Doubt about whether a client-lawyer relationship still exists should be clarified by the lawyer, preferably in writing, so that the client will not mistakenly suppose the lawyer is looking after the client's

affairs when the lawyer has ceased to do so. For example, if a lawyer has handled a judicial or administrative proceeding that produced a result adverse to the client and the lawyer and the client have not agreed that the lawyer will handle the matter on appeal, the lawyer must consult with the client about the possibility of appeal before relinquishing responsibility for the matter. See Rule 1.4(a)(2). Whether the lawyer is obligated to prosecute the appeal for the client depends on the scope of the representation the lawyer has agreed to provide to the client. See Rule 1.2....

[3] Communication

Model Rule 1.4 provides:

(a) A lawyer shall:

(1) promptly inform the client of any decision or circumstance with respect to which the client's informed consent, as defined in Rule 1.0(e), is required by these Rules;

(2) reasonably consult with the client about the means by which the client's objectives are to be accomplished;

(3) keep the client reasonably informed about the status of the matter;

(4) promptly comply with reasonable requests for information; and

(5) consult with the client about any relevant limitation on the lawyer's conduct when the lawyer knows that the client expects assistance not permitted by the Rules of Professional Conduct or other law.

(b) A lawyer shall explain a matter to the extent reasonably necessary to permit the client to make informed decisions regarding the representation.

The Comment to this Rule provides:

[1] Reasonable communication between the lawyer and the client is necessary for the client effectively to participate in the representation.

[2] If these Rules require that a particular decision about the representation be made by the client, paragraph (a)(1) requires that the lawyer promptly consult with and secure the client's consent prior to taking action unless prior discussions with the client have

resolved what action the client wants the lawyer to take. For example, a lawyer who receives from opposing counsel an offer of settlement in a civil controversy or a proffered plea bargain in a criminal case must promptly inform the client of its substance unless the client has previously indicated that the proposal will be acceptable or unacceptable or has authorized the lawyer to accept or to reject the offer. See Rule 1.2(a).

[3] Paragraph (a)(2) requires the lawyer to reasonably consult with the client about the means to be used to accomplish the client's objectives. In some situations—depending on both the importance of the action under consideration and the feasibility of consulting with the client—this duty will require consultation prior to taking action. In other circumstances, such as during a trial when an immediate decision must be made, the exigency of the situation may require the lawyer to act without prior consultation. In such cases the lawyer must nonetheless act reasonably to inform the client of actions the lawyer has taken on the client's behalf. Additionally, paragraph (a)(3) requires that the lawyer keep the client reasonably informed about the status of the matter, such as significant developments affecting the timing or the substance of the representation.

[4] A lawyer's regular communication with clients will minimize the occasions on which a client will need to request information concerning the representation. When a client makes a reasonable request for information, however, paragraph (a)(4) requires prompt compliance with the request, or if a prompt response is not feasible, that the lawyer, or a member of the lawyer's staff, acknowledge receipt of the request and advise the client when a response may be expected. A lawyer should promptly respond to or acknowledge client communications.

[5] The client should have sufficient information to participate intelligently in decisions concerning the objectives of the representation and the means by which they are to be pursued, to the extent the client is willing and able to do so. Adequacy of communication depends in part on the kind of advice or assistance that is involved. For example, when there is time to explain a proposal made in a negotiation, the lawyer should review all important provisions with the client before proceeding to an agreement. In litigation a lawyer should explain the general strategy and prospects of success and ordinarily should consult the client on tactics that are likely to result in significant expense or to injure or coerce others. On the other hand, a lawyer ordinarily will

not be expected to describe trial or negotiation strategy in detail. The guiding principle is that the lawyer should fulfill reasonable client expectations for information consistent with the duty to act in the client's best interests, and the client's overall requirements as to the character of representation. In certain circumstances, such as when a lawyer asks a client to consent to a representation affected by a conflict of interest, the client must give informed consent, as defined in Rule 1.0(e).

[6] Ordinarily, the information to be provided is that appropriate for a client who is a comprehending and responsible adult. However, fully informing the client according to this standard may be impracticable, for example, where the client is a child or suffers from diminished capacity. See Rule 1.14. When the client is an organization or group, it is often impossible or inappropriate to inform every one of its members about its legal affairs; ordinarily, the lawyer should address communications to the appropriate officials of the organization. See Rule 1.13. Where many routine matters are involved, a system of limited or occasional reporting may be arranged with the client.

[7] In some circumstances, a lawyer may be justified in delaying transmission of information when the client would be likely to react imprudently to an immediate communication. Thus, a lawyer might withhold a psychiatric diagnosis of a client when the examining psychiatrist indicates that disclosure would harm the client. A lawyer may not withhold information to serve the lawyer's own interest or convenience or the interests or convenience of another person. Rules or court orders governing litigation may provide that information supplied to a lawyer may not be disclosed to the client. Rule 3.4(c) directs compliance with such rules or orders.

The duty to communicate with your client is personal. Thus, the obligation is not satisfied by delegating responsibility for communicating to a subordinate, whether another lawyer, paralegal, or secretary.[34] Similarly, communicating with persons other than the client instead of directly with the client does not fulfill the obligation.[35]

The duty of communication also extends to notifying your client about your failure to act, whether that failure was the result of incompetence, lack

---

34. Mays v. Neal, 938 S.W.2d 830 (Ark. 1997); *In re* Galabasini, 786 P.2d 971 (Ariz. 1990).

35. *In re* Dreier, 671 A.2d 455 (D.C. 1996).

of diligence, or a disagreement with him about an appropriate course of action.[36] It has been held that if your failure to act would give rise to a legal malpractice claim, you have a duty to promptly notify your client about the possibility of such a claim.[37] If the failure to act was due to your belief that continuing the representation would result in violating the Rules of Professional Conduct, you must appropriately notify your client of this fact and may not simply abandon the representation without following appropriate procedures for withdrawal.[38]

§6.05 Advising the Client

Adequately advising your client is, of course, central to your counseling function. In your role as advisor, Model Rule 2.1 provides that "[i]n representing a client, a lawyer shall exercise independent professional judgment and render candid advice. In rendering advice, a lawyer may refer not only to law but to other considerations such as moral, economic, social and political factors, that may be relevant to the client's situation."

The Comment to this Rule instructively provides:

[1] A client is entitled to straightforward advice expressing the lawyer's honest assessment. Legal advice often involves unpleasant facts and alternatives that a client may be disinclined to confront. In presenting advice, a lawyer endeavors to sustain the client's morale and may put advice in as acceptable a form as honesty permits. However, a lawyer should not be deterred from giving candid advice by the prospect that the advice will be unpalatable to the client.

[2] Advice couched in narrow legal terms may be of little value to a client, especially where practical considerations, such as cost or effects on other people, are predominant. Purely technical legal advice, therefore, can sometimes be inadequate. It is proper for a lawyer to refer to relevant moral and ethical considerations in giving advice. Although a lawyer is not a moral advisor as such, moral and ethical con-

---

36. *In re* Hyde, 950 P.2d 806 (N.M. 1997); *In re* Brousseau, 697 A.2d 1079 (R.I. 1997); *In re* Glee, 472 S.E.2d 615 (S.C. 1996).

37. *See* Tallon v. Committee on Professional Standards, 447 N.Y.S.2d 50 (1982); *In re* Higginson, 64 N.E.2d 732 (Ind. 1996); Florida Bar v. Bazley, 597 So.2d 796 (Fla. 1992).

38. People v. Doherty, 945 P.2d 1380 (Colo. 1997); Florida Bar v. King, 664 So.2d 925 (Fla. 1995); State v. Batista, 492 N.W.2d 354 (Wis. App. 1992).

siderations impinge upon most legal questions and may decisively influence how the law will be applied.

[3] A client may expressly or impliedly ask the lawyer for purely technical advice. When such a request is made by a client experienced in legal matters, the lawyer may accept it at face value. When such a request is made by a client inexperienced in legal matters, however, the lawyer's responsibility as advisor may include indicating that more may be involved than strictly legal considerations.

[4] Matters that go beyond strictly legal questions may also be in the domain of another profession. Family matters can involve problems within the professional competence of psychiatry, clinical psychology or social work; business matters can involve problems within the competence of the accounting profession or of financial specialists. Where consultation with a professional in another field is itself something a competent lawyer would recommend, the lawyer should make such a recommendation. At the same time, a lawyer's advice at its best often consists of recommending a course of action in the face of conflicting recommendations of experts.

[5] In general, a lawyer is not expected to give advice until asked by the client. However, when a lawyer knows that a client proposes a course of action that is likely to result in substantial adverse legal consequences to the client, the lawyer's duty to the client under Rule 1.4 [Communication] may require that the lawyer offer advice if the client's course of action is related to the representation. Similarly, when a matter is likely to involve litigation, it may be necessary under Rule 1.4 to inform the client of forms of dispute resolution that might constitute reasonable alternatives to litigation. A lawyer ordinarily has no duty to initiate investigation of a client's affairs or to give advice that the client has indicated is unwanted, but a lawyer may initiate advice to a client when doing so appears to be in the client's interest.

Like the duty to communicate, the duty to advise your client is personal and therefore may not be delegated to someone else. The obligation extends to personally interviewing your client.[39] Generally, you should apprise your

---

39. *See In re* Pinkins, 213 B.R. 818 (E.D. Mich. 1997) (unethical for lawyer to use legal assistant to screen clients to see whether they are eligible for bankruptcy protection); Michigan Informal Ethics Opinion RI-128 (1992) (unethical for initial client interviews to be conducted by assistant with result that lawyer sometimes performed legal paperwork without ever having met client).

client of the full implications of a proposed course of action, and this includes giving candid advice about whether it would be undesirable for him to pursue a particular course of action, even if it is not illegal or morally wrong.[40] In addition, you have a duty to advise your client of all potential courses of action that are reasonably pertinent to the subject matter of the representation.[41]

In exercising "independent professional judgment" under Rule 2.1, it has been said that "[e]motional detachment is essential to the lawyer's ability to render competent legal services."[42] Thus, a number of jurisdictions categorically prohibit a lawyer from having a sexual relationship with the client during the representation,[43] and the ABA has taken the position that a "lawyer shall not have sexual relations with a client unless a consensual sexual relationship existed between them when the client-lawyer relationship commenced."[44]

Apart from exercising independent professional judgment and rendering candid advice, Rule 2.1 encourages, but does not require, you to incorporate pertinent moral, economic, social and political considerations in your advice. For example, in an appropriate case, your advice might include perspectives on how a course of action might be sensitive to preserving racial harmony or gender equity,[45] or your advice might even include a discussion of moral considerations grounded in theology[46] so long as your religious beliefs are not forced upon the client.[47] A few courts have specially commented on the desir-

---

40. *See* Summit, Rovins & Feldesman v. Fonar Corp., 623 N.Y.S.2d 245 (N.Y. Sup. Ct. App. Div. 1995) (lawyer failed to predict and explain likelihood that corporate strategy would not succeed); Dobris, Ethical Problems for Lawyers upon Trust Terminations: Conflict of Interest, 38 U. Miami L. Rev. 1, 62–63 (1983) ("a lawyer has an affirmative duty to inform the client if she believes that the proposal is improper or unwise, even if it is not illegal or morally wrong.").

41. *See* Nichols v. Keller, 19 Cal. Rptr. 601 (Ct. App. 1993) (even though attorney was hired to pursue workers' compensation claim, he had duty to advise client of potential damages claim against third parties).

42. ABA Comm. On Ethics and Professional Responsibility, Formal Op. 92-364 (1992).

43. *See, e.g.,* Bourdon's Case, 565 A.2d 1052 (N.H. 1989); Okla. Bar Ass'n. Legal Ethics Comm. Op. 308 (1994).

44. Model Rule 1.8(j).

45. *See generally,* Hing, *In the Interest of Racial Harmony: Revisiting the Lawyer's Duty to Work for the Common Good,* 47 Stan. L. Rev. 901 (1995).

46. *See generally,* Symposium, 27 Tex. Tech. L. Rev. 911 (1996) (essays by lawyers from diverse religious backgrounds describing how they reconcile their professional life with their faith); Beggs, *Laboring Under the Sun: An Old Testament Perspective on the Legal Profession,* 28 Pac. L. J. 257 (1996).

47. *See* Tennessee Formal Ethics Op. 96-F-140 (1996) (lawyer opposed to abortion on religious grounds may not pressure client into foregoing right not to first discuss the abortion

ability of counseling a client about "fairness" considerations when entering into a prenuptial agreement,[48] and the unique opportunity that a lawyer may have in a drunk driving case to urge a problem drinker to receive treatment.[49]

§6.06 Representing a Client Who Is under a Disability

A client may be under a disability or suffer from a form of diminished capacity that seriously affects his decision-making capacity due to a variety of reasons such as alcohol or drug addiction, depression, senility, retardation, or insanity. In representing a client afflicted by a disability or diminished capacity, Model Rule 1.14 provides:

> (a) When a client's capacity to make adequately considered decisions in connection with a representation is diminished, whether because of minority, mental impairment or for some other reason, the lawyer shall, as far as reasonably possible, maintain a normal client-lawyer relationship with the client.
>
> (b) When the lawyer reasonably believes that the client has diminished capacity, is at risk of substantial physical, financial or other harm unless action is taken and cannot adequately act in the client's own interest, the lawyer may take reasonably necessary protective action, including consulting with individuals or entities that have the ability to take action to protect the client and, in appropriate cases, seeking the appointment of a guardian ad litem, conservator or guardian.
>
> (c) Information relating to the representation of a client with diminished capacity is protected by Rule 1.6. When taking protective action pursuant to paragraph (b), the lawyer is impliedly authorized under Rule 1.6(a) to reveal information about the client, but only to the extent reasonably necessary to protect the client's interests.

The Comment to this Rule provides:

> [1] The normal client-lawyer relationship is based on the assumption that the client, when properly advised and assisted, is capable of

---

with her parents); Florida Bar v. Johnson, 511 So.2d 295 (Fla. 1987) (lawyer disciplined for bullying client with threats that God would visit misfortunes on client).

48. *See In re* Marriage of Foran, 834 P.2d 1081 (Wash. App. 1992).

49. *See* Friedman v. Commissioner of Public Safety, 473 N.W.2d 828 (Minn. 1991).

making decisions about important matters. When the client is a minor or suffers from a diminished mental capacity, however, maintaining the ordinary client-lawyer relationship may not be possible in all respects. In particular, a severely incapacitated person may have no power to make legally binding decisions. Nevertheless, a client with diminished capacity often has the ability to understand, deliberate upon, and reach conclusions about matters affecting the client's own well-being. For example, children as young as five or six years of age, and certainly those of ten or twelve, are regarded as having opinions that are entitled to weight in legal proceedings concerning their custody. So also, it is recognized that some persons of advanced age can be quite capable of handling routine financial matters while needing special legal protection concerning major transactions.

[2] The fact that a client suffers a disability does not diminish the lawyer's obligation to treat the client with attention and respect. Even if the person has a legal representative, the lawyer should as far as possible accord the represented person the status of client, particularly in maintaining communication.

[3] The client may wish to have family members or other persons participate in discussions with the lawyer. When necessary to assist in the representation, the presence of such persons generally does not affect the applicability of the attorney-client evidentiary privilege. Nevertheless, the lawyer must keep the client's interests foremost and, except for protective action authorized under paragraph (b), must look to the client, and not family members, to make decisions on the client's behalf.

[4] If a legal representative has already been appointed for the client, the lawyer should ordinarily look to the representative for decisions on behalf of the client. In matters involving a minor, whether the lawyer should look to the parents as natural guardians may depend on the type of proceeding or matter in which the lawyer is representing the minor. If the lawyer represents the guardian as distinct from the ward, and is aware that the guardian is acting adversely to the ward's interest, the lawyer may have an obligation to prevent or rectify the guardian's misconduct. See Rule 1.2(d).

[5] If a lawyer reasonably believes that a client is at risk of substantial physical, financial or other harm unless action is taken, and that a normal client-lawyer relationship cannot be maintained as provided in paragraph (a) because the client lacks sufficient capacity to communicate or to make adequately considered decisions in con-

nection with the representation, then paragraph (b) permits the lawyer to take protective measures deemed necessary. Such measures could include: consulting with family members, using a reconsideration period to permit clarification or improvement of circumstances, using voluntary surrogate decisionmaking tools such as durable powers of attorney or consulting with support groups, professional services, adult-protective agencies or other individuals or entities that have the ability to protect the client. In taking any protective action, the lawyer should be guided by such factors as the wishes and values of the client to the extent known, the client's best interests and the goals of intruding into the client's decisionmaking autonomy to the least extent feasible, maximizing client capacities and respecting the client's family and social connections.

[6] In determining the extent of the client's diminished capacity, the lawyer should consider and balance such factors as: the client's ability to articulate reasoning leading to a decision, variability of state of mind and ability to appreciate consequences of a decision; the substantive fairness of a decision; and the consistency of a decision with the known long-term commitments and values of the client. In appropriate circumstances, the lawyer may seek guidance from an appropriate diagnostician.

[7] If a legal representative has not been appointed, the lawyer should consider whether appointment of a guardian ad litem, conservator or guardian is necessary to protect the client's interests. Thus, if a client with diminished capacity has substantial property that should be sold for the client's benefit, effective completion of the transaction may require appointment of a legal representative. In addition, rules of procedure in litigation sometimes provide that minors or persons with diminished capacity must be represented by a guardian or next friend if they do not have a general guardian. In many circumstances, however, appointment of a legal representative may be more expensive or traumatic for the client than circumstances in fact require. Evaluation of such circumstances is a matter entrusted to the professional judgment of the lawyer. In considering alternatives, however, the lawyer should be aware of any law that requires the lawyer to advocate the least restrictive action on behalf of the client.

[8] Disclosure of the client's diminished capacity could adversely affect the client's interests. For example, raising the question of diminished capacity could, in some circumstances, lead to proceedings for involuntary commitment. Information relating to the representa-

tion is protected by Rule 1.6. Therefore, unless authorized to do so, the lawyer may not disclose such information. When taking protective action pursuant to paragraph (b), the lawyer is impliedly authorized to make the necessary disclosures, even when the client directs the lawyer to the contrary. Nevertheless, given the risks of disclosure, paragraph (c) limits what the lawyer may disclose in consulting with other individuals or entities or seeking the appointment of a legal representative. At the very least, the lawyer should determine whether it is likely that the person or entity consulted with will act adversely to the client's interests before discussing matters related to the client. The lawyer's position in such cases is an unavoidably difficult one.

[9] In an emergency where the health, safety or a financial interest of a person with seriously diminished capacity is threatened with imminent and irreparable harm, a lawyer may take legal action on behalf of such a person even though the person is unable to establish a client-lawyer relationship or to make or express considered judgments about the matter, when the person or another acting in good faith on that person's behalf has consulted with the lawyer. Even in such an emergency, however, the lawyer should not act unless the lawyer reasonably believes that the person has no other lawyer, agent or other representative available. The lawyer should take legal action on behalf of the person only to the extent reasonably necessary to maintain the status quo or otherwise avoid imminent and irreparable harm. A lawyer who undertakes to represent a person in such an exigent situation has the same duties under these Rules as the lawyer would with respect to a client.

[10] A lawyer who acts on behalf of a person with seriously diminished capacity in an emergency should keep the confidences of the person as if dealing with a client, disclosing them only to the extent necessary to accomplish the intended protective action. The lawyer should disclose to any tribunal involved and to any other counsel involved the nature of his or her relationship with the person. The lawyer should take steps to regularize the relationship or implement other protective solutions as soon as possible. Normally, a lawyer would not seek compensation for such emergency actions taken.

When representing a client who is under a form of diminished capacity, you will find Rule 1.14(a) to be largely uninstructive because it merely prescribes that "the lawyer shall, as far as reasonably possible, maintain a normal client-lawyer relationship with the client." The "normal client-lawyer relationship" referred to in the provision is defined by Rule 1.2(a) (*see* §6.03) as one in which the lawyer "shall abide by a client's decisions concerning the objectives of representation."[50] The difficult questions you will face are (1) how to determine whether and to what extent your client is under a disability;[51] and (2) if the client appears to be under a disability, whether you should act as an "advocate" and nevertheless try to abide by the client's decisions regarding the objectives of the representation, or whether you should seek the appointment of a guardian or take some other protective action under Rule 1.14(b) in the "best interest" of the client. Scholars have hotly debated whether the lawyer should serve as an advocate for his client or as a paternal protector for his client's interests.[52]

When the client's capacity or competence is in serious question, one commentator points out that there are six potential choices available to you: (1) presume the client's competence and honor his decisions about lawful objectives regardless of the consequences; (2) seek to persuade the client to make "better" choices about his objectives; (3) seek unofficial consent from a family member or close friend of the client to take protective action on the client's behalf; (4) proceed as a *de facto* guardian for the client; (5) seek the formal appointment of a guardian for the client; or (6) withdraw from the representation.[53] The choice that may be most appropriate in a particular situation will, of course, depend upon the nature and severity of your client's disability and the overall circumstances of the representation.

The choice of presuming your client's competence and honoring his decisions regardless of the consequences may run afoul of your duty as an advisor under Rule 2.1 to exercise "independent professional judgment" and render "candid" advice in connection with the representation (*see* §6.05). In addition, this option may violate your duty under Rule 1.14(b) to protect your client's interests if you reasonably believe that he cannot adequately act in his

---

50. *See In re* M.R., 638 A.2d 1274 (N.J. 1994).

51. *See generally*, Anderer, *A Model for Determining Competency in Guardianship Proceedings*, 7 Mental Health & Physical Disability L. Rep. 107 (1990); Luckasson & Ellis, *Representing Institutionalized Mentally Retarded Persons*, 7 Mental Disability L. Rep. (1983).

52. *See, e.g.*, Devine, *The Ethics of Representing the Disabled Client: Does Model Rule 1.14 Adequately Resolve the Best Interests/Advocacy Dilemma*, 49 Mo. L. Rev. 493 (1984) (criticizing option of taking protective action as being inconsistent with advocacy model of representation); Luban, *Paternalism and the Legal Profession*, 1981 Wis. L. Rev. 454, 493 (lawyer's exercise of professional judgment for disabled client is "justified paternalism").

53. Tremblay, *On Persuasion and Paternalism: Lawyer Decisionmaking and the Questionably Competent Client*, 1987 Utah L. Rev. 515, 519–20.

own interests. For example, in a criminal case, a defendant's Sixth Amendment right to effective assistance of counsel may be violated if you blindly accede to his decisions affecting his "fundamental" rights in the face of a serious question about his competency.[54] If your client's disability is only temporary (e.g., he forgot to take his medicine), you may easily be able to protect him from the adverse consequences of an ill-considered decision in accordance with Rule 1.14(b) by temporarily postponing action on the matter until he has regained the capacity to rationally reconsider his choices.[55]

In circumstances where the disability is not extreme, you may be able to attempt to persuade your client that his decisions about the objectives of the representation are unwise.[56] If persuasion is unsuccessful or the nature of your client's disability makes rational communication with him impossible, short of seeking a formal appointment of a guardian, you might temporarily act as a *de facto* guardian, or seek the consent of a family member or close friend of the client to take protective action on his behalf. However, one commentator argues that such "unilateral usurpation of client autonomy is never appropriate except in emergencies."[57] Consulting a family member or close friend about protective action is also controversial because it may constitute a violation of your duty to protect client confidences from disclosure (*see* §6.07). Although a number of authorities take the view that limited consultation with a family member or close friend may be appropriate where the third person does not have an adverse interest in your client's affairs and your client has not expressly

---

54. *See* Kilbert v. Peyton, 383 F.2d 56 (4th Cir. 1967) (ineffective assistance when lawyer, retained only ten days earlier, allowed defendant to plead guilty on the basis of defendant's mere nod of the head despite serious doubts about defendant's mental condition); Red Dog v. State, 625 A.2d 245 (Del. 1993) (lawyer who doubted client's competence to forego further appeals had duty to timely inform the court and request judicial determination about competency); Speedy v. Wyrick, 702 F.2d 723 (8th Cir. 1983) (ineffective assistance not to entertain competency hearing when lawyer was aware of obvious indications of defendant's mental illness). *See also, ABA Standards for Criminal Justice*, Standard 7-4.2 (1984) (defense counsel must raise competency issue whenever there is a good-faith doubt about competency, regardless of client's wishes).

55. *See* N.Y. City Bar Ass'n. Op. 83-1 (lawyer's options properly include maintaining the *status quo* until client is capable of making a considered judgment); Iowa Ethics Op. 81-15 (lawyer unable to locate alcoholic client in personal injury action may not dismiss case, but should seek continuance and attempt to locate client, or seek appointment of guardian *ad litem* to make decisions in the case).

56. *See* Genden, *Separate Legal Representation for Protecting the Rights and Interests of Minors in Legal Proceedings*, 11 Harv. C.R.—C.L.L. Rev. 565, 588–89 (1976).

57. Tremblay, *On Persuasion and Paternalism: Lawyer Decisionmaking and the Questionably Competent Client*, 1987 Utah L. Rev. 515, 584.

forbidden you to consult with the third person,[58] other authorities flatly prohibit such consultation when it would involve the disclosure of client confidences.[59] Rule 1.14(c) allows disclosure, "but only to the extent reasonably necessary to protect the client's interests."

The option of seeking the formal appointment of a guardian is expressly authorized by Rule 1.14(b). If you reasonably believe your client cannot adequately act in his own interest, this option may be pursued even if your client objects.[60] In the litigation context, jurisdictions typically require the appointment of a guardian *ad litem* for minors and other persons suffering from certain mental disabilities.

Finally, while neither Rule 1.14 nor its Comment refer to the option of withdrawing from the representation, withdrawal may be permissible if you believe that your client's irrational behavior and incapacity to act in his own interests are making the representation "unreasonably difficult."[61] (*See also* §6.11). However, it has been said that withdrawal is the least desirable option because it leaves the client without representation at a time when the protection of his interests is often most needed, and he is least able to hire other counsel.[62]

§6.07 Preserving Confidentiality of Information

Your duty to preserve confidential communications of your client is a central aspect of the attorney-client relationship.[63] The duty is given effect not only through the Rules of Professional Conduct, but also through the attorney-client privilege, the work product doctrine, and the law of evidence.[64] The obligation encourages people to seek early legal assistance, encourages them to

---

58. *See, e.g.*, Me. Bar Bd. of Overseers, Professional Ethics Comm., Op. 84 (1988); ABA Comm. On Ethics and Professional Responsibility, Informal Op. 89-1530 (1989); Neb. State Bar Ass'n, Advisory Comm. Op 91-4 (1991).

59. *See, e.g.*, Nassau County (N.Y.) Ethics Op. 90-17 (1990); California Ethics Opinion 1989-112.

60. *See* Fla. Bar, Professional Ethics Comm., Op. 85-4 (1985); Ala. Bar, Op. 87-137 (1987).

61. *See* Ill. Bar Ass'n Comm. On Professional Ethics, Op. 89-12 (1990).

62. *See* Me. Bar Bd. of Overseers, Comm. On Professional and Judicial Ethics, Op. 84 (1988); N.Y. City Bar Ass'n, Comm. On Professional Ethics, Op. 83-1.

63. AG GRO Servs. Co. v. Sophia Land C. Inc., 8 F.Supp. 2d 495 (D. Md. 1997).

64. Comment to Rule 1.6 at paragraph [3].

communicate fully and frankly with a lawyer, and facilitates the full development of facts essential to proper client representation.[65]

Model Rule 1.6 provides:

> (a) A lawyer shall not reveal information relating to the representation of a client unless the client gives informed consent, the disclosure is impliedly authorized in order to carry out the representation or the disclosure is permitted by paragraph (b).
>
> (b) A lawyer may reveal information relating to the representation of a client to the extent the lawyer reasonably believes necessary:
>
> (1) to prevent reasonably certain death or substantial bodily harm;
>
> (2) to prevent the client from committing a crime or fraud that is reasonably certain to result in substantial injury to the financial interests or property of another and in furtherance of which the client has used or is using the lawyer's services;
>
> (3) to prevent, mitigate or rectify substantial injury to the financial interests or property of another that is reasonably certain to result or has resulted from the client's commission of a crime or fraud in furtherance of which the client has used the lawyer's services;
>
> (4) to secure legal advice about the lawyer's compliance with these Rules;
>
> (5) to establish a claim or defense on behalf of the lawyer in a controversy between the lawyer and the client, to establish a defense to a criminal charge or civil claim against the lawyer based upon conduct in which the client was involved, or to respond to allegations in any proceeding concerning the lawyer's representation of the client;
>
> (6) to comply with other law or a court order; or
>
> (7) to detect and resolve conflicts of interest arising from the lawyer's change of employment or from changes in the composition or ownership of a firm, but only if the revealed information would not compromise the attorney-client privilege or otherwise prejudice the client.

Because the duty of confidentiality embraces all information "relating to the representation," the duty covers not only information learned from your client,

---

65. Comment to Rule 1.6 at paragraph [2].

but also information obtained from others and even information which is available from public sources.[66] Disclosure is prohibited regardless of your motivation and regardless of whether a judicial proceeding is involved. For example, it is unethical for you to disclose a client's confidences without his consent when asking for assistance in the case from a lawyer outside your firm.[67]

The duty of confidentiality will usually be triggered once a prospective client consults you in good faith for the purpose of obtaining legal advice, even if you do not end up representing him.[68] The duty continues after the attorney-client relationship is terminated.[69] If you practice in a law firm, you may disclose client confidences to other lawyers or employees in the firm unless your client has instructed you otherwise,[70] and the other employees of your firm also have a duty to protect your client's confidences from disclosure.[71]

Rule 1.6(a) recognizes that your disclosure of confidential information may be impliedly authorized to carry out the representation. For example, in a real estate transaction, information such as the purchase price of the property, the amount of an offer, the amount accepted, and the condition of the property would typically be matters that could be disclosed as being impliedly authorized by the representation.[72] When your client is under a disability, limited disclosure

---

66. Comment to Rule 1.6 at paragraph [3]. *See also In re* Anonymous, 654 N.E.2d 1128 (Ind. 1995).

67. *See, e.g., In re* Mandelman, 514 N.W.2d 11 (Wis. 1994). *See also* ABA Comm. on Ethics and Professional Responsibility, Op. 98-411 (1998) (encouraging consultation with other lawyers by means of hypotheticals when possible); Comment to Rule 1.6 at paragraph [4] ("A lawyer's use of a hypothetical to discuss issues relating to the representation is permissible so long as there is no reasonable likelihood that the listener will be able to ascertain the identity of the client or the situation involved.").

68. Rule 1.18(b); ABA Comm. on Ethics and Professional Responsibility, Formal Op. 90-358 (1990). *See* Gilmore v. Goedecke, 954 F. Supp. 187 (E.D. Mo. 1996) (law firm could not represent defendant in age discrimination case because plaintiff had previously consulted another member of the firm by telephone).

69. Comment to Rule 1.6 at paragraph [20]; United States v. Standard Oil Co., 136 F. Supp. 345 (S.D. N.Y. 1955).

70. Comment to Rule 1.6 at paragraph [5].

71. *See* Pennsylvania v. Mrozek, 657 A.2d 997 (Pa. 1995); State Bar of Mich. Comm. on Professional and Judicial Ethics, Op. RI-123 (1992) (information received by non-lawyer assistant is protected and may be basis for disqualification of lawyer even if assistant never conveyed the information to the lawyer). *See also* Me. Bar Bd. of Overseers Professional Ethics Comm'n Op 134 (1993) (lawyer must adequately train, monitor, and discipline non-lawyer employees to maintain confidentiality or be subject to discipline for disclosures).

72. Ark. Bar Ass'n. Standing Comm. on Professional Ethics and Grievances, Op. 96-1 (1996).

of confidential information may be appropriate when consulting with a family member or close friend of your client (*see* § 6.06), or when consulting with your client's physician concerning a medical condition that is interfering with your client's ability to communicate or make decisions.[73]

Although the Comment to Rule 1.6 recognizes that "other law may require that a lawyer disclose information about a client,"[74] there is no circumstance under the Rule that ever *mandates* the disclosure of a client's confidences.[75] Rather, Rule 1.6(b) authorizes *permissive* disclosure, in your discretion,[76] in only limited circumstances: (1) to prevent reasonably certain death or substantial bodily harm and (2) to prevent the client from committing (or to prevent, mitigate or rectify the results of) a crime or fraud that is reasonably certain to result (or has resulted) in substantial injury to the financial interests or property of another and in furtherance of which the client has used your services; (3) to defend yourself on a civil, criminal, or ethical charge, or to establish a claim that you may have in a controversy between you and your client; or (4) to secure legal advice about your compliance with your ethical obligations or to comply with other law or a court order; or (5) to detect and resolve conflicts of interest resulting from your change of employment or the change of composition or ownership of your firm. The first two of these exceptions are widely recognized.[77] The third exception is also well recognized, but you must scrupulously avoid revealing confidential information not nec-

---

73. ABA Comm. on Ethics and Professional Responsibility, Informal Op. 89-1530 (1989).

74. Comment to Rule 1.6 at paragraph [12]. *See, e.g.,* United States v. Goldberger & Dubin, P.C., 935 F.2d 501 (2d Cir. 1991) (requirement in Internal Revenue Code, 26 U.S.C. § 6050 I, that every person who receives more than $10,000 in cash in connection with a trade or business must file a report with the IRS does not violate the federal constitution or the attorney-client privilege).

75. *See* Utah State Bar Ethics Advisory Comm. Op. 97-12 (1998) (although lawyer who suspects client of committing child abuse may be legally obligated to report information pursuant to statute, lawyer is not ethically mandated to report such information).

76. *See* Comment to Model Rule 1.6 at paragraph [7].

77. *See, e.g.,* Purcell v. District Attorney for Suffolk County, 676 N.E.2d 436 (Mass. 1997) (lawyer could properly alert authorities when client stated intent to burn down a building); State v. Hansen, 862 P.2d 122 (Wash. 1993) (lawyer could advise judge that person who called lawyer to retain him had threatened to kill judge); ABA Comm. on Ethics and Professional Responsibility, Informal Op. 83-1500 (1983) (lawyer may disclose client's intent to commit suicide). As to whether a lawyer may reveal to a client's sexual partner that the client has Acquired Immune Deficiency Syndrome (AIDS), *see generally*, Isaacman, The Conflict Between Illinois Rule 1.6(b) and the AIDS Confidentiality Act, 25 J. Marshall L. Rev. 727 (1992).

essary to your defense or claim and limit disclosure only to those having a need to know the information.[78]

With the widespread use of e-mail, some have proposed the use of encryption to protect the confidentiality of messages involving client communications. Others have argued encryption is not necessary because the expectation of privacy for electronic mail is the same as that for ordinary telephone calls, and unauthorized interception of electronic messages is unlawful.[79] However, in unusual circumstances involving extraordinarily sensitive information, you should seriously consider employing security measures such as encryption, just as you would take other precautions in communicating highly sensitive information such as not using a cell phone in certain circumstances.[80]

§6.08 Serving as an Intermediary between Clients

Lawyers are sometimes asked to represent multiple clients who, despite potential conflicts of interest, desire to achieve a common or group objective. Generally, this type of multiple representation is permissible so long as the common representation will not adversely affect any one of the clients and all of them consent after full consultation. The following Comments to Model Rule 1.7 (otherwise discussed in §6.09) explain:

> [29] In considering whether to represent multiple clients in the same matter, a lawyer should be mindful that if the common representation fails because the potentially adverse interests cannot be reconciled, the result can be additional cost, embarrassment and

---

78. *See, e.g.,* Ohio Sup. Ct. Bd. of Comm'rs on Grievances and Discipline, Op. 91-16 (1991) (firm using collection agency to collect fee should reveal confidences only to degree necessary for that purpose); N.Y. County Lawyer's Ass'n Comm. on Professional Ethics, Op. 722 (1997) (lawyer may reveal confidences to rebut charges of actionable misconduct to extent reasonably necessary to defend against accusations); *In re* National Mortgage Equity Corp. Litig., 120 F.R.D. 687 (C.D. Cal. 1988) (law firm may disclose confidential information from client to establish firm was not aware that client issued misleading securities statement).

79. ABA Comm. on Ethics and Professional Responsibility, Op. 99-413 (1999).

80. *See* Ariz. State Bar Comm. on Rules of Professional Responsibility, Op. 97-04 (1997) (lawyers should use e-mail cautiously, consider encryption, and include cautionary statement that information is confidential; S.C. Bar Ethics Advisory Comm. Op. 97-08 (1997) (lawyers may communicate with clients by e-mail but should discuss encryption options); Ark. Bar Ass'n Ethics Comm. Op. 98-2 (1998).

recrimination. Ordinarily, the lawyer will be forced to withdraw from representing all of the clients if the common representation fails. In some situations, the risk of failure is so great that multiple representation is plainly impossible. For example, a lawyer cannot undertake common representation of clients where contentious litigation or negotiations between them are imminent or contemplated. Moreover, because the lawyer is required to be impartial between commonly represented clients, representation of multiple clients is improper when it is unlikely that impartiality can be maintained. Generally, if the relationship between the parties has already assumed antagonism, the possibility that the clients' interests can be adequately served by common representation is not very good. Other relevant factors are whether the lawyer subsequently will represent both parties on a continuing basis and whether the situation involves creating or terminating a relationship between the parties.

[30] A particularly important factor in determining the appropriateness of common representation is the effect on client-lawyer confidentiality and the attorney-client privilege. With regard to the attorney-client privilege, the prevailing rule is that, as between commonly represented clients, the privilege does not attach. Hence, it must be assumed that if litigation eventuates between the clients, the privilege will not protect any such communications, and the clients should be so advised.

[31] As to the duty of confidentiality, continued common representation will almost certainly be inadequate if one client asks the lawyer not to disclose to the other client information relevant to the common representation. This is so because the lawyer has an equal duty of loyalty to each client, and each client has the right to be informed of anything bearing on the representation that might affect that client's interests and the right to expect that the lawyer will use that information to that client's benefit. See Rule 1.4. The lawyer should, at the outset of the common representation and as part of the process of obtaining each client's informed consent, advise each client that information will be shared and that the lawyer will have to withdraw if one client decides that some matter material to the representation should be kept from the other. In limited circumstances, it may be appropriate for the lawyer to proceed with the representation when the clients have agreed, after being properly informed, that the lawyer will keep certain information confidential. For example, the lawyer may reasonably conclude that failure to disclose one client's trade se-

crets to another client will not adversely affect representation involving a joint venture between the clients and agree to keep that information confidential with the informed consent of both clients.

[32] When seeking to establish or adjust a relationship between clients, the lawyer should make clear that the lawyer's role is not that of partisanship normally expected in other circumstances and, thus, that the clients may be required to assume greater responsibility for decisions than when each client is separately represented. Any limitations on the scope of the representation made necessary as a result of the common representation should be fully explained to the clients at the outset of the representation. See Rule 1.2(c).

In what is often cited as the leading case in support of the lawyer's role as intermediary, the Court in *Lessing v. Gibbons*, 45 P.2d 258, 261 (Cal. App. 1935) summarized some of the more common situations in which you may properly represent multiple clients in the same transaction even if they have potentially conflicting interests:

> The position of an attorney who acts for both parties to the knowledge of each, in the preparation of papers needed to effect their purpose, and gives to each the advice necessary for his protection, is recognized by the law as a proper one. Were this not the rule, the common practice of attorneys in acting for both partners in drawing articles of copartnership or drawing agreements for the dissolution of copartnership, in acting for both the grantor and the grantee in the sale of real property, in acting for both the seller and purchaser in the sale of personal property, in acting for both the lessor and lessee in the leasing of property, and in acting for both the lender and the borrower in handling a loan transaction would be prohibited even though done in the utmost good faith and with the full consent of all parties concerned.

In addition to these situations, you may—albeit in more cautious circumstances—act as an intermediary between clients in uncontested family-law matters such as divorce, custody, child support, alimony or property division,[81] or in estate and probate matters.[82] On the other hand, although

---

81. *See, e.g.,* Klemm v. Superior Court of Fresno County, 142 Cal. Rptr. 509 (Cal. Ct. App. 1977); Levine v. Levine, 436 N.E.2d 476 (N.Y. 1982); *In re* Eltzroth, 679 P.2d 1369 (Or. Ct. App. 1984).

82. *See* Kidney Association of Oregon Inc v. Ferguson, 843 P.2d 442 (Or. 1992); Alaska Ethics Opinion 91-2 (1991). *See generally,* Collett, *The Ethics of Intergenerational Representation,* 62 Fordham L. Rev. 1453 (1994).

the Model Rules do not *expressly* prohibit you from serving as an intermediary between clients who are in litigation, it is essentially inconceivable that such representation would be permissible in light of the general conflict-of-interest Rule 1.7 (*see* §6.09), which prohibits common representation of opposing parties in litigation.[83] Most authorities also prohibit common representation of clients in an adoption case even if the natural parents and the adopting parents consent.[84]

Although many jurisdictions permit you to represent consenting spouses in an uncontested family-law matter (e.g., in the preparation of a separation agreement),[85] other jurisdictions flatly prohibit such representation notwithstanding full consultation and consent.[86] Even in jurisdictions where common representation of clients in a family-law matter is permitted, the dangers of such representation are often noted by the courts in language such as the following:

> Divorces are frequently uncontested; the parties may make their financial arrangements peaceably and honestly.... Even in that situation the attorney's professional obligations do not permit his descent to the level of a scrivener.... Representing the wife in an arm's length divorce, an attorney of ordinary professional skill would demand some verification of the husband's financial statement; or, at the minimum, inform the wife that the husband's statement was unconfirmed, that wives may be cheated, that prudence called for investigation and verification.[87]

Therefore, whenever you are considering representing both spouses in what appears to be an uncontested separation agreement, you should be especially

---

83. *See* Comment to Model Rule 1.7 at paragraph [17]; Pearce, *Family Values and Legal Ethics: Competing Approaches to Representing Spouses*, 62 Fordham L. Rev. 1253, 1265 (1994) (most commentators have determined that Rule 2.2 is limited by Rule 1.7).

84. *See, e.g., In re* Petrie, 742 P.2d 796 (Ariz. 1987); Rushing v. Bosse, 652 So.2d 869 (Fla. 1995); ABA Informal Ethics Opinion 87-1523 (1987); Indiana Ethics Opinion 2 (1988); Pennsylvania Ethics Opinion 95-59 (1995).

85. *See* Levine v. Levine, 436 N.E.2d 467 (N.Y. 1982).

86. *See, e.g., In re* Breen, 552 A.2d 105 (N.J. 1989); Walden v. Hoke, 429 S.E.2d 504 (W. Va. 1993); Wisconsin Ethics Opinion E-88-4 (1988); Alaska Rule of Professional Conduct 2.2(d); Iowa Code of Professional Responsibility for Lawyers DR 5-105(A). *See generally,* Gibbard & Hartmeister, *Mediation and Wyoming Domestic Relations Cases — Practical Considerations, Ethical Concerns and Proposed Standards of Practice,* 27 Land & Water L. Rev. 435, 454 (1992); Collett, *And the Two Shall Become as One ... Until the Lawyers are Done,* 7 Notre Dame J. Legal Ethics & Pub. Policy 101, 129 (1993).

87. Ishmael v. Millington, 50 Cal. Rptr. 592, 596 (Ct. App. 1996).

alert to any obvious inequities on the face of their proposed agreement or other matters that may raise questions or conflicts about the substance of their agreement. If such inequities or potential conflicts are apparent, you should decline the common representation and advise the clients to obtain independent counsel.[88]

§6.09 Conflicts of Interest

The Model Rules contain six separate rules dealing with conflict-of-interest situations in which you must decline to represent a client or withdraw from the representation if it has already been undertaken. Rules 1.7 and 1.9(a), discussed below, primarily address the circumstances under which you may represent a client whose interests are adverse to one of your existing or former clients. The four other rules, which are beyond the scope of this book, address conflict-of-interest situations where a lawyer engages in certain transactions respecting a client (Rule 1.8), where the disqualification of one lawyer in a firm will be imputed to other lawyers in the firm (Rule 1.10), where a lawyer engages in successive government and private employment (Rule 1.11), and where a lawyer formerly participated in a matter as a judge or arbitrator (Rule 1.12).

Rule 1.7, the "general" conflict-of-interest Rule, provides:

(a) Except as provided in paragraph (b), a lawyer shall not represent a client if the representation involves a concurrent conflict of interest. A concurrent conflict of interest exists if:

(1) the representation of one client will be directly adverse to another client; or

(2) there is a significant risk that the representation of one or more clients will be materially limited by the lawyer's responsibilities to another client, a former client or a third person or by a personal interest of the lawyer.

(b) Notwithstanding the existence of a concurrent conflict of interest under paragraph (a), a lawyer may represent a client if:

(1) the lawyer reasonably believes that the lawyer will be able to provide competent and diligent representation to each affected client;

(2) the representation is not prohibited by law;

---

88. *See In re* Eltzroth, 679 P.2d 1369, 1373 n. 7 (Or. App. 1984). *See also* Charles W. Wolfran, *Modern Legal Ethics* 730 (1996).

(3) the representation does not involve the assertion of a claim by one client against another client represented by the lawyer in the same litigation or other proceeding before a tribunal; and

(4) each affected client gives informed consent, confirmed in writing.

Under this Rule, you are prohibited from representing a client whose interests are directly adverse to those of a current client, or if there is a significant risk that your representation will be materially limited as a result of your other responsibilities or interests, even if the two representations are unrelated, unless you believe that you can provide competent and diligent representation to each client and both clients consent. The prohibition apples when an opponent of a current client retains you to represent him in a matter unrelated to your representation of the current client,[89] or when you accept representation that requires you to bring suit on behalf of the new client against an existing client.[90] The rationale for the Rule is to preserve your loyalty to your clients,[91] and to prevent you from diminishing the vigor of your representation of one client to avoid antagonizing the other client.[92]

Representation of dual clients is never permissible when the two clients oppose each other in the same litigation.[93] In contrast to this clear-cut situation, however, the Comment to the Rule states that an impermissible conflict does not exist when the simultaneous representation concerns an unrelated matter involving clients "whose interests are only economically adverse, such as representation of competing economic enterprises." In such a situation, the conflict is so diffused and general that client consent is not even required.[94]

Current ethics opinions are divided about whether a disqualifying conflict arises when you are called upon to advocate a legal position that would benefit one client but would have negative consequences for another client in a different case.[95] That is, a lawyer sometimes faces the situation of urging the court to

---

89. *See, e.g., In re* Hansen, 586 P.2d 413 (Utah 1978).

90. *See, e.g.,* Unified Sewerage Agency v. Jelco Inc., 646 F.2d 1339 (9th Cir. 1981).

91. *See* Jeffry v. Pounds, 67 Cal. App.3d 6, 136 Cal. Rptr. 373 (Cal. App. 1977); ABA Informal Ethics Opinion 1495 (1982); Comment to Rule 1.7 at paragraph [1].

92. *See* Cinema 5 Ltd. v. Cinerama Inc., 528 F.2d 1384 (2d Cir. 1976); International Business Machines Corp. v. Levin, 579 F.2d 271 (3d Cir. 1978).

93. Comment to Rule 1.7 at paragraph [17]. *See, e.g.,* GATX/Airlog Co. v. Evergreen Int'l Airlines, Inc., 8 F. Supp. 2d 1182 (N.D. Cal. 1998); *In re* Ireland, 706 P.2d 352 (Ariz. 1985); Florida Bar v. Milin, 502 So.2d 900 (Fla. 1986).

94. Comment to Rule 1.7 at paragraph [6].

95. *See generally,* Dzienkowski, *Positional Conflicts of Interest,* 71 Tex. L. Rev. 457 (1993).

interpret unsettled law in a way that would favor one client while representing another client who, in an unrelated matter, would benefit from a contrary interpretation of the law. The ABA has taken the position that you may not concurrently represent clients whose matters would require you to argue a directly contrary position in the same jurisdiction, unless neither case is likely to lead to precedent harmful to the other and each client consents. If the cases are pending in different jurisdictions, the concurrent representations are permitted if both clients consent and you reasonably believe that neither representation will be adversely affected by the other.[96] Other ethics opinions take the view that there is no conflict in arguing opposite sides of the same legal issue before the same judge when representing two different clients in separate cases,[97] or that a conflict only arises when the two cases are pending at the same time in an appellate court.[98]

Under subsection (a)(2) of Rule 1.7, you are prohibited from representing a client when the representation would be "materially limited" by your responsibilities to another client. This proscription often arises when representing multiple clients in a single matter, especially in criminal cases. Although single representation of codefendants in a criminal case is not a *per se* violation of the constitutional guarantee of effective assistance of counsel,[99] the Comment to Rule 1.7 states that "[t]he potential for conflict of interest in representing multiple defendants in a criminal case is so grave that ordinarily a lawyer should decline to represent more than one codefendant."[100] For example, a serious conflict arises from joint representation of codefendants when the prosecution offers a plea to one of the codefendants in exchange for his testimony against the other. Obviously, a lawyer who is representing the codefendants is then placed in the untenable position of giving advice to the codefendant who has been offered the plea while fighting against the anticipated testimony when representing the other codefendant. Most authorities agree with the general rule expressed in the Comment to Rule 1.7 that lawyers should ordinarily decline to represent more than one codefendant in a criminal case.[101]

---

96. ABA Comm. on Ethics and Professional Responsibility, Formal Op. 93-377 (1993).

97. *See, e.g.,* State Bar of Cal. Standing Comm. on Professional Responsibility and Conduct, Op. 1989-108.

98. *See* Philadelphia Bar Ass'n Professional Guidance Comm., Op. 89-27 (1990).

99. Holloway v. Arkansas, 435 U.S. 475 (1978).

100. Comment to Rule 1.7 at paragraph [23].

101. *See, e.g.,* United States v. Hawkins, 139 F.3d 902 (7th Cir. 1998); Armstrong v. People, 701 P.2d 17 (Colo. 1985); Shongutsie v. State, 827 P.2d 361 (Wyo. 1992). *See generally,* Annotation, Circumstances Giving Rise to Prejudicial Conflict of Interests Between Criminal Defendants and Defense Counsel: State Cases, 18 A.L.R.4th 360 (1982).

Multiple representations of clients by a single lawyer can also create impermissible conflicts of interest in civil cases. For example, a number of cases have held that it is generally impermissible for a lawyer to represent both the buyer and seller in a complex real estate transaction.[102] Numerous cases also hold that when an insurance company hires an attorney to represent the carrier and the insured in a personal injury case, the dual representation will be prohibited if the interests of the company become at odds with those of the insured,[103] as where a lawyer representing the insured brings a separate declaratory judgment action asserting that the plaintiff's claims fall outside the policy's coverage.[104] Similarly, when there is a non-frivolous dispute about liability in an automobile-accident personal injury case, it is generally considered to be improper for a lawyer to represent both the plaintiff-driver and his passenger in a suit against the driver of the of the adverse vehicle who claims that the plaintiff driver was at fault in causing the accident.[105] In addition, as pointed out in Section 6.08, impermissible conflicts of interest may arise when representing both spouses in a seemingly uncontested family-law matter.

Subsection (a)(2) of Rule 1.7 also prohibits you from representing a client if the representation may be materially limited by your own interests. Many of the most common situations in which the representation of a client may be compromised by a lawyer's personal interests are addressed by other specific rules. For example, lawyers may not enter into certain business transactions with clients except under certain circumstances (Rule 1.8(a)); lawyers are prohibited from preparing certain instruments giving them or their immediate relatives substantial gifts from clients (Rule 1.8(c)); lawyers are prohibited during the representation of a client from obtaining literary or media rights to a portrayal or account based in substantial part on information relating to the representation (Rule 1.8(d)); lawyers are prohibited from providing financial assistance to clients in connection with litigation except in limited circumstances (Rule 1.8(e)); lawyers are prohibited from accepting fees paid by third parties except in certain circumstances (Rule 1.8(f)); lawyers are pro-

---

102. *See, e.g.,* Florida Bar v. Belleville, 591 So.2d 170 (Fla. 1991); *In re* Pohlman, 604 N.Y.S.2d 61 (N.Y. App. Div. 1993); Baldasarre v. Butler, 625 A.2d 458 (N.J. 1993).

103. *See* Nelson Elec. Contracting Corp. v. Transcontinental Co., 660 N.Y.S.2d 220 (N.Y. App. Div. 1997).

104. State Farm v. Armstrong Extinguisher Serv., 791 F. Supp. 799 (D.S.D. 1992).

105. *See, e.g., In re* Thornton, 421 A.2d 1 (D.C. App. 1980); Fugnitto v. Fugnitto, 452 N.Y.S.2d 976 N.Y. Sup. Ct. App. Div. 1982. *Compare* Alabama Ethics Opinion 82-662 (such representation of plaintiff-driver and passenger not prohibited if no possibility of liability on plaintiff-driver's part, and both driver and passenger consent to the common representation after disclosure of potential conflicts).

hibited from entering into agreements with clients that limit the lawyers' liability for malpractice (Rule 1.8(h)); lawyers may not acquire proprietary interests in the subject matter of litigation (Rule 1.8(i); lawyers are prohibited from having a sexual relationship with a client unless such a relationship existed between them when the client-lawyer relationship began (Rule 1.8(j)); and lawyers are prohibited from undertaking representation in certain cases where they have switched from government to private employment or vice versa (Rule 1.11), or when they have participated in certain cases as a former judge or arbitrator (Rule 1.12).

The general conflict-of-interest provisions in subsection (a) of Rule 1.7 are, however, subject to a significant exception. Even if the particular circumstances present a conflict of interest, the representation is not improper if (1) you reasonably believe that you will be able to provide competent and diligent representation to each affected client, and (2) your client gives informed consent to the other representation in writing. Under Model Rule 1.0(e), "informed consent" means that you have "communicated adequate information and explanation about the material risks of and reasonably available alternatives to the proposed course of conduct." As mentioned previously, the only circumstance in which consent cannot serve as an exception to Rule 1.7(a) is set out in subsection (b)(3) where "the representation [involves] the assertion of a claim by one client against another client represented by the lawyer in the same litigation or other proceeding before a tribunal."

While Rule 1.7 addresses the circumstances under which you may represent a client whose interests are adverse to one of your *existing* clients, Rule 1.9(a) addresses when you may properly represent a client whose interests are adverse to one of your *former* clients.[106] Rule 1.9(a) provides:

> A lawyer who has formerly represented a client in a matter shall not thereafter represent another person in the same or a substantially related matter in which that person's interests are materially adverse to the interests of the former client unless the former client gives informed consent, confirmed in writing.

Under this Rule, after your representation of a client is over, your continuing duty of loyalty to preserve his confidences prohibits you from representing another client in the "same or a substantially related matter" in which the new

---

106. Rule 1.9 also contains subsections (b) and (c) which deal with the protection of client confidences gained by a lawyer in a prior affiliation with a law firm and after termination of the attorney-client relationship. These subsections are not discussed here.

client's interests are materially adverse to those of your former client, unless your former client consents in writing. That is, you have an obligation not to use confidential information about the former client to his disadvantage in the subsequent representation of another client.

The Rule may even be triggered to protect a former *prospective* client whom you advised during an initial consultation but ended up not representing. For example, the Rule would be applicable if the prospective client disclosed confidential information to you during an initial office visit or phone conversation under circumstances where an attorney-client relationship would be implied.[107] (*See also* §6.02.) To guard against this disqualifying situation, it has been pointed out that you can warn the prospective client in the initial conference to reveal only enough information to enable you to determine whether you have a conflict of interest. Then, after you have determined that no conflict exists, you would allow the potential client to discuss his confidential situation with you.[108]

In determining whether the representation of a new client involves the "same or a substantially related matter" (i.e., subject matter, case, cause of action, or legal work) involved in the representation of the former client, courts variously consider the similarity of the legal issues, the similarity of the factual settings, the identity of the parties, and whether actual confidential information obtained from a former client could be used to his detriment in the representation of the new client.[109] For example, one court provided the following list of factors appropriate to consider:

> whether the liability issues presented are similar; whether any scientific issues presented are similar; whether the nature of the evidence is similar; whether the lawyer had interviewed a witness who was a key witness in both causes; the lawyer's knowledge of the former client's trial strategies, negotiation strategies, legal theories, business practices and secrets; the lapse of time between causes; the duration and intimacy of the lawyer's relationship with the clients; the functions being performed by the lawyer; the likelihood that actual conflict will arise; and the likely prejudice to the client if conflict a does arise.[110]

---

107. *See* Marshall v. State of New York Div. of State Police, 952 F. Supp. 103 (N.D. N.Y. 1997); Richardson v. Griffiths, 560 N.W.2d 430 (Neb. 1997).

108. *See* ABA Formal Ethics Opinion 90-358 (1990).

109. *See generally*, Wolfran, Former Client Conflicts, 10 Geo. J. Legal Ethics 67 (1997).

110. State ex rel. Wal-Mart Stores, Inc v. Kortum, 559 N.W.2d 496, 501 (Neb. 1997).

Many courts hold that "[o]nce the former client proves that the subject matters of the present and prior representations are 'substantially related,' the court will irrebutably presume that relevant confidential information was disclosed during the former period of representation."[111] Other courts engage in the circular reasoning of saying, "[i]f there is a reasonable probability that confidences were disclosed which could be used against the former client in the later adverse representation, ... a substantial relationship between the two cases will be presumed."[112] These fictional and circular approaches to the "substantial relationship" test are the product of an effort to spare the former client from the self-defeating necessity of having to reveal the confidential information he imparted to his lawyer when seeking to disqualify the lawyer from representing another client, and it has the practical benefit of reducing the need for courts to hold *in camera* or *ex parte* proceedings every time a disqualification motion is filed. In essence, the test allows the courts to infer that, if there is a good deal of similarity between the matter handled for the former client and the matter on which the lawyer is now representing another client, then it is likely that the information learned by the lawyer from the former client would be useful to the new client and adverse to the former one, and therefore the lawyer should be disqualified from representing the new client.

Even if the substantial relationship test is met and the representation of the new client would be materially adverse to the confidentiality interests or other interests of the former client, your representation of the new client is not prohibited if the former client consents in writing. Usually, you will not be permitted to treat the former client's bare knowledge of the new representation as consent to it.[113] Your consultation in connection with obtaining his consent

---

111. Duncan v. Merrill Lynch, Pierce, Fenner & Smith, Inc., 646 F.2d 1020, 1028 (5th Cir. 1981). *See also* Brotherhood Mut. Ins. Co. v. National Presto Indus. Inc, 846 F. Supp. 57 (M.N. Fla. 1994); Rogers v. Pittston Co., 800 F. Supp. 350 (W.D. Va. 1992); Sullivan County Reg'l Refuse Disposal v. Acworth, 686 A.2d 755 (N.H. 1996); Marshall v. State of New York Div. of State Police, 952 F. Supp. 103 (N.D. N.Y. 1997).

112. Thomas v. Municipal Court of Antelope Valley Judicial District of California, 878 F.2d 285, 288 (9th Cir. 1988).

113. *See* Manoir-Electroalloys Corp. v. Amalloy Corp, 711 F. Supp. 188 (D.C. N.J. 1989); Marketti v. Fitzsimmons, 373 F. Supp. 637 (W.D. Wis. 1974). Sometimes implied consent will be found, as where the former client knew of the new representation, failed to object to it after having ample opportunity to object, and there would be great hardship to the new client if disqualification were ordered. See, e.g., River West Inc. v. Nickel, 234 Cal. Rptr. 33 (Cal. App. 1987); Cox v. American Cast Iron Pipe Co., 847 F.2d 725 (11th Cir. 1988); Donohoe v. Consolidated Operating & Production Corp., 691 F. Supp. 109 (N.D. Ill. 1988).

should involve not only an explanation of the conflicts that may arise, but also their implications.[114]

Finally, it is important to emphasize that although conflict-of-interest questions might be raised by the trial judge or opposing counsel, the primary responsibility for resolving such questions rests with you, and you are obligated to adopt reasonable office procedures to determine in both litigation and non-litigation matters the parties and issues involved and to determine whether there are actual or potential conflicts of interest.[115] If a disqualifying conflict arises after you have undertaken the representation, you should take appropriate steps to withdraw (*see* §6.11). If more than one client is involved and a conflict arises after representation, you may even have to withdraw from the representation of *both* clients if required by Rule 1.16.[116]

§6.10 Setting Attorney's Fees

Entering into a fee agreement with your client is an integral part of establishing the attorney-client relationship in terms of clarifying the services you will render and how your client will pay for them. This Section discusses setting fees on an hourly rate or in a fixed amount. Ethical considerations in connection with contingent fees are discussed in Section 6.14.

Model Rule 1.5 provides in part:

> (a) A lawyer shall not make an agreement for, charge, or collect an unreasonable fee or an unreasonable amount for expenses. The factors to be considered in determining the reasonableness of a fee include the following:
>
> (1) the time and labor required, the novelty and difficulty of the questions involved, and the skill requisite to perform the legal service properly;
>
> (2) the likelihood, if apparent to the client, that the acceptance of the particular employment will preclude other employment by the lawyer;
>
> (3) the fee customarily charged in the locality for similar legal services;

---

114. *See* First Wisconsin Mortgage Trust v. First Wisconsin Corp., 422 F. Supp. 493 (E.D. Wis. 1976); Florida Insurance Guaranty Association Inc. v. Carey Canada Inc., 749 F. Supp. 255 (S.D. Fla. 1990).

115. Comment to Rule 1.7 at paragraph [3].

116. Comment to Rule 1.7 at paragraph [5].

(4) the amount involved and the results obtained;

(5) the time limitations imposed by the client or by the circumstances;

(6) the nature and length of the professional relationship with the client;

(7) the experience, reputation, and ability of the lawyer or lawyers performing the services; and

(8) whether the fee is fixed or contingent.

(b) The scope of the representation and the basis or rate of the fee and expenses for which the client will be responsible shall be communicated to the client, preferably in writing, before or within a reasonable time after commencing the representation, except when the lawyer will charge a regularly represented client on the same basis or rate. Any changes in the basis or rate of the fee or expenses shall also be communicated to the client.

The Comment to the Rule instructs in part:

[1] Paragraph (a) requires that lawyers charge fees that are reasonable under the circumstances. The factors specified in (1) through (8) are not exclusive. Nor will each factor be relevant in each instance. Paragraph (a) also requires that expenses for which the client will be charged must be reasonable. A lawyer may seek reimbursement for the cost of services performed in-house, such as copying, or for other expenses incurred in-house, such as telephone charges, either by charging a reasonable amount to which the client has agreed in advance or by charging an amount that reasonably reflects the cost incurred by the lawyer.

[2] When the lawyer has regularly represented a client, they ordinarily will have evolved an understanding concerning the basis or rate of the fee and the expenses for which the client will be responsible. In a new client-lawyer relationship, however, an understanding as to fees and expenses must be promptly established. Generally, it is desirable to furnish the client with at least a simple memorandum or copy of the lawyer's customary fee arrangements that states the general nature of the legal services to be provided, the basis, rate or total amount of the fee and whether and to what extent the client will be responsible for any costs, expenses or disbursements in the course of the representation. A written statement concerning the terms of the engagement reduces the possibility of misunderstanding....

[4] A lawyer may require advance payment of a fee [i.e., a retainer], but is obligated to return any unearned portion. See Rule 1.16(d)....

[5] An agreement may not be made whose terms might induce the lawyer improperly to curtail services for the client or perform them in a way contrary to the client's interest. For example, a lawyer should not enter into an agreement whereby services are to be provided only up to a stated amount when it is foreseeable that more extensive services probably will be required, unless the situation is adequately explained to the client. Otherwise, the client might have to bargain for further assistance in the midst of a proceeding or transaction. However, it is proper to define the extent of services in light of the client's ability to pay. A lawyer should not exploit a fee arrangement based primarily on hourly charges by using wasteful procedures.

The touchstone of a valid fee is reasonableness. In this regard, the eight factors enumerated in Rule 1.5(a) are general guidelines to be considered in setting the amount of a fee. Although the factors do not add up to some mandatory formula that must be followed in establishing either the type of amount of your fee, courts routinely consider these factors when reviewing the reasonableness of a fee agreement.[117]

A court always has the inherent power to review the reasonableness of fees and to refuse to enforce any contract involving excessive or unreasonable fees.[118] For example, a contract calling for a fee in excess of that permitted by statute will not be enforced.[119] In addition, courts have consistently prohibited lawyers from charging general overhead expenses to clients in addition to a fee, or from separately charging clients for rote "housekeeping" activities such as organizing and labeling files or delivering documents.[120]

---

117. *See* Fourchon Docks, Inc. v. Milchem, Inc., 849 F.2d 1561 (5th Cir. 1988).

118. Pfeifer v. Sentry Ins., 745 F. Supp. 1434 (E.D. Wis. 1990); Beatty v. NP Corp., 581 N.E.2d 1311 (Mass. App. 1991); *In re* Kidney Ass'n of Oregon, Inc. v. Ferguson, 843 P.2d 442 (Or. 1992).

119. *See, e.g., In re* Harney, 3 Cal. St. Bar Ct. Rptr. 266 (Review Dep't 1995) (fee in excess of state-law cap on fees in medical malpractice case); Committee on Legal Ethics of W. Va. State Bar v. Burdette, 445 S.E.2d 733 (W. Va. 1994) (fee in excess of that permitted in workers' compensation case); *In re* Estate of Konopka, 498 N.W.2d 853 (Wis. App. 1993) (fee in excess of that permitted by statute in estate matter).

120. *See, e.g.,* Spicer v. Chicago Bd. Options Exch., 844 F. Supp. 1226 (N.D. Ill. 1993); Keith v. Volpe, 644 F. Supp. 1317 (C.D. Cal. 1986).

Comment [4] above allows you to require your client to advance money for legal fees or to pay a retainer fee. There are three types of retainers:

1. With a special retainer, a client agrees to pay a specified fee for a specified service, which can be calculated on an hourly or percentage basis, and may be paid in advance or as billed.

2. A nonrefundable retainer permits a lawyer to keep advance payments regardless of the specified services provided.

3. Under a general retainer, the client agrees to pay a lawyer a fixed sum in exchange for the lawyer's promise to be available to perform legal services at an agreed price during a specific period. Because a general retainer is given in exchange for the lawyer's availability, it is a charge separate from the fee incurred for services actually provided.[121]

A special retainer is essentially an advance fee payment where the outstanding balance of the advance is reduced as you perform legal services for your client and earn the fee. If you withdraw from the representation or are discharged, you must return any unearned portion of the advance fee payment.[122] A nonrefundable retainer, by definition, need not be returned to your client if you withdraw or are discharged and have not yet earned the advance payment.[123] However, many jurisdictions prohibit nonrefundable retainers on public-policy grounds and require the unearned portion of the fee to be returned to the client in the event of your withdrawal or discharge.[124] A general retainer, sometimes called a "classic" or "true" retainer,[125] is a payment that is considered separate from a fee for services rendered and is provided solely to ensure your availability to handle the client's case. The nonrefundable nature of such a retainer is recognized in a number of jurisdictions.[126]

Although Rule 1.5 does not require that the fee agreement with your client be in writing, the safest practice is to provide your client with a simple letter

---

121. Wong v. Michael Kennedy, P.C., 853 F. Supp. 73 (E.D. N.Y. 1994).

122. Comment to Rule 1.5 at paragraph [4]; Rule 1.16(d) (see §6.11).

123. See Pa. Bar Ass'n Comm. on Legal Ethics and Professional Responsibility, Formal Op. 85-120 (1985); Alaska Bar Ass'n Ethics Comm., Op. 87-1 (1987).

124. See, e.g., In re Cooperman, 591 N.Y.S.2d 855 (App. Div. 1993); Jennings v. Backmeyer, 569 N.E.2d 689 (Ind. App. 1991); Texas Ethics Opinion 431 (1986); Ala. State Bar Gen. Counsel. Op. RO-93-21 (1993).

125. See In re National Magazine Publishing Co., 170 B.R. 329 (Bankr. Ohio 1994).

126. See, e.g., Mass Bar Ass'n Ethics Comm., Op. 95-2 (1995); In re Disciplinary Action Against Lochow, 469 N.W.2d 91 (Minn. 1991); Richmond v. Nodland, 501 N.W.2d 759 (N.D. 1993).

or memorandum concerning the fee to reduce the possibility of any misunderstanding.[127] Whether your agreement is made orally or reduced to writing, it should clearly specify (1) the specific client or clients you are representing;[128] (2) the services you have agreed to provide on your client's behalf;[129] (3) any limits on the scope of your services,[130] such as whether your representation includes any appeal;[131] (4) how the fee will be computed and how your client will be billed;[132] (5) any anticipated change in the fee rate in the future, and what different rates will be charged for paralegals or other lawyers who work on the case;[133] and (6) what costs and expenses (e.g., charges for court filings, expert witnesses, investigators, stenographers, transcriptions, photocopying, travel, computer assisted research, etc.) your client will be responsible for paying.[134]

§6.11 Declining or Withdrawing from Representation

Except when you are appointed by the court to represent a client, ordinarily you have no obligation to accept the representation of a client and may even limit the scope of your representation as a condition of agreeing to accept the client's case.[135] However, once you undertake to represent a client, the discretion

---

127. Comment to Rule 1.5 at paragraph [2].

128. *See* Stern v. Wonzer, 846 S.W.2d 939 (Tex. App. 1993).

129. *See* Connecticut Informal Ethics Op. 92-31 (1992); Iowa Ethics Op. 86-13 (1987).

130. *See, e.g.,* New York State Ethics Op. 604 (1989) (representation may be limited to discreet matter or particular stage of proceedings).

131. *Compare,* Joseph E. Di Loreto Inc. v. O'Neill, 1 Cal. Rptr.2d 636 (Cal. App. 1991) (fee contract specified lawyer was not obligated to pursue appeal) *with* Maryland Attorney Grievance Comm. v. Korotki, 569 A.2d 1224 (Md. App. 1990) (appeal should be pursued if fee contract silent about the matter).

132. *See* Comment to Rule 1.5 at paragraph [2]; ABA Formal Ethics Opinion 93-379 (1993); Kansas Ethics Opinion 81-28 (1981).

133. *See* Severson, Werson, Berke & Melchior v. Bolinger, 1 Cal. Rptr.2d 531 (Cal. App. 1991); ABA Business Law Section, Task Force on Lawyer's Business Ethics, "Statement of Principles in Billing for Legal Services" (1995); New Mexico Ethics Op. 1990-4 (1990); Los Angeles County Ethics Op. 391 (1981).

134. *See* ABA Business Law Section Task Force on Lawyer Business Ethics, "Statement of Principles in Billing for Disbursements and Other Charges" (1995); Alaska Ethics Op. 93-5 (1993).

135. Model Rule 1.2(c) (*see* §6.03).

to decline the case is replaced with a duty to diligently pursue your client's objectives until you have completed the matter you were retained to undertake.[136] Notwithstanding this duty, there are certain circumstances in which you are *required* to decline representation or withdraw from representing your client, and there are other circumstances in which you *may*, but are not required to, withdraw from the representation. Regardless of whether the grounds for withdrawal are mandatory or permissive, if you are the client's attorney of record in litigation, your withdrawal is subject to the approval of the court.[137]

Model Rule 1.16 provides:

> (a) Except as stated in paragraph (c), a lawyer shall not represent a client or, where representation has commenced, shall withdraw from the representation of a client if:
>
> (1) the representation will result in violation of the Rules of Professional Conduct or other law;
>
> (2) the lawyer's physical or mental condition materially impairs the lawyer's ability to represent the client; or
>
> (3) the lawyer is discharged.
>
> (b) Except as stated in paragraph (c), a lawyer may withdraw from representing a client if:
>
> (1) withdrawal can be accomplished without material adverse effect on the interests of the client;
>
> (2) the client persists in a course of action involving the lawyer's services that the lawyer reasonably believes is criminal or fraudulent;
>
> (3) the client has used the lawyer's services to perpetrate a crime or fraud;
>
> (4) the client insists upon taking action that the lawyer considers repugnant or with which the lawyer has a fundamental disagreement;
>
> (5) the client fails substantially to fulfill an obligation to the lawyer regarding the lawyer's services and has been given reasonable warning that the lawyer will withdraw unless the obligation is fulfilled;

---

136. *See* Model Rule 1.3 and Comment to that Rule at paragraph [4] (*See also* §6.04[b]); Tormo v. Yormark, 398 F.Supp. 1159 (D.C. N.J. 1975); Anderson, Calder & Lembke v. District Court, 629 P.2d 603 (Colo. 1981).

137. *See* Vander Voort v. Texas State Bar, 802 S.W.2d 332 (Tex. App. 1990); Lutes v. Alexander, 421 S.E.2d 857 (Va. App. 1992).

(6) the representation will result in an unreasonable financial burden on the lawyer or has been rendered unreasonably difficult by the client; or

(7) other good cause for withdrawal exists.

(c) A lawyer must comply with applicable law requiring notice to or permission of a tribunal when terminating a representation. When ordered to do so by a tribunal, a lawyer shall continue representation notwithstanding good cause for terminating the representation.

(d) Upon termination of representation, a lawyer shall take steps to the extent reasonably practicable to protect a client's interests, such as giving reasonable notice to the client, allowing time for employment of other counsel, surrendering papers and property to which the client is entitled and refunding any advance payment of fee or expense that has not been earned or incurred. The lawyer may retain papers relating to the client to the extent permitted by other law.

The Comment to the Rule provides in part:

[1] A lawyer should not accept representation in a matter unless it can be performed competently, promptly, without improper conflict of interest and to completion ...

[2] A lawyer ordinarily must decline or withdraw from representation if the client demands that the lawyer engage in conduct that is illegal or violates the Rules of Professional Conduct or other law. The lawyer is not obliged to decline or withdraw simply because the client suggests such a course of conduct; a client may make such a suggestion in the hope that a lawyer will not be constrained by a professional obligation.

[3] When a lawyer has been appointed to represent a client, withdrawal ordinarily requires approval of the appointing authority ... Difficulty may be encountered if withdrawal is based on the client's demand that the lawyer engage in unprofessional conduct. The court may request an explanation for the withdrawal, while the lawyer may be bound to keep confidential the facts that would constitute such an explanation. The lawyer's statement that professional considerations require termination of the representation ordinarily should be accepted as sufficient ...

[4] A client has a right to discharge a lawyer at any time, with or without cause, subject to liability for payment for the lawyer's services ...

[5] Whether a client can discharge appointed counsel may depend on applicable law. A client seeking to do so should be given a full ex-

planation of the consequences. These consequences may include a decision by the appointing authority that appointment of successor counsel is unjustified, thus requiring self-representation by the client.

[6] If the client has severely diminished capacity, the client may lack the legal capacity to discharge the lawyer, and in any event the discharge may be seriously adverse to the client's interests. The lawyer should make special effort to help the client consider the consequences and may take reasonably necessary protective action as provided in Rule 1.14. [See §6.06].

[7] A lawyer may withdraw from representation in some circumstances. The lawyer has the option to withdraw if it can be accomplished without material adverse effect on the client's interests. Withdrawal is also justified if the client persists in a course of action that the lawyer reasonably believes is criminal or fraudulent, for a lawyer is not required to be associated with such conduct even if the lawyer does not further it. Withdrawal is also permitted if the lawyer's services were misused in the past even if that would materially prejudice the client. The lawyer may also withdraw where the client insists on taking action that the lawyer considers repugnant or with which the lawyer has a fundamental disagreement.

[8] A lawyer may withdraw if the client refuses to abide by the terms of an agreement relating to the representation, such as an agreement concerning fees or court costs or an agreement limiting the objectives of the representation.

For the most part, the provisions of Rule 1.16 are fairly self-explanatory. The most ambiguous provisions concern the permissive withdrawal situations where the "client insists upon taking action that the lawyer considers repugnant or with which the lawyer has a fundamental disagreement" under subsection (b)(4), where "the representation ... has been rendered unreasonably difficult by the client" under subsection (b)(6), and where "other good cause for withdrawal exists" under subsection (b)(7).

It has been suggested that the "repugnant" language provides you with a certain degree of professional independence to withdraw when the client's conduct, though not unlawful, violates community interests or your sense of public policy or personal morals.[138] For example, it has been held that a lawyer could properly withdraw on grounds of repugnancy where he could not in good con-

---

138. *See* Gillers, *What We Talked About When We Talked About Ethics: A Critical View of the Model Rules*, 46 Ohio St. L. J. 243, 260 (1985).

science continue to represent a defendant who wanted to forgo appeals and accept the death penalty.[139] Similarly, repugnancy may permit you to withdraw if your client insists on a course of action or objective that is contrary to your advice and your client would not be prejudiced by your withdrawal.[140]

Withdrawal on the ground that your client has rendered the representation "unreasonably difficult" may be justified when your client refuses to communicate or cooperate in the case,[141] or tensions between you and your client have led to a complete breakdown of the trust and loyalty necessary for an effective attorney-client relationship.[142] An antagonistic breakdown in the attorney-client relationship may also constitute "other good cause" for withdrawal.[143] In addition, it has been held that "other good cause" for withdrawal may exist when it has become clear that the client's case is without merit,[144] the client has filed a grievance against the lawyer,[145] or the client has deliberately disregarded a fee obligation.[146]

If you are discharged by your client or withdraw from the representation, you have a duty under subsection (d) of the Rule to take reasonable steps to

---

139. Red Dog v. State, 625 A.2d 245 (Del. 1993). *See also* Tenn. Sup. Ct. Bd. of Professional Ethics Comm., Op. 96-F-140 (1996) (withdrawal may be permitted if lawyer's representation impaired by his moral or religious beliefs).

140. *See* Spero v. Abbott Laboratories, 396 F. Supp. 321 (D. Ill. 1975); Kannewurf v. Johns, 632 N.E.2d 711 (Ill. App. 1994) (refusal to follow advice regarding settlement). But see May v. Seibert, 264 S.E.2d 643 (W. Va. 1980) (acceptance of settlement terms is solely within client's province, and thus client's refusal to settle is not adequate ground for lawyer's withdrawal).

141. *See, e.g.,* Statute of Liberty-Ellis Island Foundation Inc. v. International United Industries, 110 FRD 395 (S.D. N.Y. 1986) (refusal to cooperate); Sobol v. District Court of Aprahoe County, 619 P.2d 765 (Colo. 1980) (client withheld material information, repeatedly contacted opponent's lawyers, and was critical of counsel); Hancock v. Mutual of Omaha Insurance, 472 A.2d 867 (D.C. App. 1984) (client unresponsive to phone calls and letters).

142. *See, e.g.,* McGuire v. Wilson, 735 F. Supp. 83 (S.D. N.Y. 1990) (client alleged lawyer mishandled case, coupled with vituperative letters between client and counsel evidencing "sad state" of relationship); *In re* Admonition Issued in Panel File No. 94-24, 533 N.W.2d 852 (Minn. 1995) (client's anger and refusal to cooperate with lawyer showed client had no confidence in lawyer); Kolomick v. Kolomick, 518 N.Y.S2d 413 (N.Y. App. Div. 1987) (breakdown of relationship made representation impossible).

143. *See, e.g.,* McGuire v. Wilson, 735 F. Supp. 83 (S.D. N.Y. 1990); Chaleff v. Superior Court, 138 Cal. Rptr. 735 (Cal. App. 1977); Lasser v. Nassau Community College, 457 N.Y.S.2d 343 (N.Y. App. Div 1983).

144. *See* Kirsch v. Duryea, 146 Cal. Rptr. 218 (Cal. App. 1978).

145. *See In re* Anonymous, 379 S.E.2d 723 (S.C. 1989).

146. Commonwealth v. Sheps, 523 A.2d 363 (Pa. 1987).

mitigate any damage to your client's interests. As that subsection states, this means giving your client reasonable notice of your intent to withdraw, allowing time for your client to employ other counsel, surrendering papers and property to which your client is entitled, and refunding any advance payment of a fee not yet earned. In addition, you should advise your client about the importance of hiring substitute counsel,[147] and diligently cooperate with substitute counsel in responding to inquiries and handing over the client's file.[148]

§6.12 Dealing with Persons Other Than Your Own Client

In representing a client, Model Rule 4.2 addresses the extent to which you may communicate with another person who is represented by counsel in the same legal matter, and Model Rule 4.3 addresses your dealings with unrepresented persons. Model Rule 4.4 otherwise deals with your conduct towards third persons.

Model Rule 4.2 provides that "[i]n representing a client, a lawyer shall not communicate about the subject of the representation with a person the lawyer knows to be represented by another lawyer in the matter, unless the lawyer has the consent of the other lawyer or is authorized to do so by law or a court order." The Comment to the Rule explains in part:

> [2] This Rule applies to communications with any person who is represented by counsel concerning the matter to which the communication relates.
>
> [3] The Rule applies even though the represented person initiates or consents to the communication. A lawyer must immediately terminate communication with a person if, after commencing communication, the lawyer learns that the person is one with whom communication is not permitted by this Rule.
>
> [4] This Rule does not prohibit communication with a represented person, or an employee or agent of such a person, concerning matters outside the representation. For example, the existence of a controversy between a government agency and a private party, or be-

---

147. *See In re* Palmer, 380 S.E.2d 813 (S.C. 1989); *In re* Kaufman, 567 P.2d 957 (Nev. 1977).

148. *In re* Tos, 576 A.2d 607 (Del. 1980); *In re* Sumner, 665 A.2d 986 (D.C. App. 1995); *In re* Dils, 646 N.E.2d 667 (Ind. 1995); *In re* Swerine, 513 N.W.2d 463 (Minn. 1994).

tween two organizations, does not prohibit a lawyer for either from communicating with nonlawyer representatives of the other regarding a separate matter. Nor does this Rule preclude communication with a represented person who is seeking advice from a lawyer who is not otherwise representing a client in the matter. A lawyer may not make a communication prohibited by this Rule through the acts of another. See Rule 8.4(a). Parties to a matter may communicate directly with each other, and a lawyer is not prohibited from advising a client concerning a communication that the client is legally entitled to make. Also, a lawyer having independent justification or legal authorization for communicating with a represented person is permitted to do so....

[7] In the case of a represented organization, this Rule prohibits communications with a constituent of the organization who supervises, directs or regularly consults with the organization's lawyer concerning the matter or has authority to obligate the organization with respect to the matter or whose act or omission in connection with the matter may be imputed to the organization for purposes of civil or criminal liability. Consent of the organization's lawyer is not required for communication with a former constituent. If a constituent of the organization is represented in the matter by his or her own counsel, the consent by that counsel to a communication will be sufficient for purposes of this Rule ...

[8] The prohibition on communications with a represented person only applies in circumstances where the lawyer knows that the person is in fact represented in the matter to be discussed. This means that the lawyer has actual knowledge of the fact of the representation; but such actual knowledge may be inferred from the circumstances. See Rule 1.0(f). Thus, the lawyer cannot evade the requirement of obtaining the consent of counsel by closing eyes to the obvious.

This Rule, sometimes called the "anti-contact" rule, is designed first to prevent lawyers from taking advantage of laypersons, and second to preserve the integrity of the attorney-client relationship.[149] Although the Rule applies only when you have "actual knowledge" that the person is represented, Comment [8] above makes clear that you cannot avoid the Rule by simply "closing [your]

---

149. *See* United States v. Lopez, 4 F.3d 1455 (9th Cir. 1993); Polycast Tech. Corp. v. Uniroyal Inc, 129 F.R.D. 621 (S.D. N.Y. 1990); Michaels v. Woodland, 988 F. Supp. 468 (D. N.J. 1997); ABA Comm. on Ethics and Professional Responsibility, Formal Op. 95-396.

eyes to the obvious" in circumstances where there is substantial reason to believe that the other person is represented.[150] Accordingly, some cases have held that in doubtful situations you have a duty to ask the layperson whether he is represented.[151]

The Rule does not prohibit represented parties from speaking with one another without lawyer consent, but you cannot "mastermind" the inter-party communications by, for example, using your client as a conduit to initiate a conversation with the other party and then take over the conversation with the other party without his lawyer's consent.[152] Nor can you get around the Rule by claiming that you just "listened" to the represented person. It has been held that a lawyer who merely "listens" to an adverse party who initiates a conversation with the lawyer violates the Rule if the interaction occurs without the consent of the adverse party's lawyer.[153]

The Rule, however, does not preclude you from interviewing witnesses of another party.[154] Also, when a governmental agency is the represented party, the Fifth Amendment right of petition permits you to discuss the controversy with government officials without consent of counsel for the Government.[155]

In criminal cases, the courts have repeatedly held that the Rule is inapplicable to communications entered into by a prosecutor, his agents, or informants with a represented criminal suspect, so long as those communications occur in a *non-custodial* setting and *before* the initiation of formal charges.[156] With respect to federal prosecutors, the United States Justice De-

---

150. ABA Standing Committee on Ethics and Professional Responsibility, Formal Op. 95-396 (1995).

151. *See, e.g.,* Monsanto Co. v. Aetna Cas. & Sur. Co., 539 A.2d 1013 (Del. 1990); Upjohn v. Aetna Cas. & Sur. Co., 768 F. Supp. 1186 (W.D. Mich. 1990). Contra Colo. Bar Ass'n Comm. on Professional Ethics, Rev. Op. 69 (1987) (no duty to inquire).

152. *See* Trumball County Bar Ass'n v. Makridis, 671 N.E.2d 31 (Ohio 1996) (lawyer for plaintiff reprimanded when he suggested his client call defendant, and during call, plaintiff handed phone to lawyer who continued conversation with defendant). *Cf.* State Bar of Cal. Standing Comm. on Professional Responsibility and Conduct, Formal Op. 1993-131 (1993) (lawyer may confer with client about strategy to be pursued in client's communications with other party, but content of communication must originate with client, not lawyer).

153. *See, e.g., In re* Howes, 940 P.2d 159 (N.M. 1997).

154. *See* McCallum v. CSX Transp. Inc., 149 F.R.D. 104 (M.D. N.C. 1993); Cole v. Appalachian Power Co., 903 F. Supp. 975 (S.D. W. Va. 1995).

155. *See* Camden v. State of Maryland, 910 F. Supp. 1115 (D. Md. 1996); N.C. State Bar Ass'n Ethics Comm., Op. 219 (1995).

156. *See* United States v. Marcus, 849 F. Supp. 417 (D. Md. 1994); United States v. Balter, 91 F.3d 427 (3d Cir. 1996).

partment has established specific guidelines governing prosecutor contacts with represented persons.[157]

In dealing with an unrepresented person, Rule 4.3 provides:

> In dealing on behalf of a client with a person who is not represented by counsel, a lawyer shall not state or imply that the lawyer is disinterested. When the lawyer knows or reasonably should know that the unrepresented person misunderstands the lawyer's role in the matter, the lawyer shall make reasonable efforts to correct the misunderstanding. The lawyer shall not give legal advice to an unrepresented person, other than the advice to secure counsel, if the lawyer knows or reasonably should know that the interests of such a person are or have a reasonable possibility of being in conflict with the interests of the client.

It is important to note that this Rule covers any communications directed to *any* unrepresented person by a lawyer acting on a client's behalf, including other parties to a proposed transaction, potential witnesses, and opposing parties in planned or pending litigation.

If the person's interests might conflict with those of your client, Rule 4.3 prohibits you from giving advice to an unrepresented person other than the advice to obtain counsel.[158] In addition, although the Rule does not prohibit you from interviewing an unrepresented person (whether a witness or prospective adverse party),[159] when seeking or conducting an interview you should clearly identify your role as lawyer for your client.[160] A number of jurisdictions have held that if the unrepresented person is a potential adverse party, you should notify him that a lawsuit is possible or contemplated;[161] and if a lawsuit

---

157. *See* 28 C.F.R. §77 (1994) (permitting, before charge, arrest, or indictment, *ex parte* contacts with persons known to be represented in the matter being investigated).

158. Comment to Rule 4.3 at paragraph [2].

159. *See, e.g.,* Pennsylvania Ethics Opinion 96-145 (1996); Mississippi Ethics Opinion 141 (1988); New York State Ethics Opinion 607 (1990).

160. *See, e.g.,* Arizona Ethics Opinion 87-25 (1987); Pennsylvania Ethics Opinion 93-156 (1993).

161. *See, e.g.,* Arizona Ethics Opinion 87-25 (1987); Pennsylvania Ethics Opinion 93-156 (1993). When interviewing an unrepresented present or former employee, some jurisdictions have established special protocols to be followed by lawyers. *See, e.g.,* McCallum v. CSX Transp. Inc., 149 F.R.D. 104 (M.D. N.C. 1993) (requiring interviewing lawyer to disclose his representative capacity, nature of interview, and to inform employee of right to refuse interview and have counsel present). *See also* Kan. Bar Ass'n Ethics/Advisory Services Comm., Op. 97-07 (1992).

has already been filed and the unrepresented party does not know about it, you should reveal that information.[162]

Finally, Rule 4.4(a) provides that "[i]n representing a client, a lawyer shall not use means that have no substantial purpose other than to embarrass, delay, or burden a third person, or use methods of obtaining evidence that violate the legal rights of such a person." This Rule essentially commands that, when representing a client, you must act with civility towards all third persons including opposing counsel,[163] the opposing party,[164] witnesses,[165] and the court.[166] In dealing with third persons, you are also obligated to be truthful when making any statements "of material fact or law." (*See* Rule 4.1.)

§6.13 Attorney's Authority to Settle and Advising the Client

Rule 1.2(a) of the Model Rules provides, in part, that "[a] lawyer shall abide by a client's decisions concerning the objectives of representation ... [and] shall consult with the client as to the means by which they are to be pursued." This provision has been interpreted as making a distinction between the client's objectives and the means for achieving them, whereby the lawyer is in charge of "procedural" decisions such as tactics and strategy and the client has the final decision over matters directly affecting the ultimate resolution of the case.[167] However, as a lawyer you generally have no authority to enter into a final agreement to settle a case on behalf of a client merely by virtue of the attorney-client relationship or because you have been given general authority to enter into negotiations.[168] Rather, except in rare emergency situations where prompt action by you is necessary to protect your client's interests and consultation with the

---

162. *See* Brew v. Stern, 603 A.2d 126 (N.J. 1991).

163. *See, e.g.,* St. Paul Fire & Marine Ins. Co., 828 F. Supp. 594 (C.D. Ill. 1992); *In re* Belue, 76 P.2d 206 (Mont. 1988); Principe v. Assay Partners, 586 N.Y.S2d 182 (N.Y. 1992).

164. *See, e.g., In re* Golden, 496 S.E.2d 619 (S.C. 1998); *In re* Bechhold, 771 P.2d 563 (Mont. 1988).

165. *See, e.g., In re* Golden, 496 S.E.2d 619 (S.C. 1998).

166. *See, e.g.,* Kentucky Bar Ass'n v. Waller, 929 S.W.2d 184 (Ky. 1996); *In re* Vincenti, 704 A.2d 927 (N.J. 1998).

167. *See* State v. Debler, 856 S.W.2d 641 (Mo. 1993); State v. Ali, 407 S.E.2d 183 (N.C. 1991); Blanton v. Womancare, Inc., 696 P.2d 645 (Cal. 1985).

168. *See* Faris v. J.C. Penney Co., 2 F. Supp. 2d 695 (E.D. Pa. 1998); Kaiser Foundation v. Doe, 903 P.2d 375 (Or. App. 1995).

client is impossible,[169] most courts require that you have *express* authority from your client to enter into a binding agreement or compromise of an action; and Rule 1.2(a) adopts this position by mandating that "[a] lawyer shall abide by a client's decision whether to settle a matter." In many states, this express authority is otherwise prescribed by statute or local court rule.[170]

Generally, the special authority you need to settle your client's claim can be obtained only when a specific offer is proposed, or when you have been given prior authority to settle within certain limits.[171] This, of course, presupposes appropriate communication between you and your client. Model Rule 1.4 provides, in part:

> (a) A lawyer shall:
>
> (1) promptly inform the client of any decision or circumstance with respect to which the client's informed consent … is required by these Rules;….
>
> (3) keep the client reasonably informed about the status of the matter;
>
> (4) promptly comply with reasonable requests for information;….
>
> (b) A lawyer shall explain a matter to the extent reasonably necessary to permit the client to make informed decisions regarding the representation.

The official Comment to Model Rule 1.4 explains, in pertinent part:

> [2] If these Rules require that a particular decision about the representation be made by the client, paragraph (a)(1) requires that the lawyer promptly consult with and secure the client's consent prior to taking action unless prior discussions with the client have resolved what action the client wants the lawyer to take. For example, a lawyer who receives from opposing counsel an offer of settlement in a civil controversy or a proffered plea bargain in a criminal case must promptly inform the client of its substance unless the client has previously indicated that the proposal will be acceptable or unacceptable or has authorized the lawyer to accept or to reject the offer. See Rule 1.2(a)….

---

169. *See* Sockolof v. Eden Point North Condominium Assoc., 421 So.2d 716 (Fla. App. 1982); Schumann v. Northtown Ins. Agency, Inc., 452 N.W.2d 482 (Minn. App. 1990); Midwest Federal Savings Bank v. Dickinson Econo-Storage, 450 N.W.2d 418 (N.D. 1990).

170. *See generally,* Annotation, *Authority of Attorney to Compromise Action—Modern Cases,* 90 ALR 4th 326 (1991).

171. *See* Lord v. Money Masters, Inc., 435 S.E.2d 247 (Ga. 1993).

[5] The client should have sufficient information to participate intelligently in decisions concerning the objectives of the representation and the means by which they are to be pursued, to the extent the client is willing and able to do so. Adequacy of communication depends in part on the kind of advice or assistance that is involved. For example, when there is time to explain a proposal made in a negotiation, the lawyer should review all important provisions with the client before proceeding to an agreement. In litigation a lawyer should explain the general strategy and prospects of success and ordinarily should consult the client on tactics that are likely to result in significant expense or to injure or coerce others. On the other hand, a lawyer ordinarily will not be expected to describe trial or negotiation strategy in detail. The guiding principle is that the lawyer should fulfill reasonable client expectations for information consistent with the duty to act in the client's best interests....

Thus, you have a duty to disclose to your client all good faith settlement offers,[172] and to adequately explain all ramifications of a proposed agreement or settlement so that your client can make an informed decision.[173] If you settle your client's case without authority, fail to communicate a settlement offer to your client, or fail to adequately advise your client about a potential settlement, you may be subject to discipline by the bar[174] and be liable to the client for malpractice.[175]

§6.14 Contingent Fees

Many settlements occur in personal injury cases, whether arising out of common law negligence, an intentional tort, or a breach of a duty of care defined by statute. Lawyers often take these cases on a contingent fee basis, whereby the attorney's fee is a percentage of the total monetary amount or in-

---

172. *See In re* Cardenas, 791 P.2d 1032 (Ariz. 1990); *In re* Baehr, 744 P.2d 799 (Kan. 1987).

173. *See generally*, Perschbacher, *Regulating Lawyers Negotiations*, 27 Ariz. L. Rev. 76, 115–119 (1985).

174. *See generally*, Annotation, *Conduct of Attorney in Connection with Settlement of Client's Case as Ground for Disciplinary Action*, 92 ALR3d 288 (1979).

175. *See, e.g.*, Moores v. Greenberg, 834 F.2d 1105 (1st Cir. 1987) (attorney may be liable for malpractice for failing to inform client of settlement offer, permitting client to recover damages in the amount of that offer).

terest in property[176] recovered for the client (usually one-third), or a combination of a percentage and an hourly fee.[177] The rationale for contingent fees
is that they provide a means by which clients who cannot afford to pay an
hourly or fixed fee may compensate their lawyers by giving the lawyer a portion
of the winning result. The fact that a lawyer might earn a larger sum of money
in charging a contingent fee than would otherwise be earned from a fixed fee
or at an hourly rate is balanced against the risk that the lawyer will receive no
fee at all if no recovery is obtained for the client.

Model Rule 1.5 provides, in pertinent part:

> (c) A fee may be contingent on the outcome of the matter for which
> the service is rendered, except in a matter in which a contingent fee
> is prohibited by paragraph (d) or other law. A contingent fee
> agreement shall be in a writing signed by the client and shall state the
> method by which the fee is to be determined, including the percentage
> or percentages that shall accrue to the lawyer in the event of settlement,
> trial or appeal; litigation and other expenses to be deducted from the
> recovery; and whether such expenses are to be deducted before or after
> the contingent fee is calculated. The agreement must clearly notify the
> client of any expenses for which the client will be liable whether or
> not the client is the prevailing party. Upon conclusion of a contingent
> fee matter, the lawyer shall provide the client with a written statement
> stating the outcome of the matter and, if there is a recovery, showing
> the remittance to the client and the method of its determination.
>
> (d) A lawyer shall not enter into an arrangement for, charge, or
> collect:
>> (1) any fee in a domestic relations matter, the payment or
>> amount of which is contingent upon the securing of a divorce or
>> upon the amount of alimony or support, or property settlement
>> in lieu thereof; or
>> (2) a contingent fee for representing a defendant in a criminal
>> case.

Like other types of fees, a contingent fee must be reasonable in terms of the
percentage the lawyer will receive of the monetary amount recovered for his

---

176. *See, e.g.,* Beatie v. Delong, 561 NYS2d 448 (N.Y. Sup. Ct. App. Div. 1990)
(upholding 30% of revenues generated by patents whose rights the lawyer recaptured for
the client).

177. *See, e.g.,* Boston and Maine Corp v. Sheehan, Phinney, Bass & Green P.A., 778 F.2d
890 (1st Cir. 1985) (upholding hourly fee plus reduced contingent fee).

client; and the courts retain overall supervisory power to monitor the reasonableness of such fees.[178] Even when this percentage falls within the usual range of percentages charged in similar types of cases, a court may find the percentage unreasonable if the risk of no recovery by the client is virtually nonexistent or the lawyer can easily resolve the matter without much effort.[179] For example, the courts have repeatedly warned that contingent fees are usually inappropriate in cases involving the collection of insurance proceeds when the client's right to that money is clear and it will take little effort to collect it.[180] On the other hand, even a 50% contingent fee may be permissible if the case is very complicated, liability is highly questionable, or a favorable outcome of the case will depend upon considerable skill by the lawyer.[181] In addition, by statute or local court rule, some jurisdictions limit the percentages that may be charged in matters such as workers' compensation cases, social security cases, medical malpractice[182] or civil rights actions,[183] or in cases involving the representation of children.[184] These statutory limitations may never be exceeded in a contingent fee contract.

Rule 1.5(c) requires that the contingent fee contract be in writing and signed by the client. The agreement must state the percentage or percentages of the

---

178. Thornton, Sperry & Jensen Ltd. v. Anderson, 352 N.W.2d 467 (Minn App. 1984); West Virginia State Bar Committee on Legal Ethics v. Taterson, 352 S.E.2d 107 (W.Va. Sup.Ct.App. 1986).

179. *See, e.g., In re* Gerard, 548 N.E.2d 1051 (Ill. 1989) (lawyer disciplined for collecting contingent fee of 35.2% to locate and collect client's assets to which no adverse claims were made, where it took the lawyer no more than 160 hours to perform the task and contingent fee amounted to approximately $1000 per hour of work).

180. *See In re* Hanna, 362 S.E.2d 632 (S.C. 1987); West Virginia State Bar Committee on Legal Ethics v. Tatterson, 352 S.E.2d 107 (W.Va. Sup. Ct. App. 1986); Maryland Attorney Grievance Commission v. Kemp, 496 A.2d 672 (Md. App. 1985).

181. *E.g.,* Sweeney v. Athens Regional Medical Center, 917 F.2d 1560 (11th Cir. 1990); Fraidin v. Weitzman, 611 A.2d 1046 (Md. Ct. Spec. App. 1992). Cf. West Virginia State Bar Committee on Legal Ethics v. Gallaher, 376 S.E.2d 346 (W.Va. Sup. Ct. App. 1988) (50% contingent fee excessive where lawyer achieved modest settlement of client's case in less than seventeen hours; one-third fee would have been more appropriate); Maryland Attorney Grievance Commission v. Korotki, 569 A.2d 1224 (Md. App. 1990) (even though case was complex and involved a trial and two appeals, successive contracts adding up to 75% contingent fee constituted excessive fee).

182. *See generally,* Annotation, *Validity of Statute Establishing Contingent Fee Scale for Attorneys Representing Parties in Medical Malpractice Actions,* 12 ALR4th 23 (1982).

183. *See* Federal Tort Claims Act, 28 USC 2678, limiting contingent fees to 25% (or 20% if the case is settled at the administrative level).

184. *See generally* Annotation, *Court Rules Limiting Amount of Contingent Fees or Otherwise Imposing Conditions on Contingent Fee Contracts,* 77 ALR2d 411 (1961).

recovery to which you will be entitled if your client's case (1) is settled (making clear whether a different percentage applies if the case is settled during trial, as opposed to prior to trial); (2) goes to trial (or is retried); and (3) is appealed. If a structured settlement is possible, you should state whether the fee will be based on a percentage of the lump sum immediately received by your client plus the present value of the future payments to which your client is entitled, or on a percentage of each future payment received by your client when it is received. In addition, the agreement must state generally the "litigation and other expenses to be deducted from the recovery," and whether your percentage of the recovery will be taken from the gross amount before deduction of expenses or the net amount after deduction of expenses.[185] The agreement might also contain a clause that, in the event you are discharged from the case without good cause, you will be entitled to a fee amounting to the reasonable value of your services under *quantum meruit*, expressed as either a reduced percentage of the amount recovered by your client or a fee based on an hourly rate.[186]

Rule 1.5(d)(1) states explicitly that you cannot charge a contingent fee if the contingency is your client's obtaining a divorce, or if the amount of the fee is dependent on what your client is awarded as alimony or child support or in a "property settlement" in lieu of alimony or child support. However, in most states you are permitted to charge a contingent fee where your client's right to alimony or child support has *already* been established judicially and the aim of the representation is the collection of past-due payments of alimony or child support. Jurisdictions are divided about whether the Rule's prohibition against contingent fees in "property settlement" matters embraces equitable distribution cases. Some courts holding that a contingent fee in an equitable distribution case is permissible so long as the contract does not simultaneously provide for compensation contingent on securing a divorce, or obtaining alimony or child support.[187]

Finally, Rule 1.5(c) provides that, at the conclusion of the contingent fee representation, you are obligated to provide your client with a written financial accounting of the monies to be disbursed in connection with the case. The dis-

---

185. *See* Louisiana State Bar Assoc. v. St. Romain, 560 So.2d 820 (la. 1990) (attorney privately reprimanded for using retainer agreement that did not specify how expenses would be deducted).

186. *See generally*, Annotation, *Limitation to Quantum Meruit Recovery, Where Attorney Employed Under Contingent Fee Contract is Discharged Without Cause*, 92 ALR3d 690 (1979); Annotation, *Circumstances Under Which Attorney Retains Right to Compensation Notwithstanding Voluntary Withdrawal from Case*, 88 ALR3d 246 (1978).

187. *See* Williams v. Garrison, 411 S.E.2d 633 (N.C. App. 1992).

bursement statement must state "the outcome of the matter and, if there is a recovery, show[] the remittance to the client and method of its determination." A failure to abide by this requirement may result in disciplinary action.[188]

§6.15 Example of Contingent Fee Contract

Contingent Fee Contract

The law firm of _____ (Attorneys) is retained and employed by _____ (Client) to represent Client in a claim for damages against _____ or any others who may be liable for injuries that Client sustained on _____ [Date] _____.

1. This is a contingent fee contract and it is agreed that if Attorneys recover no compensation for Client, Client owes Attorneys no fee until a favorable recovery is obtained. If a recovery is obtained on behalf of Client, Attorneys shall receive as attorneys' fees _____% of any recovery obtained, whether by settlement or trial. If an appeal is taken or proceedings are necessary to collect any judgment, the attorneys' fees shall increase to _____%. These percentages shall be calculated and paid based on the gross amount recovered for Client, and before deduction of any costs, litigation expenses, or medical charges and expenses as provided for in paragraphs 3 and 4.

2. If settlement of this case is made by a structured settlement, attorneys' fees shall be based on the present cash value of the settlement as determined by actuarial experts, and such fees shall be paid out of the initial cash lump sum payment.

3. In addition to attorneys' fees, all court costs, expert witness fees, subpoena costs, photographs, depositions, court reporter fees, reports, witness statements, photocopying, telephone, travel and all other out-of-pocket expenses directly incurred in investigating, preparing or litigating this claim shall be paid by client irrespective of the outcome of this case, and Attorneys may deduct those amounts from the Client's share of the proceeds of any recovery.

---

188. *See* Florida Bar v. Rood, 633 So.2d 7 (Fla. 1994).

4. All medical expenses and charges of any nature made by doctors, hospitals, clinics, or other health-care providers in connection with the diagnosis or treatment of Client's injuries shall be paid by Client. In the event that Attorneys recover damages on Client's behalf, Client authorizes Attorneys to pay all such expenses and charges that are unpaid as of that date from Client's share of the recovery.

5. Client agrees not to make any settlement of this case without Attorneys being present and receiving all payments due them under this Contract.

6. Client agrees that Attorneys have made no promises or guarantees about the outcome of this case.

7. Client and Attorneys each have a copy of this Contract, and its terms are acceptable.

This the _____ day of _____, [year].

_____

by: _____

[Client]

[Attorneys]

Chapter Seven

Interviewing Witnesses

SYNOPSIS

§7.01 Introduction

Witnesses typically fall into one of three categories: the "friendly" witness, who is sympathetic to or aligned with your client's cause; the "neutral" witness, who has "no ax to grind" one way or another; and the "adverse" witness, who is unsympathetic or even hostile to your client's cause. Regardless of the type of witness you interview, the *ABA's Model Rules of Professional Conduct* set out five pertinent proscriptions on your conduct.

First, you must not "communicate about the subject of the representation with a person [you know] to be represented by another lawyer in the matter, unless [you have] the consent of the other lawyer or [are] authorized to do so by law or a court order" (Rule 4.2). Second, you are prohibited from "mak[ing] a false statement of material fact or law" (Rule 4.1(a)), and from "engag[ing] in conduct involving dishonesty, fraud, deceit or misrepresentation" (Rule 8.4(c)). Third, you cannot "state or imply [to a person not represented by counsel] that [you, as a lawyer, are] disinterested" or "give legal advice to an unrepresented person, other than the advice to secure counsel, if [you] know or reasonably should know" that there is "a reasonable possibility" of a conflict of interest between the unrepresented person and your client (Rule 4.3). Fourth, you cannot "request a person other than a client to refrain from voluntarily giving relevant information to another party unless: (1) the person is a relative or an employee or other agent of a client; and (2) [you] reasonably believe[] that the person's interests will not be adversely affected by refraining from giving such information" (Rule 3.4(f)). And fifth, you must not "falsify evidence, counsel or assist a witness to testify falsely, or offer an inducement to a witness that is prohibited by law" (Rule 3.4(b)). As to this last prohibition, it has been said that "when a lawyer discusses the case with a witness, the lawyer must not try to bend the witness's story or put words in the witness's mouth."[1]

All of the foregoing apply to your interaction with any kind of witness. Likewise, all of the "Types of Questions" and "Information-Gathering Techniques" discussed in Sections 4.05 and 4.06 should be employed, as appropriate, when interviewing a witness. However, because you have no attorney-client relationship with a witness, effective witness interviewing also requires an understanding of who should conduct the interview, how to prepare for the interview, how to arrange the interview and develop rapport with the witness, what techniques are best suited for interviewing neutral or adverse witnesses, and how to preserve the witness's testimony for future use. These matters are discussed below.

§7.02 Who Should Interview the Witness

Most lawyers prefer to interview a witness themselves, sometimes taking along an associate lawyer or paralegal to hear the witness's story and take notes. This is so because, as the client's attorney, you are the person most familiar with the facts and law affecting your client's case and therefore are in the best position to know what to ask the witness. In addition, as the attorney who will try the case if it goes to trial, you are in the best position to evaluate the witness's effect on a judge or jury. Having an associate or paralegal accompany you to the interview is also helpful not only for note-taking purposes, but will allow you to call the associate attorney or paralegal to testify in court to impeach the witness if the witness testifies differently at trial.[2]

---

1. Richard C. Wydick, *The Ethics of Witness Coaching*, 17 Cardozo L. Rev. 1 (1995).

2. Under Rule 3.7(b) of the Model Rules of Professional Conduct, an associate lawyer in your firm is not, for that reason alone, prohibited from testifying at a trial where you are the client's principal attorney. The testimony of a paralegal in your law office would not be barred under this Rule in any event.

Alternatively, you might choose to send an associate lawyer, paralegal, or private investigator to conduct the interview. Attorneys often hire private investigators to conduct witness interviews in criminal cases. Finally, you may decide to send someone to conduct a witness interview because you think the witness will feel more comfortable answering questions posed by someone of the same race, gender or age.

Regardless of whom you send to conduct the interview, you must thoroughly brief the interviewer about your client's case and what you need to know from the witness. In addition, to comply with Model Rule 5.3(b), you must "make reasonable efforts to ensure that the person's conduct is compatible with [your] professional obligations [as a] lawyer," which include all of the ethical proscriptions set out at the beginning of this Section.

§7.03 Preparing for the Interview

Before interviewing a witness, whether a fact witness or an expert witness, you must be thoroughly prepared about what to ask. Ideally, you should already have a good grasp of all salient, adverse, disputed, and unknown facts and legal theories bearing upon your client's case. Based on these matters, you should be able to formulate questions that elicit what you need to find out from the witness. Because the best advocates are their own best "devil's advocates," this includes discovering information that undercuts the factual or legal theories of your client's case as well as those that bolster your client's case. That is, because you will have to formulate a strategy for dealing with adverse facts, the information you obtain from a witness that hurts your client's case is as important as the information you obtain that helps your client's case.

Thus, prepare an outline of what you need to find out from the witness based upon (1) everything your client has told you, (2) all facts you have otherwise obtained, (3) all documentary and physical evidence, and (4) all legal principles pertinent to the case (including applicable burdens of proof and evidentiary considerations). Be sure to include in your outline rote inquiries about how to contact the witness in the future, whether the witness has talked with anyone else about the case, whether the witness has given any written statements, and whether the witness has knowledge of any other matters bearing on the case that you have not covered.

For example, before lawyer Larry Odden interviewed Police Officer Boles (see §5.10 at lines 3 through 15), Larry might have prepared an outline of what he needed to find out from Boles as follows:

Contact and Background Information for Boles

- Boles's work and home address; regular telephone number; pager/cell phone numbers; email addresses.
- Boles's rank on the police force; how long he has been on the force; and a general description of his duties.

How Boles Came to the Accident Scene

- What caused him to go to the accident scene?
- Dispatcher? What did the dispatcher say? When did he get the call to go to the scene?
- When did he arrive at the scene?

What Boles Observed at the Accident Scene

- Ask him to describe and explain what he observed.
- Go over the accident report with him: all details about the positions of the vehicles when he arrived, weather conditions, road conditions, traffic conditions, tire skid marks on the road, etc.
- Describe any damage to the vehicles; were any driveable?

Did Any Other Officers Arrive at the Scene?

- If so, who and when?
- What did they do?
- Who did they speak to, and what was said?
- What did they tell Boles?
- What did Boles tell them?
- Obtain all contact information for the other officers.

Explain How the Accident Scene Was Cleared to Resume Regular Traffic

- How were the vehicles moved from the intersection?
- Who called the wrecker? What is the name and address of the wrecker service? When did the wrecker arrive? When did the wrecker remove the vehicles? Where did the wrecker take the vehicles?

Ask About Boles's Conversations with All Persons Involved in the Accident and Any Other Witnesses to the Accident

- Who did Boles talk to about how the accident happened? Where and when?
- What did each person say? What was each person's demeanor? What did Boles say in response?
- If any other officer talked with persons involved in the accident or any other witness to the accident, what does Boles know about those conversations?

Show Photos of Accident Scene to Boles
- Ask Boles to mark and show on the photos the position of the vehicles as he saw them at the time he arrived at the accident scene.

Why Did Boles Not Issue a Citation to Any Driver?

Did Boles Observe Any Injuries to Any Person as a Result of the Accident?
- If so, detail all injury complaints and who made those complaints.

Is there Anything Else Boles Can Say About How the Accident Happened?

§7.04 Arranging the Interview and Developing Rapport

Arranging an interview of a friendly witness will usually be easy. With a simple telephone call, such a witness may readily meet with you at your office, at the witness's home, or at work during a "break." However, a neutral or adverse witness will usually be much less accommodating. In this situation, you must be particularly tactful, personable, and mindful of the witness's sensibilities and availability for the interview.

Thus, the key to arranging an interview with a neutral or adverse witness is to do so in as personable and convenient way as possible, consistent with your professional obligations to identify yourself as a lawyer for your client. Generally, the best approach is to first telephone the witness. In a likeable and non-threatening tone, tell the witness that you need his/her help in understanding all of the facts of the situation. For example, in a telephone call to Officer Boles to arrange an interview, Larry Odden might say:

Officer Boles, I'm Larry Odden, an attorney representing Clara Miles in connection with an automobile accident that you investigated on February 8 of last year. She was a passenger in her husband Dan's car, which was hit broad-side by another car at the intersection of Franklin and Estes Drive. To more fully understand what happened, I would like to talk with you about the accident. I know your time is limited, but I could meet with you at your office or even at the accidence scene, whenever and wherever it would be most convenient for you. Can you help me with this?

Don't try to coerce the witness to meet with you by threatening to subpoena or depose the witness. Threats or coercion may turn a neutral witness into an adverse one and an adverse witness into an even more hostile one. Similarly, don't promise the witness that, if he agrees to be interviewed, he won't be deposed or subpoenaed to testify at a trial. This is a promise that you can never guarantee, if only because the opposing party may decide to depose the witness or subpoena him to trial.

Make every effort to interview the witness in person rather than over the telephone. This is important because your ability to obtain maximum information, as well as your ability to assess the demeanor and credibility of the witness, is greatly enhanced by a face-to-face meeting. In addition, meeting personally with the witness will provide you with a greater opportunity to build rapport with the witness when he perceives you as courteous, respectful, and friendly.

Accordingly, whenever possible, tactfully resist a mere telephone interview. Volunteer your willingness to meet with the witness at any time and place most convenient to him. If you have documentary or physical evidence to show the witness, explain that reviewing these matters will be less time consuming in a face-to-face meeting. If the witness has no particular preference about where to meet, suggest the location that you believe is most likely to maximize your efforts to obtain information. Depending upon the particular circumstances, this may be at the witness's home or office, the accident scene, or your office.

Finally, when you are successful in arranging a time and place for the interview, be sure to thank the witness with an expression of non-canned gratitude—again to help build rapport. For example, when Officer Boles agreed to meet with Larry Odden, Larry may have concluded the telephone conversation with Boles by saying, "*Thank you, Officer; I appreciate your professionalism and time on this. I look forward to seeing you.*" If the witness declines your request for an interview, maintain your civility. If necessary, in a civil case you can always depose the witness; and, in a civil or criminal case, you can always subpoena the witness to testify at trial.[3] If Officer Boles turned down Larry's request for an interview, Larry might say, "*I understand and respect your decision; I'm only trying to do my job for my client. If your schedule frees up, please feel free to give me a call at any time and I will be happy to meet with you at any time or place that would be best for you.*"

---

3. The refusal of a witness to talk with you may be used at trial to impeach the witness.

§7.05 Interviewing the Neutral or Adverse Witness

As mentioned in the introduction to this Section, all of the "Types of Questions" and "Information-Gathering Techniques" discussed in Sections 4.05 and 4.06 are generally applicable to interviewing witnesses, particularly friendly witnesses. However, unlike friendly witnesses who will usually give you the time to question through a series of open, follow-up, closed, leading, and summary questions under "The Funnel Technique," neutral or adverse witnesses may not tolerate the time required for, nor have the disposition to accommodate, the Funnel-Technique approach. Under these circumstances, you must be prepared (see the outline in §7.03 above) to take a more focused and "to-the-point" approach to the interview.

Basically, this approach suggests that you (1) begin the interview (i.e., after preliminary "small talk") with questions about non-controversial matters that will not offend the witness and will help build rapport with him, and (2) then employ mostly closed and leading questions (*without* the tag lines beginning with "It's true that …?" or ending with "… that's correct, isn't it?") during the information-gathering stage of the interview.

As for beginning with non-controversial and rapport-building questions, you might start the interview by first asking some questions about certain flattering or endearing matters that are important to the witness based on what you learned from your preliminary small talk—i.e., questions about one or more significant accomplishments of the witness, whether vocationally or avocationally; how the witness's children are doing in school, sports, or their careers; how an ill relative or spouse is faring, etc. The overall goal here is to try to put the witness at ease and to have him appreciate you as a "person," rather than as a mere interviewer-advocate.

Next, when you proceed to the more substantive topics of the interview, (i.e., the facts of what happened), try starting with open questions, such as "What happened?" or "Could you describe … or explain …?" If the witness is glib or reticent (as may be the case for a neutral or adverse witness), use a combination of closed and non-adversarial leading questions to flesh out the witness's story.

For example, if Officer Boles (as a neutral witness) was not particularly responsive to an open question by Larry Odden as to what Boles observed when he arrived at the accident scene, Larry's (L) questioning of the Officer (B) might proceed as follows:

L: Sergeant Boles, let's look at your accident report.

B: Okay.

L: On it, you have drawn Dan's car here [pointing to accident report] and Mr. Smith's car here [pointing to accident report].

B: Yes.

L: Was that the position of the vehicles when you first saw them?

B: Yes.

L: So, Dan's car was approximately two-thirds of the way through the intersection at the time of impact?

B: Yes; that's about right.

L: Would you say that Dan's car was almost through the intersection when the accident occurred?

B: I think that's fair.

L: Was the damage to Dan's car on the front passenger side of the car [pointing to accident report]?

B: Yes; that's what I saw.

L: If the traffic light turned yellow when Dan entered the intersection, would he have three seconds to clear the intersection before the light turned red?

B: That's about right, about three seconds.

L: After the light on Franklin Street turns from yellow to red, is there a one- or two-second delay before the Estes Drive light turns green?

B: Yes, it's about a one- or two-second delay based on standard Department of Transportation guidelines. You can check with them to confirm.

L: So this gave Dan up to five seconds to fully clear the intersection before the light turned green?

B: Yes; well, maybe, depending upon whether there is a one- or two-second delay for the light on Estes.

L: I want to be fair. Would you be able to say that Dan had approximately four to five seconds to clear the intersection before the Estes light turned green?

B: Yeah, I'd agree that's fair to say; four to five seconds.

Bearing in mind the ethical proscription that you must not "counsel or assist a witness to testify falsely" (*see* Model Rule 3.4(f)), your questions still might suggest or lead to a favorable modification of a neutral or adverse witness's initial story. If the facts relayed by the witness point to a different opinion or conclusion than the one initially held by the witness, it is not unethical for you to point this out in a fair way.[4]

For example, in light of Larry's colloquy with Officer Boles above, Larry might question Boles's decision not to give a citation to Ronald Smith as follows:

> L: Based on what we've talked about, it would appear that Mr. Smith entered the intersection on a red light—
>
> B: Well, that may be true; but I'm not sure of that.
>
> L: I understand you have to call the balls and strikes as you see them.
>
> B: Yes, that's a good way of putting it; I do the best I can.
>
> L: Let me be upfront with you, Sergeant. From everything I've been told and have been able to look at, it seems that Dan had more than enough time to go through the intersection on a yellow light before Mr. Smith had a green light and proceeded into the intersection from a stopped position that would have added yet another second or two to the four to five seconds we have been talking about.
>
> B: Well, that may be a good theory.
>
> L: I suppose what I am asking is whether you think my theory is plausible?
>
> B: Sure, it's plausible; and that may well be what actually happened.
>
> L: You chose not to issue a citation to anyone—
>
> B: Yes; and I stand by that. There were conflicting stories about what happened: Mr. Miles said he had a green or yellow light; Mr. Smith said he had a green light.
>
> L: I fully understand, and I don't fault your decision on this in any way. But let me clarify something for my own purposes. If asked, would you be comfortable in saying that, based on everything you know about this accident, it is more likely than not that Mr. Miles ran a red light?
>
> B: I would be willing to say that my investigation is consistent with your version about what happened.

---

4. *See, e.g.*, D.C. Bar Ethics Opinion No. 79 (December 18, 1979) ("… [T]he fact that the particular words in which testimony, whether written or oral, is cast originated with a lawyer rather than the witness whose testimony it is has no significance so long as the substance of that testimony is not, so far as the lawyer knows or ought to know, false or misleading."). *See also* State v. McCormick, 298 N.C. 788, 791–92 (N.C. 1979) (preparation of a witness by an attorney so that the witness' testimony at trial is presented in the most effective manner is not improper "so long as the attorney is preparing the witness to give the witness' testimony at trial and not the testimony that the attorney has placed in the witness' mouth and not false or perjured testimony").

L: Do you mean that my version is the most likely scenario about what happened?

B: I would say that it is a likely version of what happened, but I stand on my decision not to charge any of the drivers involved.

L: You would be able to say that my version is, quote, "likely" based on everything you know.

B: Yes; I would say that.[5]

Finally, if the witness's testimony remains equivocal, contradictory, or otherwise nonsensical in light of undisputed facts, resist any temptation to argue with the witness. The interview is not a time to give the witness a rehearsal of what cross-examination may be like. Instead, take careful notes on the matters about which the witness may be impeached. These impeachment matters might be raised in a deposition,[6] and certainly you will bring them up at a trial.

§7.06 Preserving the Witness's Testimony

At the conclusion of your interview with a witness (or one conducted solely by an associate lawyer, paralegal, or private investigator), you must appropriately preserve the witness's testimony for future evidentiary use. Most lawyers recast their notes from the interview to prepare a typewritten statement or affidavit for the witness's subsequent signature. If the witness's testimony is relatively brief, some lawyers will draft a handwritten statement in the presence of the witness and have him or her review and sign the statement on the spot. When using either method, be sure that the typewritten affidavit or handwritten statement contains the witness's signature, date of signature, and a recital to the following effect: "I [name of witness] have carefully read the foregoing and adopt it as my own statement, based upon my personal knowledge and belief."

---

5. Officer Boles's opinion would not be admissible at trial for lack of personal knowledge (*i.e.*, he did not actually see the accident happen) and because he would not qualify as an accident-reconstruction expert. Nevertheless, his opinion that it is "likely" that Mr. Smith ran the red light (even though Smith was not cited for that violation) may be of value to Larry in settlement discussions with Smith's insurance carrier.

6. In an ordinary discovery deposition, as opposed to one taken on tape or disk for full replay at trial, it is also generally unwise to give the deponent a rehearsal of what it will be like to be cross-examined.

There is one caveat that you should keep in mind when you are drafting a witness statement. If the case you are investigating eventually ends up in litigation, a "statement" is discoverable under Rule 26(b)(3)(c) of the Federal Rules of Civil Procedure if it is "a written statement signed or otherwise adopted by the person making it, or a stenographic, mechanical, electrical, or other recording, or a transcription thereof, which is a substantially verbatim recital of an oral statement by the person making it and contemporaneously recorded." If what the witness says appears helpful to your case, there should be no problem in drafting a statement for the witness to sign that you will eventually produce in discovery if the case goes into litigation. However, if the witness's statement is unfavorable to your case, you should weigh the value of a written statement that you can use to impeach the witness if his trial testimony is worse than his statement against the likelihood that your opponent will demand copies of all statements in discovery.

Sometimes, but quite rarely, the witness will agree to have his testimony recorded. In that event, you (or any other person recording the interview) must ensure an appropriate "chain of custody" of the recording. In many circumstances, however, recording the witness's testimony will make the witness uncomfortable and inhibit the interviewer's efforts to obtain maximum and forthright information.

Chapter Eight

Counseling and Decision-Making in Special Contexts

SYNOPSIS

§8.01 Introduction

The specific content of your counseling depends, of course, on the particular situation or problem presented by your client. Chapters 3 and 5 discuss your counseling function as part of the client's decision-making process in all types of client representation. This Chapter discusses counseling in certain special contexts: (1) when counseling about wise objectives and non-litigation options;

(2) when counseling about settlement; (3) when counseling through opinion letters; (4) when counseling the client as a deponent; and (5) when counseling the criminal defendant.

§8.02 Counseling about Wise Objectives and Non-Litigation Options

Good judgment is "the [lawyer's] principal stock in trade [and is] the most valuable thing a lawyer has to offer clients—more valuable than legal learning or skillful analysis of doctrine."[1] Good judgment involves counseling about "precisely the right thing at precisely the right moment" and includes "appreciating the hidden complexity in questions that seem easy when they are posed in the abstract."[2]

Many lawyers, in their early years of practice, lack the quality of the "good judgment" described above. This has less to do with lack of experience (although that is a factor) as it has to do with the vestiges of three years of repetitive legal training in the rigid paradigm of "legal analysis"—i.e., identifying the relevant facts, identifying the issue(s) to be decided, researching the pertinent principles of law, and then applying the facts to the law to reach a result. Thus, many young lawyers are constrained to think exclusively in this "box of the law." This sometimes tends to cause them to jettison their practical sense and broader imagination in counseling a client about her situation or problem.

In contrast, older and more experienced lawyers tend to consider how a client's problem might be addressed or resolved outside of the mere "box of the law." This does not mean that legal considerations bearing upon the client's problem are ignored or considered unimportant, but the lawyer's initial focus is often on how best to achieve the client's underlying goals and objectives outside the strictures of the law and the attendant expense of protracted litigation. That is, experienced lawyers place a premium on "not only [the] law but [on] other considerations such as moral, economic, social and political factors, that may be relevant to the client's situation" (Model Rule 2.1). In short, experienced lawyers know that, frequently, there is a wholly different way to "skin the cat" in dealing with a client's problem than what might be provided by the law alone.

---

1. David Luban and Michael Millemann, *Good Judgment: Ethics Teaching in Dark Times*, 9 Geo. J. Leg. Ethics 31, 34 (1995).

2. *Id.* n. 7 at 71; Thucydides, *History of the Peloponnesian War*, I. 138 (R. Warner trans. 1954).

This preface about experienced client representation and "good judgment" raises two issues addressed in this Section: in counseling your client: (1) what general tests should be considered in identifying wise objectives? and (2) what general tests should be considered in choosing best options for achieving those objectives?

[1] General Tests for Identifying Wise Objectives

As discussed in § 3.06, it is important at the initial client meeting to obtain at least a sense of your client's objectives—i.e., what he would like to accomplish or how he believes his situation or problem might best be resolved. These potential objectives should be explored by you through questions about the client's feelings, needs, concerns, motivations, hopes and desires, and his psychological, social, economic, and moral or ideological interests (*see* § 5.06[1]). In subsequent meetings and counseling sessions, you will revisit these matters to help your client more clearly define his objectives and the best options for achieving them. (*See* §§ 5.04 and 5.07.)

In this process, there are four tests you might employ to help your client define his objectives. In general, a "wise" objective:

(1) is based on the client's more rational sensibilities, rather than upon the influence of extreme emotion (such as anger or hurt);
(2) will not result in long-term loss for the sake of short-term gain;
(3) is reasonably achievable in terms of cost and time; and
(4) generally seeks "less" rather than "more," because a greater objective usually involves more risk, expense, and time.

For example, a client who is under the influence of anger and hurt stemming from a bitter divorce may seek sole custody of the parties' children merely as a form of "revenge" against his former spouse. When he cools down, the client is likely to realize that any short-term psychological satisfaction he might obtain by going to court and testifying about his spouse's failings is far outweighed by the long-term harm this might cause his children. In addition, he may be able to understand your advice that obtaining sole custody in lieu of joint custody or expansive visitation is not reasonably achievable. Similarly, a real estate developer who is outraged by a city's denial of his rezoning or special use permit application to build a project may have difficulty realizing that contesting the action in court may be more risky and more costly in time and money than developing a strategy to revise the scope of his project to address the concerns of objecting neighbors and then make another application for zoning approval.

In your role as your client's "advisor," not his "dictator," you have an obligation to "exercise independent professional judgment and render candid advice" (*see* § 6.05); and this means exercising your professional judgment and rendering candid advice about your client's objectives. If you believe that your client's objectives are unwise, you might:

- Share with the client your experience about how similarly situated clients have formulated their objectives.
- Ask the client what he sees as being the short-term and long-term consequences of the proposed objective.
- Reassure the client that you are on "his side" and want him to pursue an objective that he will be comfortable with and benefit from in the long run.
- Ask the client how he might define his objectives if he were considering them months or years from now.
- Spend ample time, if necessary, allowing the client to "vent" his feelings of anger, hurt, fear, frustration or the like.
- Ask the client what he would have done about the problem or situation on his own, had he not consulted you.
- Share with the client your best judgment about the extent to which his proposed objectives are achievable in terms of his personal and financial cost, time and risk.
- If appropriate, tactfully share with the client the wisdom of the adage that "less is often better than more," and that sometimes we should "be careful about what we wish for."

[2] General Tests for Choosing Best Options

Closely related to defining wise objectives is developing the most realistic and efficacious options, including extra-legal or non-litigation options, for achieving those objectives. For many clients, particularly (though not exclusively) corporate, governmental, or institutional clients, the best option is often the one that, compared with alternative options, best satisfies four general tests.[3] Under these tests, the best option:

(1) is, as a first step, peaceful rather than warlike;
(2) is least expensive to execute in terms of money, time and effort;
(3) results in the least adverse publicity or public exposure; and

---

3. *See* Paul J. Zwier, *Legal Strategy* at 115–124 (NITA 2005).

(4) carries the least risk in terms of being wrong about the assumptions made, the facts, and the law.

Thus, when helping your client to identify potential options and the likely outcomes of each option (*see* §§ 5.05 and 5.06), each of these tests might be applied to each potential option. In the end, the option that fares best on these tests may be the one to choose at the outset, followed by the second or third best options if the first one is unsuccessful in achieving the objective.

For example, suppose you represent Parkwood Homes, a company that constructs mobile homes and operates mobile home parks in your state and in various other states throughout the country. Parkwood's primary competitor in your state is Delmar Homes, which is engaged in the same business and has embarked on a strategy to monopolize the mobile-home-living market in your state. As part of its promotional literature, Delmar has recently been distributing a flyer to prospective lessees/owners of the company's homes; and Parkwood believes that Delmar may repeat the representations made in the flyer in a forthcoming statewide newspaper advertising campaign. The flyer says, in part:

> The homes by Delmar beat out Parkwood homes any day! If you want first-rate construction, complaint-free living, and beautiful landscaping, choose Delmar as your first-choice living experience. Parkwood can't give you that and won't give you that. But Delmar can and will!

Parkwood contends that these representations are defamatory and also may violate the state's Unfair and Deceptive Trade Practices statute. Parkwood's objective is to stop Delmar from continuing to make these disparaging statements now and in the future.

However, Parkwood admits to you that three years ago it had to replace the roofing on about twenty of its homes after the roofs were damaged by an unusually severe thunderstorm. Two years ago, the siding on about fifty homes had to be replaced due to a manufacturing defect in the siding, which was not caused by Parkwood or its construction of the homes. Last year, Parkwood received numerous calls from homeowners in one of its parks in the state, complaining that the Management Company hired by Parkwood to maintain the common areas of the park was neglecting to maintain the landscaping. Parkwood has since been assured by the Management Company that these complaints have been addressed.

Assume that, based on your discussions with Parkwood, you and your client have come up with a list of the following potential options. Under each option is a summary of its pros and cons, particularly in light of the four tests described above:[4]

- Sue Delmar for defamation and Unfair and Deceptive Trade Practices, seeking preliminary and permanent injunctive relief and damages.

This option "declares war." Assuming that the mere filing of suit would not cause Delmar to altogether abandon its derogatory advertising, the option is highly expensive in terms of lawyers' fees and costs and in the long run will take considerable time and effort to execute. Winning the suit on the merits is a risky proposition under the facts and the law. Parkwood is unlikely to establish the requisite likelihood of success on the merits, irreparable harm, and balancing of the equities in its favor to justify preliminary injunctive relief. On the defamation claim, a court or jury might conclude that the assertions in the flyer are mere expressions of opinion, rather than actionable statements of fact that are either true or false. In addition, Delmar might succeed with the complete defense of "truth" of its statements. To the extent the Unfair and Deceptive Trade Practices statute requires proof that consumers were misled by Delmar's false statements, Parkwood currently has no evidence to support that element of the statutory claim. Even if Parkwood ultimately prevailed on the merits, its damages may be entirely speculative or otherwise not justify the expense of litigation. Finally, suing Delmar may result in adverse publicity for Parkwood insofar as one of the issues in the case will be whether Delmar's statements were true.

- Send a demand letter to Delmar, demanding that it cease its false statements or risk a lawsuit.

This option is less warlike than immediately filing suit. It is neither expensive nor particularly time-consuming, and it will not result in adverse public exposure unless Delmar publicizes the letter (which would be unlikely). On the other hand, the letter may provoke Delmar into vigorously defending its statements and quickly escalate the matter into litigation, which will carry all of the risks on the facts and the law previously mentioned. In addition, Parkwood does not want to threaten legal action unless it is willing to take such action if Delmar continues to make its false statements.

---

4. The hypothetical is a variation of one used in Paul J. Zwier, *Legal Strategy* at 117–124 (NITA 2005). The facts in the hypothetical are quite abbreviated. The point here is to merely get a basic understanding of how to apply the four tests for choosing the best option among multiple potential options.

- Propose informal mediation with Delmar.

Parkwood might propose that the matter be discussed between the companies through a mediation session conducted by, for example, the president or other representative of the state's homebuilders' association or by some other mediator agreed to by the parties. This is a peaceful option that involves minimal time, cost and effort. Under typical mediation and evidentiary rules, the matters discussed at the mediation would remain confidential and inadmissible in any court proceeding. Mediation is otherwise a low-risk option because a skilled mediator may be able to diffuse tensions, correct misunderstandings, and allow the parties to save face in resolving the situation.

- Use informal persuasion to convince Delmar to stop its derogatory advertising.

Parkwood's CEO could arrange a meeting with Delmar's CEO to try to resolve the matter, or Parkwood might instruct you to call or meet with Delmar's lawyer toward the same end. This is a peaceful option if handled skillfully. It is low cost in terms of money, time, and effort to execute; and it is unlikely to result in adverse public exposure. Of course, the success of this option (as against exacerbating the controversy) will depend heavily upon the interpersonal approach taken by the parties' representatives in discussing the matter.

- Engage in negative advertising, criticizing Delmar's mobile home parks.

This option is not peaceful and will involve significant cost, time and effort to execute. Delmar may retaliate by expanding the scope of its own negative advertising, thus increasing adverse public exposure for Parkwood and the likelihood of an eventual lawsuit between the parties.

- Engage in positive advertising, extolling the virtues of Parkwood's mobile home parks.

Although this option is peaceful, it also involves significant cost, time and effort. Moreover, although a positive advertising campaign may enhance Parkwood's image in the market, those gains may be offset by an ongoing negative advertising campaign waged by Delmar.

- Hire a new Management Company to replace the one that failed to maintain the landscaping.

Choosing this option assumes that the existing Management Company that failed to properly maintain the landscaping in one of Parkwood's mobile home parks has failed to correct the problem. The option is peaceful and may be low in cost and simple to execute if other competent management companies are available to do the job and Parkwood's contract with the existing Management Company allows Parkwood to make the change. However, Parkwood has not recently received further complaints from homeowners about its existing Management Company, and Delmar's derogatory statements allege second-rate construction in addition to customer complaints about unkempt landscaping. Thus, hiring a new Management Company is unlikely to stop Delmar's disparaging statements and may even give Delmar an additional basis for asserting that Parkwood's mobile home parks are poorly managed.

- Sell Parkwood's existing business in the State or "spin off" the existing operation into a new company under a different name.

Both of these options are peaceful and have the advantage of disassociating Parkwood's national name from the mobile home business in this State. The advantage of selling assumes the existence of a buyer who is willing to pay a reasonable price for the business in the face of having to deal with Delmar's aggressive, competitive tactics in the future. A sale may also entail significant expense and time to execute. Although a spin off of the existing operation into a new company under a different name is less complicated than a sale, a spin off may attract adverse speculation about the true motives for the corporate maneuver; and it risks providing Delmar with yet another ground for disparaging Parkwood's good name.

- Do nothing and wait to see the contents of Delmar's newspaper advertising campaign.

This option is peaceful and, by itself, involves no cost or public exposure. If Delmar's newspaper advertisements are not disparaging, Parkwood might decide not to pursue the matter further. On the other hand, taking no immediate action risks substantial adverse publicity if Delmar's newspaper advertisements continue to disparage Parkwood. Moreover, in that event, Parkwood may have to pursue a more costly option to stop Delmar than would otherwise be the case had Parkwood acted sooner.

Based on the foregoing analysis of each potential option—particularly in light of the tests of peacefulness, least expense, least adverse publicity, and least risk—you can help your client decide upon the best option (or combination of options) to pursue at the outset, followed by a strategy of what to do in the event the initial option is unsuccessful in achieving the client's objective. Because different clients have different dispositions, values, and levels of aversion to risk (and thus will weigh the four tests differently), reasonable minds may differ markedly about the best option to choose on the same set of facts.

That being said, it would be reasonable for Parkwood to conclude that filing a lawsuit is the least desirable option at the outset, and that the options of negative or positive advertising, hiring a new Management Company, selling or spinning off the existing business, or doing nothing may be of little benefit at this time to stop Delmar's behavior. Parkwood may conclude that the best strategy is to start with some form of informal persuasion that will leave open the door for mediation if direct talks with Delmar are unsuccessful. If either of these efforts do not resolve the matter, the other options could be reassessed, and the circumstances at that time may even give rise to entirely new options.

In sum, the foregoing hypothetical underscores the reality that in many cases a strictly law-based or litigation option may not be the most efficacious way of dealing with your client's situation. This reality should not be misunderstood to mean that experienced lawyers eschew a thorough legal analysis of the client's problem and assessment of the legal processes available for addressing that problem. Rather, it means that exercising good judgment in counseling a client requires you to resist being entrapped into thinking solely within "the box of the law" and to actively consider whether there are extra-legal or non-litigation options that may be more effective to accomplish your client's objections.

§8.03 Counseling about Settlement

Approximately 95% of all civil cases are settled, either by negotiation, mediation, or some other alternative dispute resolution process; and most state and federal jurisdictions require that, after a lawsuit has been filed, the parties engage in some form of mediation. The *ABA Model Rules of Professional Conduct* in Rule 1.2 and its Commentary instruct that you must (1) inform your client about all settlement offers; (2) provide your client with sufficient information to participate intelligently in decisions regarding settlement, including general negotiation strategy; and (3) abide by your client's decision whether to settle a matter. (*See* §6.13.)

In connection with these obligations, effective representation about settlement involves counseling your client about the ten matters given below.[5] All

---

5. For a more expansive discussion of these matters, *see* G. Nicholas Herman & Jean M. Cary, *Legal Counseling, Negotiating, and Mediating: A Practical Approach* at Chapters 8, 11–12, and 16 (2d ed. LexisNexis 2009).

these matters are pertinent to decisions about negotiation and mediation strategy and whether to settle a dispute. They are also relevant to deal making when no dispute is involved. Of course, however, the extent to which you will need to counsel your client about these ten matters will vary widely depending upon the particular circumstances of your client's situation.

[1] Discuss the Most Appropriate Strategy for the Negotiation: "Adversarial" or "Problem-Solving"

Generally, there are two strategies or models of negotiation: the "adversarial" model and the "problem-solving" model. Each has its own advantages and disadvantages depending upon the particular matter being negotiated; and sometimes the models are combined in the same negotiation. Choosing the most appropriate model for the particular negotiation is essential for enhancing the prospects of settlement.

[a] The Adversarial Model

The adversarial model of negotiation, which is the most commonly used approach to legal negotiations, focuses on "winning" in the sense of maximizing the likelihood the client will prevail and the amount the client will receive upon prevailing. Each side strives to get as much of the thing bargained for (usually money), with the result that the more one side gets, the less the other side gets. Adversarial negotiators engage in a largely competitive and manipulative process in which a series of concessions is made from initial, polarized positions to arrive at a compromise point that is perceived to be either roughly equivalent to what a court would award or more desirable than taking the risk of what might happen in court.

Adversarial negotiation usually involves five stages. First, each party prepares for the negotiation by establishing "target" and "resistance" points, and estimating the target and resistance points for the other side. The "target point" is the best result a party *realistically* expects can be obtained, and the "resistance point" is the point below which the party will not make any further concessions and will resort to the party's best alternative to negotiation such as going to trial. From these target and resistance points, the parties plan their first offers (which are se t somewhere beyond their target points), and establish their concession patterns in light of the ultimate "settlement zone" created by the overlap between the parties' resistance points. (See subsection [6] below.)

In the second stage, the parties define the issues and often make their first offers or proposals. Third, the parties exchange information in the course of presenting their varying positions and arguments in support of those positions. Fourth, they bargain toward compromise by analyzing and making concessions. And fifth, the parties conclude the negotiation by executing settlement documents or releases if an agreement has been reached, or, if no agreement can be reached, by resorting to their best alternative to a negotiated agreement (BATNA) such as going to trial.

Critics of the adversarial model contend that its underlying assumptions and method of negotiating often limit the quality of the solution to the parties' problem or dispute. By assuming that the parties desire the same goals, items, or values (such as money) and therefore are limited to bargaining over the same scarce resource, the parties may overlook the fact that they really value these goals or items unequally or have completely different goals in mind. When these differences are not taken into account, the parties may fail to consider alternative solutions, such as trading a smaller sum of money for the performance of an act or service by the other side. Moreover, by assuming that the matters to be bargained for are limited to those that a court would award, the parties often limit their solutions to purely "legal" ones without considering extra-legal alternatives that may better satisfy both parties' goals, values, or needs.

For example, assume that a former husband and wife are in dispute about an appropriate increase in the amount of alimony the wife should receive. If the wife contends she needs $300 more per month than the husband says he is able to afford without straining his cash-flow situation, a strict application of the adversarial model may result in the parties splitting the difference at $150 more a month or some other amount they think a court might award. However, if the wife's underlying need for the additional $300 is to allow her to make payments on a new car over a two-year period, and the former husband is the owner of a car dealership, he may be able to give her a car from his inventory in exchange for the wife's agreement to forego a $300 increase in monthly support payments. In this way, the wife receives the item that is of greater value to her (the immediate use of a dependable car), and the husband obtains the goal that is most important to him (preserving his future cash-flow situation).

Critics of the adversarial model also contend that the process by which adversarial negotiations are conducted tends to undermine the quality of potential solutions in two ways. First, the process of exchanging offers, counteroffers, and concessions may not be helpful when the parties are faced with multiple issues. Second, the competitive nature of adversarial negotiation tends to result in argumentation, manipulation, and deception that may inhibit creativity in finding solutions, leave the parties resentful even if an agreement is reached, and impair their future relationship.

[b] The Problem-Solving Model

In contrast to the adversarial model, the problem-solving model of negotiation focuses on identifying the parties' underlying interests or needs to develop a broad range of potential solutions from which an agreement can be fashioned that satisfies as many of the parties' mutual needs as possible. Unlike the adversarial model, which emphasizes maximizing individual gain at the expense of the other side, problem solving emphasizes maximizing the parties' joint gain. Problem-solving negotiators engage in a largely cooperative and collaborative process that strives to create a mutually satisfactory solution that is not necessarily limited to traditional judicial remedies.

The problem-solving model is based on four assumptions. First, the model assumes that the usual objective of obtaining money damages is actually a proxy for more basic interests or needs apart from merely those things that money can buy. Second, the model assumes that the parties' interests or needs are often not mutually exclusive. Third, it assumes that by identifying the parties' underlying interests or needs, the parties can come up with a greater number of possible solutions. And fourth, the model assumes that by exploring a greater number of possible solutions, the parties are more likely to find a solution that satisfies their respective interests or needs.

The problem-solving model is usually applied in five stages of so-called "principled negotiation." First, the parties plan for the negotiation by identifying each side's underlying interests or needs. These interests, which essentially constitute the underlying *reasons* for the parties' objectives or goals, are identified in light of all considerations affecting the parties—their financial situation, their social and psychological needs, their moral perspectives, and the factual and legal issues in the case.

Second, the parties make a conscientious effort to "separate the people from the problem," a mindset that attacks the problem, not each other. Instead of focusing on stated "positions," they discuss and share information about each other's interests or needs to see which are shared and which are in conflict.

Third, the parties seek to generate as many solutions as possible that may satisfy the interests or needs of both parties. Fourth, the parties choose the most reasoned solution that maximizes their mutual gain. Concessions might be made by trading off different interests or needs; and, where interests conflict, the parties might try to resolve their differences based on some objective standard (such as market values, expert opinions, customs, industry standards, or the law) which is independent of the mere naked will of either side. Finally, the parties conclude the negotiation by executing settlement documents or releases if an agreement is reached, or, if no agreement can be reached, by resorting to their "best alternative to a negotiated agreement" (BATNA) such as going to trial.

Many negotiations involve neither a purely adversarial nor a purely problem-solving approach. Thus, negotiators sometimes use more than one of these approaches in a single negotiation. For example, the parties might start with an adversarial approach and then move to a problem-solving one, or they might apply different approaches to distinct issues in the case. While it may sometimes be psychologically difficult to shift between approaches (particularly when a highly competitive adversarial approach is taken at the outset and the parties then try to engage in problem solving after egos have been frayed or inflated), the willingness to be flexible in shifting one's approach often makes the difference between reaching and not reaching a satisfactory agreement.

[c] Choosing the Most Appropriate Model

In deciding which negotiating model may be most effective in a particular case, you should consider the following factors:

[i] The Nature of the Dispute or Problem

The nature of the parties' dispute or problem often has a significant impact on the relative effectiveness of the adversarial or problem-solving approach. For example, the adversarial model may be better suited when the parties are bargaining solely over a fixed and finite matter such as money. If the only issue is how much one party will pay the other, and the gain to one party will necessarily be at the expense of the other, this "zero-sum" controversy rarely provides an opportunity or incentive for the parties to collaborate in expanding the resources they might divide or trade to their mutual gain. Thus, if the only issue between a buyer and seller is the price of a single item, or the only issue between the plaintiff and the defendant is the amount of damages to be paid, the adversarial model is likely to be more appropriate.

On the other hand, the problem-solving model may be more useful to the extent the nature of the dispute or problem does not have zero-sum aspects. This is particularly true if the parties are negotiating over multiple issues that they value differently. For example, if the parties are in dispute over the issues of child custody, visitation, and support, it is more likely that a problem-solving approach will produce a more mutually satisfactory solution if the parties consider options such as joint or split custody, and how various visitation arrangements may affect appropriate amounts of child support. Similarly, if the issue between a buyer and seller is not merely price, but involves considerations such as quantity, time of delivery and manner of payment, the problem-solving approach may be more productive in reaching an agreement addressing these multiple elements.

[ii] The Other Side's Negotiating Approach

A party's negotiating approach will often be affected by the particular approach taken by the other side. For example, if the other side is unwilling to engage in a problem-solving approach, attempts to employ that model will be largely ineffective because the model presupposes information sharing and collaboration between the parties. This does not mean that a problem-solving negotiator should not try to encourage the other side to use a problem-solving approach. However, if the effort is unsuccessful, it is unlikely the problem solver will be able to make any headway in the negotiation unless he is willing to match the other side's adversarial bargaining.

Sometimes the other side's negotiating approach conforms to some generally accepted convention or norm that is endemic to a particular type of case. In personal injury cases, for example, most lawyers and insurance adjusters routinely engage in adversarial bargaining; and plaintiffs' lawyers who enter into contingency fee arrangements, whereby their fee is a percentage of the monetary amount received in settlement or at trial, may be less motivated to engage in problem solving if that approach would produce a settlement that is not exclusively resolved by the payment of money.

In addition, the parties may be reluctant to share their true needs or interests upon which expanded options for a resolution might be explored. For example, a party might be psychologically or financially distressed as a result of the dispute and not want to reveal these matters out of embarrassment or fear of demonstrating weakness. Similarly, particularly when litigation is contemplated or has already commenced, a party might not want to reveal certain information to give "free discovery" to the other side. In either of these circumstances, the parties may be more likely to resort to adversarial bargaining than problem solving.

[iii] Differences in Bargaining Leverage

Negotiating leverage stems from the perception of the negative consequences that a party can inflict on his opponent if an agreement is not reached, or from the benefits that a party can bestow on the other if an agreement is reached. The extent of this leverage is largely dependent upon the alternatives available to each party in the absence of an agreement. Generally, the side that possesses the most viable alternative in the event that an agreement is not reached will have greater power over the other side.

A negotiator who possesses greater bargaining leverage over his opponent may adopt an adversarial approach on the theory that his threats will be perceived as more credible, and he will thus be able to extract greater concessions from his opponent. Conversely, the negotiator with less bargaining power will often choose the problem-solving model to offset or neutralize the adversarial bargainer's emphasis on a purely concession-based settlement. In essence, the lower-power negotiator will attempt to appeal to the more powerful negotiator's sense of fairness and justice to counteract the latter's tendency to believe that his bargaining position is superior and that any concessions on his part are unwarranted.

When both negotiators have high aspiration levels and possess relatively equal bargaining leverage, rigid adherence to the adversarial model may often result in deadlock. On the other hand, deadlock may motivate the parties to abandon an adversarial approach and adopt a problem-solving one.

[iv] Future Dealings between the Parties

The extent to which the parties are likely to have an ongoing relationship after the negotiation ends often affects the incentive for adopting an adversarial or problem-solving approach. The adversarial model sometimes gives rise to distrust and ill will, and thus the problem-solving approach is more frequently used when the parties or their representatives expect to have future dealings with one another. On the other hand, if the parties are merely engaged in a one-time transaction or encounter, there will be less incentive to avoid the adversarial model with its concomitant risk of impairing future relations.

[v] Pressures to Reach an Agreement

The pressures placed on the parties to reach an agreement may affect their choice of negotiating approach. For example, a party might want to settle quickly because she needs the settlement proceeds immediately, desires to limit legal fees or other expenses, or wants to avoid the psychological stress of a protracted controversy. Similarly, court deadlines or heavy caseloads may pressure the lawyer negotiators to expedite an agreement.

Generally, the problem-solving model's emphasis on sharing information to identify the interests or needs of the parties and collaborating to develop possible solutions is more time consuming than the offer-counteroffer and response-counterresponse method of adversarial negotiation. Thus, the greater the time pressure placed on the parties, the more likely they are to

resort to adversarial bargaining through the swifter device of making recip-
rocal concessions.

———————

Based on the foregoing, discuss with your client the best negotiating
approach for the particular situation—whether adversarial or problem solving,
or a combination of the two. In this regard, be wary of the client who perceives
that the problem-solving model conveys a posture of "weakness" rather than
"strength." Properly applied, there is nothing "weak" or "strong" about this
model or the adversarial one. In choosing between the models, the overall
question is which approach will most likely enhance the prospects for a satisfactory agreement.

[2] Discuss Your Client's "Interests" and "Objectives"

Conceptually, your client's "interests" are to be distinguished from her negotiation "objectives," even though the two often overlap or end up being the
same. Your client's negotiation objectives are the specific matters she wants to
obtain from the negotiation, whereas her interests are the underlying *reasons*
for those objectives. There may be multiple interests underlying any one objective, or multiple objectives that are related to a single interest.

To identify the interests of your client, ask "why" she desires a particular
objective. Focus on her underlying needs, desires, concerns, fears, philosophies,
and feelings. What are the personal, psychological, ideological, and emotional
motivations behind her goals? Does she have any special needs for power, pres-
tige, acceptance, security, economic well being, belonging, or control over her
life? When discussing the interests of your client, you might rank those interests
from most important to least important, and note which interests may be
shared by the other side and which may conflict with the other side.

For example, suppose your client is the plaintiff in a defamation or wrongful
death case. While in both cases the single "legal" objective would be money,
the primary interest of your client in the defamation case might be to restore
her reputation; and the primary interest of your client in the wrongful death
case might be to ensure that the accident that killed the decedent will not
happen again. These interests may give rise to alternative objectives and
solutions apart from the mere payment of money. In the defamation case, your
client's interest in restoring her reputation might give rise to the objective of
obtaining a public retraction and apology. This might not be at odds with the

defendant's interests if the retraction and apology are styled in terms of the defendant having made a "mistake" in making the defamatory statement, and if a payment of a smaller sum is made to the plaintiff in exchange for making the recantation public. Similarly, in the wrongful death case, the interests of your client and the defendant in preventing a future accident will undoubtedly be shared, and this may lead to a possible solution in which the defendant promises to undertake specific steps to correct the product's defect in exchange for paying a smaller sum to your client.

Thus, based on your client's interests, identify her primary, secondary and incidental negotiation objectives. A "primary" objective is a specific matter that must be obtained for your client if an agreement is to be reached at all. A "secondary" objective is an important but not necessarily vital matter that your client may choose to forgo if the primary objective is resolved in a satisfactory manner. An "incidental" objective is a lower-priority goal that your client would be pleased to obtain, but which will not have a substantial effect on the overall success or failure of reaching a final agreement. In addition, an incidental objective may serve as a matter to trade or exchange with the other party for something of greater value.

[3] Discuss All Potential Solutions

In light of your client's interests and negotiation objectives (and those that might be held by the other side), discuss all potential solutions. In formulating potential solutions, consider the interests and objectives of each side that are shared or do not conflict and those which do conflict.

Particularly when thinking about solutions to the parties' conflicting objectives, try to discuss solutions based on objective criteria that are fair and independent of each party's mere wishes. For example, in a property damage dispute, a reasonable solution is more likely to be found if the parties focus on objective criteria such as appraisals or "book values" to establish fair market value, rather than on a sum that one party merely wants to receive or the other is merely willing to pay. Similarly, in a construction contract dispute, a solution might be based on industry-wide standards, rather than on the mere preferences or practices of the particular parties. Depending upon the case, other sources of objective criteria might include what a court might decide, professional standards, moral standards, expert opinions, precedent, costs, efficiency, custom, and the like.

In discussing potential solutions with your client, it is particularly important to canvass all possibilities, bearing in mind your client's alternatives in the event an agreement cannot be reached. Potential solutions will later be refined into more concrete offers or proposals (see subsection [8] below).

[4] Discuss What Information to Obtain from the Other Side, What Information to Reveal to It, and What Information to Protect From Disclosure

An integral aspect of the negotiating process is finding out information from the other side that you have been unable to obtain independently. Having as complete information as possible about the other party's interests, negotiation objectives, possible solutions, and best alternatives to a negotiated settlement is essential in shaping your particular approach to the negotiation. Thus, discuss with your client what information you need to find out from the other side, whether through discovery if a lawsuit has been filed or by asking the other side during the negotiation or mediation process.

In addition, discuss with your client particular information you might expressly want to reveal or exchange with the other party. Information to reveal may consist of your client's strong factual or legal leverage points (see subsection [5] below), or other important information bearing upon your client's interests, objectives, possible solutions, and offers or proposals.

Finally, discuss information you want to protect from disclosure to the other side. Information to protect may include damaging factual or legal points or sensitive or privileged information such as trade secrets, work product, or the like.

[5] Discuss Your Client's Factual and Legal Leverage Points (Strong and Weak)

Factual and legal leverage points are the strong and weak factual and legal aspects of the case that affect your client's target and resistance points (see subsection [6] below), and the rationale for her offers or proposals (see subsection [8] below). As such, these factual and legal leverage points are used in arguing for or against various terms of an agreement.

Therefore, you should discuss with your client the most important factual and legal leverage points (both the strong points and the weak points) that bear upon the merits of her case and a realistic settlement. Just as strong points should not be overemphasized, weak points should not be de-emphasized. Your client needs to fully understand both.

[6] Discuss Your Client's Potential "Target" and "Resistance Points"

As mentioned previously, your client's "target point" is the best result she realistically hopes to achieve from the negotiation. It is not to be confused with her opening offer (see subsection [8] below), which is the point at which she begins negotiations and thereafter moves, through a series of concessions, toward her target point but not below her "resistance" point. Your client's "resistance" point is her "bottom line"—the point below which she will cut off negotiations and resort to her Best Alternative to a Negotiated Agreement (BATNA). In other words, it is the point below which she is unwilling to make any further concessions or compromises.

Estimating target and resistance points depends upon an overall evaluation of the case in light of all the matters discussed in subsections [2] through [5] above. In addition, when monetary damages are involved, you must be prepared to advise your client about potential target and resistance points in light of a "reasonable settlement range" for her case so that she can make informed decisions not only about what offers and counter offers to make during negotiations, but also whether to accept a final statement offer or take the case to trial.

Although there are a variety of approaches to estimating the reasonable settlement range for a case, the basic analysis employed by most lawyers is to (1) begin with an estimate of what a jury would most likely award the plaintiff assuming liability and all damages are established, (2) adjust that verdict expectancy by the probability (expressed as a percentage) that the plaintiff will be successful in actually obtaining that amount, and (3) then further adjust the expected outcome by all non-shiftable litigation expenses and any special intangible factors that may induce the parties to settle. More specifically, one method you might employ (whether you represent the plaintiff or the defendant) is the "Reasonable Settlement Range Formula." It consists of the following five steps:

(1) Estimate the "Average Verdict Expectancy" (AVE) of the case based on the assumption that the plaintiff will fully prevail on liability and damages.

The Average Verdict Expectancy (AVE) for a case is your best estimate of the amount of money that a jury would award the plaintiff assuming she fully prevails on liability and damages. In other words, ask yourself, "If everything went the plaintiff's way at trial, what sum of money would a jury most likely award to her?" In making this estimate, assume that the plaintiff can establish her claimed special damages, and draw upon your experience (and the experiences of other skilled trial lawyers) to estimate what the jury might likely award in terms of general, compensatory damages (e.g., pain and suffering and permanent injury) and for punitive damages, if applicable. For example, if you estimate that a jury might reasonably award the plaintiff between $70,000 and $90,000, the Average Verdict Expectancy (AVE) would be $80,000.

(2) Estimate the "Probability the Plaintiff Will Win" (PPW) the Average Verdict Expectancy based on the law and facts of the particular case, and multiply that probability (expressed as a percentage) by the Average Verdict Expectancy (AVE) to arrive at an "expected outcome."

Taking into account any uncertainties in the law about the extent to which the case is actionable or damages are recoverable, and the relative strength of the evidence in support of and in opposition to establishing liability and damages, estimate the relative probability (in terms of a percentage) that the jury will actually award the plaintiff the Average Verdict Expectancy. Then multiply this Probability the Plaintiff Will Win (PPW) by the Average Verdict Expectancy (AVE) to calculate an "expected outcome" for the case. For example, if you estimate that there is a 50% chance on the law and the particular facts that the plaintiff will be awarded the Average Verdict Expectancy (AVE) of $80,000, the resulting "expected outcome" is $40,000.

(3) Estimate the amount of all non-shiftable litigation costs and hourly attorney's fees. If you represent the plaintiff, subtract the "Plaintiff's Costs" (PC) from the "expected outcome;" and, if you represent the defendant, add the "Defendant's Costs" (DC) to the "expected outcome" to arrive at a revised "net outcome."

Non-shiftable litigation costs and non-shiftable hourly attorney's fees are costs and fees that a court would not tax to the losing party. If you represent the plaintiff, these costs and fees (PC) are subtracted from the "expected outcome;" and if you represent the defendant, these costs and fees (DC) are added to the "expected outcome." For example, if you represent the plaintiff and estimate that her non-shiftable costs and fees would be $8,000, this amount would be subtracted from the "expected outcome" of $40,000 to arrive at a revised "net outcome" of $32,000. (If you represented the defendant, the $8000 would be added to the $40,000 to arrive at a "net outcome" or $48,000.)

(4) Place a monetary amount on all "Special Intangible Factors" (SIF) about the case; and, depending upon whether these factors increase or reduce the value of the case, add that amount to, or subtract it from, the "net outcome" to arrive at a "Reasonable Settlement Value" (RSV).

Special Intangible Factors (SIF) are special factors you have not previously taken into account in your analysis that affect the value of the case and your client's relative inclination or disinclination to settle rather than go to trial. For example, if you represent the plaintiff, you might conclude that she has far greater "jury appeal" than the defendant has and is not particularly "risk averse" (see also subsection [7] below). You might also estimate that the defendant's total costs and fees for going to trial would be $10,000, and that the insurance carrier for the defendant would be willing to contribute $6,000 of those costs and fees towards settlement (thereby saving $4,000). Thus, you and your client might place a monetary value of $16,000 on these factors and add that amount to the "net outcome" of $32,000 to arrive at a Reasonable Settlement Value (RSV) of $48,000.

(5) Calculate 10% of the Reasonable Settlement Value (RSV). Add that calculation to the RSV to establish an "upper end" of a "Reasonable Settlement Range" (RSR), and subtract that calculation to establish a "lower end" of a "Reasonable Settlement Range" (RSR).

If the Reasonable Settlement Value of your case is estimated at $48,000, then 10% of that value is $4,800. To establish an upper end of a Reasonable Settlement Range (RSR), adding $4,800 to $48,000 results in $52,800, which the plaintiff might set as her "target point." To establish a lower end of a Reasonable Settlement Range (RSR), subtracting $4,800 from $48,000 results in $43,200, which the plaintiff might set as her "resistance point."

In summary, the components of the Reasonable Settlement Range Formula are as follows:

AVE = The Average Verdict Expectancy assuming the plaintiff will fully prevail on liability and damages.

PPW = The Probability the Plaintiff Will Win the Average Verdict Expectancy, considering the law and particular facts of the case.

PC = The Plaintiff's Cost of going to trial, including non-shiftable attorney's fees.

DC = The Defendant's Cost of going to trial, including non-shiftable attorney's fees.

SIF = Special Intangible Factors (expressed as a $ amount) that may increase or decrease the verdict or affect the parties' propensity to settle or go to trial.

RSV = <u>The Reasonable Settlement Value</u> of the case.

RSR = <u>The Reasonable Settlement Range</u> of the case.

The formula may be expressed as follows:

$(AVE \times PPW) - PC \pm SIF = RSV$ **(if you represent the <u>plaintiff</u>)**

$(AVE \times PPW) + DC \pm SIF = RSV$ **(if you represent the <u>defendant</u>)**

Then, RSV + (10% of RSV) = RSR (upper end of range)

RSV − (10% of RSV) = RSR (lower end of range)

For example, drawing upon the hypothetical estimates given above for the plaintiff, the figures that would be computed in the formula would be:

- AVE = $80,000.
- PPW = 50% (.50).
- PC = $8,000.
- SIF = $16,000 in favor of plaintiff.

Applying these figures to the formula yields the following:

$(AVE \times PPW) - PC + SIF = RSV$
- ($80,000 \times .50) - $8,000 \pm $16,000 = $48,000

Then, to establish a Reasonable Settlement Range, 10% of the Reasonable Settlement Value is added to and subtracted from that Value to arrive at a range:

RSV + (.10 × RSV) = RSR (upper end of range)
- $48,000 + (.10 \times $48,000) = $52,800 (upper end of range), and

RSV − (.10 × RSV) = RSR (lower end of range)
- $48,000 − (.10 \times $48,000) = $43,200 (lower end of range).

As mentioned previously, based on your discussion with the plaintiff about the foregoing variables and analysis, she might set her resistance point at $43,200 and her target point at $52,800. She might then make an opening offer of $100,000. Almost always, the defendant's calculation of the formula will be quite different from the plaintiff's calculation. However, assuming the defendant arrives at the same Reasonable Settlement Range arrived at by the plaintiff, the defendant might set his resistance point at $52,800 and target point at $43,200, and make an opening offer of $10,000.

Finally, in counseling your client about target and resistance points, emphasize that your estimates about these matters are no more than mere "estimates." That is, reasonable minds might well arrive at different estimates.

Moreover, your estimates are highly fact sensitive and assumption sensitive. Changes in the facts and assumptions about the case warrant an ongoing assessment about appropriate target and resistance points. In sum, initial estimates of target and resistance points merely serve as the basis for formulating an *initial* strategy for the negotiation. Properly viewed, they are not unyielding and inflexible numbers. As negotiations progress and new information is learned, these numbers should be reassessed.

[7] Discuss the Extent of Your Client's Aversion to Risk

The Reasonable Settlement Range Formula discussed in the preceding subsection largely assumes that the client's decision to settle or go to trial will be made solely on the basis of which course of action will yield the best result from a rote economic standpoint. However, choosing between settlement and trial is not purely an economic process. Whether a client will accept a final settlement offer or take her chances at trial depends integrally on the client's psychological propensity or aversion to risk—that is, how willing the client is to gamble on losing at trial versus the certainty of receiving the amount offered in final settlement.

This risk averseness varies from individual to individual and will often vary for each individual at different points in time. For example, most people are less willing to "roll the dice" with an "all or nothing" outcome at trial where liability is questionable if the amount at stake is a million dollars versus $10,000. Similarly, a wealthy client is more likely to gamble on her chances at trial when the amount at stake is $10,000, whereas an indigent client faced with the same amount at stake may be content to settle for the certainty of receiving $5,000.

In addition, risk aversion largely explains why many settlements occur on the eve of trial and some occur literally on the courthouse steps. When a trial is a year or more away, the consequences of an adverse verdict appear more abstract and hypothetical.[6] On the other hand, those consequences often take on a starker reality during the weekend before trial, with the result that many clients will at that time prefer the certainty of a settlement to the risk of an undesirable verdict.

Clients also have various motivations that will affect their decision to settle the case or take it to trial. For example, settlement may be preferred to avoid

---

6. *See* D. Waterman & M. Peterson, *Evaluating Civil Claims: An Expert System Approach* 8 (1985) (one study found that the value of a personal injury case just before trial may be as much as 20% greater than the value of the case two years before trial).

the emotional strain and time demands of a trial, to preserve the personal or business relationship between the parties, to avoid unwanted publicity, to avoid an adverse legal or factual precedent, or to obtain an immediate source of funds if the client is in financial distress. On the other hand, a client might prefer a trial over settlement out of a desire to inflict punishment on the opposing party, to publicly vindicate a principle by having one side declared the winner and the other the loser, to establish a legal precedent or policy (e.g., to discourage nuisance suits), or to simply delay payment of a claim for lack of sufficient funds to pay it.

Thus, you should always discuss with your client the extent of her aversion to risk and other motivations that may affect the desirability of settling the case or trying it. These factors may be explored by (1) identifying the various risks and personal motivations bearing upon the choice between settlement and trial; (2) reducing these to a set of consequences of settling the case on the one hand, and trying it on the other; and (3) asking your client to place a monetary value on the overall consequences in light of her preferences and values to determine how much she is willing to accept or forgo for those consequences.[7] This amount, if it has not otherwise already been taken into account as a "Special Intangible Factor" under the Reasonable Settlement Range Formula, might then be applied to increase or decrease the client's resistance point established under the formula.

For example, in the hypothetical given in subsection [6] above, if the plaintiff does not want to go through the emotional trauma of a bitter trial, she might lower her resistance point of $43,200 by an additional $10,000. On the other hand, if the defendant in the same case is more willing to take the case to trial because he has received adverse publicity from the suit and wants to vindicate himself from any wrongdoing, he might adjust his resistance point of $52,800 such that he will pay no more than $40,000 to settle the case.

[8] Discuss Potential Offers or Proposals

The specific offers or proposals that your client intends to make during negotiations should be formulated in light of all the matters discussed in subsections [1] through [7] above. In advising your client about an opening offer and fall-back offers to a final offer, the target and resistance points developed in subsection [6] above are particularly important. In addition, for every offer or proposal made, you should draw upon the factual and legal leverage points

---

7. *See* P.T. Hoffman, *Valuation of Cases for Settlement: Theory and Practice*, 1 J. Disp. Res. 38–40 (1991).

discussed in subsection [5] above to back up each offer or concession with reasoned rationales.

In counseling your client about an opening offer or proposal, it is important to note that a number of studies have shown that negotiators sometimes obtain more satisfactory outcomes when they start with more extreme rather than more moderate demands (i.e., higher initial demands by plaintiffs or lower initial offers by defendants). In this regard, experience has shown that in choosing an initial offer, many successful negotiators first forecast the best result they reasonably might expect to achieve in the negotiation, and then deliberately *increase* this goal or target point in setting an opening offer.[8]

On the other hand, if the initial offer or proposal is too extreme and cannot be backed up with sensible reasons, you and your client are likely to quickly lose credibility with the opposing party. In that event, the negotiation may collapse at the outset; or, if it nevertheless proceeds, it will be more difficult for you to justify the meaningfulness of your subsequent concessions to the other side. In short, the opening offer and each subsequent offer should be supported by non-frivolous rationales, and all of these rationales need to be fully discussed with your client.

In discussing fall-back offers and concession patterns with your client, consider (1) the extent of the information possessed by each side and the extent to which the facts of the case are known and unknown; (2) how protracted the negotiation is likely to be in light of the relative complexity of the case; and (3) the particular negotiating approach of the opposing party, whether adversarial or problem-solving (see subsection [1] above). Generally, the more thoroughly developed the case is in terms of the overall information possessed by each side, the less room your client needs to leave to maneuver between the opening offer and final offer. Similarly, if the negotiation is not expected to be long or complex, and the opposing party does not take a highly adversarial approach to the negotiation, it is less important to preserve substantial maneuvering room between your client's initial proposal and bottom line. On the other hand, if the negotiations start out when the parties possess limited information about each other's interests and objectives, or if the opposing party adopts a highly adversarial strategy and competitive style, your client's concession pattern should leave ample room within which to maneuver from her opening offer to the final one.

---

8. *See* C. Karrass, *The Negotiating Game* 17–18 (1970); J. Rubin & B. Brown, *The Social Psychology of Bargaining and Negotiation* 267 (1975); M. Bazerman & M. Neale, *Negotiating Rationally* 28 (1992); Charles B. Craver, *Effective Legal Negotiation and Settlement* 63–66 (3rd ed. 1997); Herbert M. Kritzer, *The Justice Broker: Lawyers and Ordinary Litigation*, 143–155, 159–161 (1990).

[9] Discuss the Process for Negotiations and Special Tactics

Discuss with your client the particular process for how negotiations will be conducted and any special tactics. This involves deciding who will conduct the negotiations; when they will be conducted; and whether they will be conducted in writing, over the telephone, or in a face-to-face meeting. In addition, tactical decisions may have to be made, such as whether negotiations should be commenced before or after a lawsuit is filed, or whether traditional inter-party negotiations should be dispensed with at the outset in favor of negotiating through the mediation process.

[10] Discuss Your Client's Role in the Negotiation

Your client's role in the negotiation is integral to preparation and the overall approach taken to the negotiation. Some studies have indicated that the dollar outcomes of certain settlements are consistently higher when the client actively participates in the overall negotiation process, even if she is not actually present during the negotiations. Similarly, attorney-client misunderstandings have been found to be the single largest factor resulting in unsuccessful settlements.[9] In general, the more your client participates in the settlement process the more she will understand the process.

As previously mentioned, the ultimate decision whether to accept or reject a settlement negotiated by you rests with your client, and you have a duty to inform your client of all settlement offers. (*See* ABA Model Rule 1.2.) However, your client may give you broad authority not only over the process of the negotiation, but also over what offers or counteroffers to make and what proposals to accept or reject. Thus, it is imperative that there be a clear understanding between you and your client about the extent of your authority throughout the negotiation process.

In addition, you should discuss with your client how, when, and to what extent she will be involved in the actual negotiation process, either during inter-party negotiations or during mediation. In mediation, for example, decisions will have to be made about what, if anything, your client will say during the mediator's opening session with the parties, and what role she will play during the private caucuses with the mediator. If the negotiation involves the prepa-

---

9. *See* G. Williams, *Legal Negotiation and Settlement* 58–60 (1983).

ration of a demand letter or settlement brochure, or if a face-to-face negotiation will involve some form of formal presentation (e.g., a power-point presentation, slide show, video or the like), you should discuss and review the contents of these matters with your client before they are presented to the other side. Above all, consistent with your ethical obligation to "regularly provide your client with sufficient information to participate intelligently in decisions regarding settlement," as the negotiation process unfolds you should revisit with your client, as necessary, all matters set out in subsections [1] through [9] above.

§8.04 Counseling about Mediation

Mediation is an informal, non-adversarial alternative dispute resolution process, whereby a neutral third party, who is either selected by the parties or is appointed from an approved list of mediators eligible to mediate the type of case at hand, encourages and facilitates the parties to voluntarily resolve their dispute. The mediator does not decide what the outcome should be. The process is different from arbitration, in which a neutral third party hears evidence and arguments from the parties and makes a binding or non-binding decision about how the parties' dispute should be resolved. In mediation, the parties themselves make the decision; and if they do not voluntarily resolve their dispute, they may resolve it through some other alternative dispute resolution process or, if the case is actionable, litigate it.

Virtually all jurisdictions—by statute, agency rule, or court rule— mandate mediation or otherwise formally make it available in certain types of cases. Illustrative are family-law disputes, collective bargaining and other labor-law disputes, personal injury cases, medical malpractice actions, products liability cases, civil rights actions, contract cases, wrongful discharge cases and other employment-related disputes, landlord-tenant cases, small claims actions, toxic tort cases, consumer complaints, environmental disputes, professional conduct and licensing cases, neighborhood or community disputes, farm mortgage disputes, housing disputes, agricultural producer-distributor bargaining, geothermal energy development disputes, and rule-making disputes. Many jurisdictions mandate mediation in a broad range of civil cases as a prerequisite to taking the case to trial. These "court-annexed" mediation programs have burgeoned as a means of easing the backlog of cases and reducing the time and expense of litigation. In short, the "mediation explosion" has permeated our society in the both the public and private sector.

Studies have shown that mediation has a number of advantages over traditional inter-party or lawyer-to-lawyer negotiations. First, mediation provides a structured opportunity to bring the parties together, not just to exchange demands and positions, but to discuss and explain their interests, needs, and emotions in a setting where the parties can feel that another person (the mediator) has heard their side of the story and given them a "fair shake." Second, mediation structures the negotiating process in ways that increase more reliable information sharing and better understanding between the parties so that they can better decide how to resolve their dispute. Third, skilled mediators can help facilitate an agreement by breaking down cognitive and emotional barriers between the parties through a variety of tactics and techniques that help to diffuse suspicion and irrationality and help to promote reality testing and face saving. And fourth, mediation gives the parties a greater sense of participation and control over their case through a process in which they can address the issues they themselves feel are most important. In sum, the advantages of mediation are consistent with the well-established fact that clients are often at least as much concerned with how they are treated in dispute resolution as they are with its results. That is, the very *process* of how the parties go about resolving their dispute is often of integral importance to them.

Often mediation will occur after traditional negotiations have failed to produce an agreement. Sometimes, however, the parties will choose mediation as a means of first resort in trying to resolve their dispute. This Section focuses on the mediation process and matters about which the client should be counseled about that process.

[1] The Mediation Process, in General

Mediation typically occurs in a conference room at a neutral location or at a lawyer's office agreed upon by the parties and the mediator. Present are the mediator (or perhaps co-mediators in a multi-party or highly complex case), the individual parties (or a designated representative of a party if it is a corporation or governmental entity), and their lawyers. If there is insurance coverage in the case, an insurance adjuster will usually also attend. In many court-annexed mediations, all of the foregoing persons are required to attend. Sometimes, by agreement between the parties, other support persons (e.g., a spouse of a party, or a person who has some special expertise or is otherwise integrally involved in the case) might attend all or part of the mediation or be on telephone standby for consultation. Because the process is private, no stenographers, court personnel, news reporters, or other observers attend the mediation.

The mediator begins the mediation in a joint session in the presence of all participants. After the mediator introduces herself, and all participants have introduced themselves to one another, she will make some brief introductory remarks that explain her role and the overall mediation process. Typically, these remarks will explain that:

(1) Mediation is an informal process where the rules of evidence and other formal rules of procedure do not apply;

(2) The mediator is neutral and impartial in the case and has no conflict of interest;

(3) The mediator has reviewed any pre-mediation submissions that the parties may have sent to her in advance of the mediation;

(4) The mediator's role is to assist the parties in reaching a possible agreement, and not to serve as a judge or jury in the case;

(5) Generally, most things said or done during the mediation are confidential in the sense that they cannot later be used by one side against the other in litigation;

(6) If a party privately shares anything with the mediator that the party expressly states he wants kept confidential, the mediator is prohibited from disclosing that information to the other side or to anyone else unless required by law;

(7) The mediator is prohibited from giving any legal advice during the mediation;

(8) Each side will be given an opportunity at the outset to make an opening statement about the case;

(9) Each side might then wish to ask some clarifying questions of the other to bring as much non-confidential information to the table as early as possible in the mediation process;

(10) After the case is discussed in joint session, the mediator typically will hold multiple private caucuses, separately with each party, to clarify information, and to discuss underlying interests, feelings, objectives, possible solutions to the dispute, and particular proposals offered by the parties that might resolve the case;

(11) If a settlement is reached, the mediator will have all participants reconvene in a joint session at which she will summarize the terms of the agreement and make sure the parties understand what steps will be taken to prepare and execute any settlement documents;

(12) If no agreement is reached, it is the mediator's duty to declare an impasse; and

(13) The fees for the mediation will be borne equally between the parties unless they have otherwise agreed about how those fees will be paid.

After the mediator has made her introductory remarks and answered any questions about her role or the overall mediation process, each side will make an opening statement, usually beginning with the claimant. The lawyers typically give these opening statements, which generally set forth the parties' factual and legal contentions. Sometimes, however, the clients will participate in the opening statements by explaining certain parts of "the story" as further discussed below. After the opening statements, the mediator might ask some clarifying questions, might allow the parties to share further information between one another, or might let the parties engage in a free-flowing discussion of the dispute. If there are multiple issues in the case, the mediator might devote part of the joint session to establishing an appropriate agenda.

When it becomes apparent that discussions in a joint session are no longer productive, the mediator will begin private caucusing through separate, *ex parte* meetings with each side. Usually, she will hold the first private meeting with the claimant and his attorney or the side that is in the position to respond to the latest offer or proposal, and then caucus with the opposing side. In most cases, private caucusing will begin shortly after the parties have given their opening statements, and the mediator will hold numerous private meetings with each side. Indeed, in the mediation of legal disputes, it is common for the balance of the time spent during mediation to consist of these alternating private caucuses through which the mediator acts as a sort of "shuttle diplomat" between the opposing sides. On the other hand, after holding a number of private caucuses with each side, the mediator might decide to bring the parties back together in a joint session if, for example, they express a desire to do so, or if exchanging certain information or discussing a particular proposal would be more efficient in a joint meeting.

During the private caucuses, the mediator will engage in five overlapping functions or stages:

(1) Obtaining information about the facts, the law, the issues, the parties' underlying feelings, interests or needs (e.g., emotional, psychological, economic, physical, or social), the parties' primary, secondary, and incidental objectives, potential solutions or proposals, and the reasons supporting particular proposals, offers, and counteroffers;

(2) Generating and discussing potential solutions or proposals in light of the parties' interests and objectives;

(3) Assessing, selecting, and communicating specific proposals, offers, and counteroffers of the parties;

(4) Creating movement in the negotiations by encouraging the parties to compromise and consider the risks, costs, and alternatives to not reaching an agreement; and

(5) Forging and finalizing the terms of an agreement.

Throughout these stages, the mediator will engage in a variety of tactics and techniques to encourage the parties to be cooperative and realistic in the bargaining process.

Most mediation sessions last between one and five hours, but it is not uncommon for a mediation to last for a day or more in multi-party or particularly complex cases. In addition, the mediator and the parties might agree to hold more than one mediation session to allow the parties to use the time in between to formulate or consider new settlement proposals or obtain additional information.

[2] What Cases to Mediate and When to Mediate

If your client has filed a lawsuit and the jurisdiction requires that the case be mediated as a predicate to maintaining the suit, your client will have no choice but to engage in mediation unless the applicable statute, agency rule, or court rule otherwise allows the parties to waive mediation by mutual agreement or for good cause. Even if mediation is not required, it is important to decide whether to voluntarily engage in mediation either after negotiations have failed or in lieu of traditional negotiations. If you decide to pursue mediation, it is also necessary to consider at what stage of the case mediation would be most productive.

The option of mediating a case is typically not considered until after traditional negotiations have broken down. However, in circumstances where (1) the parties or their lawyers have a particularly strained relationship, (2) multiple parties are involved, or (3) there are numerous or complex issues in dispute, it may be beneficial to mediate the case at the outset in lieu of engaging in traditional negotiations. Assuming you are considering mediation, either in lieu of traditional negotiations or after they have failed, provided below are "Favorable Situations for Mediation" and "Unfavorable Situations for Mediation" to aid in client decision-making about whether to mediate and at what stage of the case mediation might be most productive.

[a] Favorable Situations for Mediation

- The parties or their lawyers are finding it difficult to engage in negotiations, or negotiations are deadlocked.
- The parties want to settle the case confidentially.
- The parties want to avoid establishing judicial precedent.
- Communication between the parties is poor, or their emotional involvement in the case is preventing settlement.
- The parties want to minimize litigation costs.
- The interests or needs of the parties are interdependent, and they would benefit from each other's cooperation in satisfying those interests or needs.
- The parties want or will have to maintain a relationship after the dispute is resolved.
- The parties have different perceptions about the facts of the case, or disagree about what data or other information is needed to resolve it.
- The parties are divided over different values or interests.
- There are multiple parties in the case, or there are a number of other persons whose input is necessary or would be desirable in resolving the dispute.
- There are multiple issues in the case and the parties disagree about the order in which the issues should be addressed.
- The parties are considering a non-monetary remedy or some other remedy that a court cannot provide.
- The parties are unable to agree on an acceptable forum or structure for negotiations.
- Stereotyping, prejudices, misunderstandings, or other misperceptions are preventing the parties from resolving their dispute.
- The parties are having difficulty evaluating the factual or legal merits of the case or its value, or have unrealistic views about those matters.
- The parties desire to resolve at least some, if not all, issues in the case.
- The parties wish to engage in informal discovery, or want to evaluate each other's credibility or jury appeal.

[b] Unfavorable Situations for Mediation

- The parties have a need for formal discovery that has not yet been completed, and they are unable to provide necessary information to one another through the mediation process.

- The parties want a judicial resolution of the dispute because they want to establish a precedent, want a court to resolve ambiguous or conflicting law, or want vindication.
- The sole issues dividing the parties are ones of "principle."
- Punitive damages are an indispensable issue in the case.
- The events giving rise to the parties' dispute were so traumatic that the parties are not yet psychologically able to discuss a possible resolution of their dispute (e.g., in the family law area, where domestic violence has been involved in the dispute).
- Negotiations have been so acrimonious or unproductive that the parties have essentially decided to take the case to trial.
- The parties stand to gain from a strategy of delay.
- There are numerous parties involved in the dispute and one or more of them is unwilling to mediate.
- The parties' dispute affects the public interest and the government is not represented.

[3] Choosing a Mediator

In jurisdictions that mandate mediation in certain types of cases, the parties are usually free to select their mediator by mutual agreement. If they cannot agree, a mediator will usually be appointed from a list of mediators eligible to mediate the particular type of case. Typically, these eligible mediators have been "certified" to mediate cases after completing a mandatory mediation-training course. Although the selection of a mediator is properly a decision for the lawyer, the choice of a mediator should be discussed with the client.

One scholar has summarized the qualities and abilities of a good mediator as a person who is "capable of appreciating the dynamics of the environment in which the dispute is occurring, intelligent, effective listener, articulate, patient, non-judgmental, flexible, forceful and persuasive, imaginative, re-sourceful, a person of professional standing or reputation, reliable, capable of gaining access to necessary resources, non-defensive, person of integrity, humble, objective, and neutral with regard to the outcome."[10] When choosing a mediator, in addition to these qualities and abilities, you should consider whether the prospects for settling the case would be enhanced by a "facilitative"

---

10. Joseph B. Stulberg, The Theory and Practice of Mediation: A Reply to Professor Susskind, 6 Vt. L. Rev. 94 (1981).

or "evaluative" mediator, and whether the particular mediator has a style and strategy that would complement the case.

Along with the foregoing considerations, it may be useful to know that, for many lawyers, the most sought-after mediators are those who are "willing and able to 'push' the parties, not in an antagonistic or hostile sense, but in the positive sense of inviting, supporting, encouraging, motivating, and urging the parties to work [toward an agreement]."[11] This overall attribute of "pushing" the parties involves pushing them (1) to obtain, disclose, and consider all information relevant to resolving the dispute; (2) to carefully assess the importance of any missing pieces of information in deciding whether and how to proceed in the absence of complete information; (3) to identify and consider all possible options for resolving the issues before focusing on specific options and making actual decisions; (4) to consider and fully understand the consequences of reaching an agreement or not reaching an agreement; (5) to articulate clearly their positions and the reasons behind them; and (6) to hear and understand each other's positions and the reasons underlying them.[12] In sum, many lawyers appreciate mediators who are willing to be persistent in the mediation process by engaging in a diligent effort to push *for* the parties to reach an agreement and push *with* them toward that end. This role of the effective mediator may be accomplished through any number of different mediator styles or strategies.

Finally, in unusually complex cases or where there are numerous parties and issues, it may be desirable to have co-mediators conduct the mediation. In selecting co-mediators, you might consider whether gender, racial, or ethnic balance would enhance the mediation. In addition, you might select one mediator for her rote skills as an effective mediator, and the other for his special expertise in the subject matter of the case to be mediated. In the end, counsel's reasons for selecting a particular mediator or co-mediators should be discussed and explained to the client.

[4] Preparing for Mediation

Preparing for mediation is much like preparing for negotiation to settle a case. All of the matters discussed in § 8.03 are pertinent to preparing your client for mediation. In addition, you will need to prepare your client for his/her participation in the mediation.

---

11. Robert A. Baruch Bush, Efficiency and Protection, or Empowerment and Recognition? The Mediator's Role and Ethical Standards in Mediation, 41 Fla. L. Rev. 277 (1989).
12. *Id.* at 278–281.

[a] Who Should Attend the Mediation

As mentioned previously, many court-annexed mediation programs require the following persons to attend the mediation: the individual parties (or a designated representative of a party if it is a corporate or governmental entity), an insurance company representative if there is insurance coverage in the case, the parties' lawyers, and the mediator (or co-mediators). The goal is to ensure that all persons necessary to reaching a workable and binding settlement be present.

However, even in jurisdictions that prescribe the persons who must attend the mediation, the parties are usually permitted, by mutual agreement and the consent of the mediator, to excuse the attendance of a person who otherwise is required to attend. For example, in automobile personal injury cases where liability is not in issue, the parties will often agree that the defendant who caused the accident need not be present, given that the defendant's insurance carrier paying the claim will be represented at the mediation by a claims adjuster and by defense counsel hired by the carrier.

When your client's attendance at the mediation is not mandatory, it is unwise for him not to attend unless there are compelling reasons for his nonattendance. In most cases, active client participation in the mediation (particularly during the private caucuses) is instrumental to reaching a settlement. Given that for many clients the very *process* of resolving a dispute is important, there can be no exposure to that "process" if your client does not attend the mediation. Moreover, your client's attendance at the mediation helps give effect to the ethical prescription that he alone must make the final decision about whether to settle the case. Finally, his attendance makes it easier for you to fulfill your ethical responsibility of ensuring that he is reasonably informed about all essential matters relevant to making that decision.

In addition to these reasons for having your client attend the mediation, his attendance may be particularly useful as an opportunity to display his credibility and likeability to the opposing side. This is important because many mediations occur before the lawyers have deposed any of the parties. Even if your client does not have a personality that readily radiates these qualities, his mere presence at the mediation will tend to humanize the case. In short, a client's demonstration of "jury appeal" can go a long way towards achieving a favorable settlement when the only alternative to settlement is taking the case to trial.

On the other hand, if your client doesn't want to attend the mediation and seems incapable of controlling negative behaviors that would impede the mediation process, you should seriously consider obtaining his consent not to attend the mediation. That is, if he is simply unable to control his distinct lack of jury appeal (even in a relatively short joint session before private caucusing), you might discuss with him the option of not attending the mediation and making himself available for private consultation with you by telephone during the mediation. Of course, discussing this option with your client is a difficult matter if he nevertheless wants to be present at the mediation. In that event, the best approach is to be straightforward but tactful about the matter, pointing out that some clients—through no fault of their own—are so emotionally affected by a dispute that their overall interests might be better served if they are not physically present at the mediation. This same explanation would be given to the other side and the mediator to obtain their consent to your client's nonattendance. However, if your client still insists on attending the mediation, you must honor that choice.

Sometimes a client will want a family member or close friend to be physically present during the mediation session as a support person. This may be permitted with the consent of the opposing party and the mediator, but rarely occurs in practice. More often, the support person will be permitted to come to the office where the mediation is being held to confer privately with the client when breaks are taken or when the mediator is holding private caucuses with the other side.

[b] Preparing the Client for Mediation

In preparing your client for mediation, you should explain the overall mediation process described above. In particular, emphasize that:

- The process is not a trial and will be conducted in an informal atmosphere that is designed to make all parties feel comfortable;
- The offers and counteroffers or proposals discussed at the mediation are not admissible as evidence at a trial;
- The mediator (even in "evaluative" mediation) does not serve as a judge or jury to decide the case, but is trained to assist both sides to consider each other's perspectives about the controversy to make an informed and voluntary decision about whether to settle the case, and if so, how to settle it;
- The ultimate decision whether to settle the case is your client's, but that you will be providing advice to your client throughout the mediation to help him make that decision;
- In the private caucuses with each side, the mediator is likely to "play the devil's advocate"—not to criticize your client's interests or positions, but to encourage a realistic assessment of the case and discussion of all possible solutions;
- Particularly in the private caucuses, the mediation process is designed to encourage free-flowing discussion and open information sharing;

- Many mediations last for the better part of the day (or even longer), and experience has shown that patience and open-mindedness in the process often leads to a satisfactory settlement of the case; and
- During the mediation session there will be ample opportunity for you and your client to confer privately.

Irrational or inflated client expectations about the value or outcome of the case are common problems that lawyers face when representing a client in mediation. If you have these problems with your client, stress the knowledge and experience of the mediator, and that the mediation process provides a unique opportunity to listen to the mediator and draw upon her special skills and experience as you and your client assess the case and the prospects for a reasonable settlement. In short, point out that consistent with the ultimate task of deciding whether it is in your client's best interests to settle the case or take it to trial, the input of an impartial and neutral mediator is worth careful consideration when one is trying to make a decision that will not later be regretted.

After explaining the overall mediation process and the role of the mediator, you should review and discuss your overall settlement strategy with your client. Be sure to emphasize to your client that this strategy is only a general "game plan" for the mediation, and not an inflexible blueprint of unalterable interests, objectives, positions, and bottom lines. Explain that it is typical to discover new information or perspectives about the case during the mediation process that may cause both parties to significantly depart from their pre-planned approach to the mediation and reconsider their earlier assessment about what would be a reasonable settlement of the dispute. In sum, emphasize that the *sine qua non* of effective advocacy in the mediation setting is to resist becoming entrapped by entrenched positions, and to keep an open mind and willingness to be flexible in considering different solutions to the case and engaging in appropriate compromise.

Next, discuss with your client the specific roles he will play during the mediation. In the joint session, this role may range from saying nothing to making pre-planned remarks as part of the opening statement or answering questions of the other side. For example, if your client is articulate, credible, likeable, and persuasive, you might have him participate in the opening statement by explaining certain facts or events in connection with the case, explaining how he has been affected by those events, or sharing his general perspectives or feelings about the dispute. Conversely, if your client's personality or emotional involvement in the case would make it inappropriate or uncomfortable for him to participate in the presentation of the opening statement or respond to questions of the other side, he should be advised to let you do all of the talking in the joint session.

Similar considerations apply in determining the extent to which your client should speak during the private caucuses. In this setting, however, your client's active participation is much "safer" in that what he says, and how he says it, is known only to the mediator and can be shielded from the other side. Therefore, it is generally a good idea to encourage your client to speak freely during the private caucuses, particularly in responding to questions asked directly to him by the mediator. This will enhance the mediator's understanding of your client's feelings and views about the case, and any "venting" or other emotional displays by your client are more likely to be viewed by the mediator as being the product of a candid attempt to respond to her questions, rather than as manifestations of an irrational or unstable personality. In any event, you can always take a recess from a private caucus if you think that your client is engaging in counterproductive or other inappropriate behavior.

Notwithstanding the usual desirability of encouraging your client to speak freely during the private caucuses, you should specifically advise your client:

- Not to reveal any information that both of you have agreed to keep confidential from the mediator;
- Not to reveal any attorney-client privileged information, such as your negotiating strategy;
- Not to get into an argument with the mediator or anyone else at the mediation session;
- Not to engage in exaggeration, hyperbole, speculation, or misrepresentation;
- Not to interrupt when another person is speaking; and
- Not to display any verbal or non-verbal reactions to any settlement proposals or offers in a way that may reveal or otherwise undermine your negotiating strategy.

These cautionary instructions also apply, of course, to any joint session during the mediation.

As for your role during the mediation, explain that your overall responsibility is to "take the lead" for your client's side. Make clear that your role as an advocate during mediation is quite different from your advocacy role at a trial or in an arbitration. That is, during mediation, you will not be engaging in the formal presentation of evidence, cross-examining any witnesses, or delivering a closing argument. Rather you will be engaging in a respectful dialogue with the other side and the mediator, where you will be doing at least as much listening as talking. Moreover, explain that consistent with your goal to advance the best interests of your client and negotiate a favorable settlement on his behalf, you will be utilizing the mediation process as part of an ongoing assessment of your client's case to give him your best judgment and advice from which he can make an informed decision about settlement.

§8.05 Counseling through Opinion Letters

Just as you must become proficient in counseling a client in person, you must also become proficient in counseling a client in writing. The latter form of counseling is typically done through opinion letters, and e-mail has otherwise made written communication with the client a convenient norm. After the initial interview with your client and one or more counseling sessions, much of your ongoing communication with your client (when not by telephone) will often be in writing.

The principal disadvantage of counseling a client in writing is that this form of communication is not immediately interactive. If the client does not understand something you wrote or otherwise has questions about what you have written, the matter cannot be addressed "on the spot" as would be the case in a face-to-face meeting or telephone conversation. On the other hand, the principal advantage of advising a client in writing (as through an opinion letter) is that the writing provides the client with a record of your advice that can be re-read, studied, and shared with other decision-makers affiliated with the client,[13] particularly when the client is a corporate, governmental, or other organizational entity. In addition, a written opinion serves to document the fact and contents of your advice, which may be important to either you or your client in the event that any question arises in the future as to what advice was given.

[1] The Function, Format and Contents of an Opinion Letter

Lawyers typically render opinions about (1) the law and its application to a particular situation (e.g., the viability of a lawsuit, defenses to a suit, what

---

13. In so-called "control group" jurisdictions, the attorney-client privilege extends only to those individuals in the organization who can make decisions on behalf of the entity or have authority to bind the entity. Other, so-called "UpJohn" jurisdictions, named after *UpJohn v. United States*, 449 U.S. 383, 101 S.Ct. 677 (1981), extend the attorney-client privilege to any employee of the organization involved for the purpose of obtaining information necessary to provide legal advice to the entity.

the law says about a particular matter, whether a particular course of action is lawful or unlawful); (2) how to deal with a client's problem or relationship with someone else (e.g., in the context of a dispute, or in the context of deal-making or engaging in a transaction); (3) how to accomplish a particular client objective (e.g., how to establish a will, trust, or corporate entity; how to satisfy a governmental regulatory requirement, or how to change particular legislation); or (4) all of the foregoing together. As emphasized in § 8.02, your opinions about these types of matters will often involve wholly extra-legal considerations and judgments, apart from or in addition to purely law-based considerations and judgments. Thus, the usual function of an opinion letter is to address in writing any one or more of the foregoing matters.

The particular format and contents of an opinion letter will, of course, vary widely depending upon the particular circumstances of the representation. In most cases, however, the format and elements of an opinion letter will have five components:

I. An Introduction or "Executive Summary"

The introduction should contain (a) a statement of what the client has asked you to provide an opinion about, and (b) a summary of how the letter is organized to render the opinion. Particularly if the letter is long, it may be useful to also include a summary of your bottom-line opinion. This is sometimes denominated as an "Executive Summary."

II. A Summary of the Facts

All facts and assumptions bearing upon your opinion should be included in the letter. This recitation of the facts might be written as a separate section of the letter, particularly if the letter asks your client to confirm the accuracy of your understanding of the facts. Alternatively, if there is no need to give a comprehensive summary of the facts, your application of the pertinent facts should be included in your discussion of the matters addressed in III and IV below. In either case, when appropriate, you should mention critical facts that are unknown and all factual assumptions bearing upon your analysis and opinion.

III. An Explanation of the Client's Options and Their Relative Advantages and Disadvantages for Achieving the Client's Objectives

The letter should identify all potentially viable options for dealing with your client's situation, along with a discussion of the relative advantages and disadvantages of each option for achieving your client's objectives. As appropriate, both litigation and extra-legal options (including settlement) should be discussed. When discussing law-based options, you will need to explain the law and how it applies to your client's factual situation.

IV. A Recommended Course of Action or Strategy for Achieving the Client's Objectives

This component of the letter sets out your opinion about the best option(s) available to your client and *why* you recommend that one or more preferred options be pursued. In addition, you should discuss, as appropriate, how your recommended course of action or strategy for achieving your client's objectives would be best implemented.

V. A Conclusion

The conclusion to the letter might invite your client to phone you or meet with you to discuss your advice after he has reviewed the letter. The conclusion might also set out what will need to be done next after your client has made a decision about your recommendation.

Stylistic Considerations

In terms of the "style" of your letter, remember that, in the usual case, your client is not a lawyer. In that connection, consider the following points:

- At the top of the letter, you might include a heading that the letter is "Attorney-Client Privileged."
- Write in plain English, preferring shorter rather than longer sentences.
- Use common terminology, avoiding unnecessary legalese. If you use a legal term or other term of art, be sure to explain its meaning.
- As appropriate, use subheadings to identify different topics discussed in your letter. This will make it easier for your client to follow your analysis.
- Don't cite or quote case law or statutes unless you have a particular reason for doing so (e.g., as where in-house counsel for your corporate client will also read the letter). This does not mean being glib about the law. For most clients, you can state the applicable law much like you would when writing a memorandum of law (albeit without citations), except that you should take extra care to define or explain legal terms.
- Don't assume that your client will understand the nuances or implications of certain words or phrases that are well known to a lawyer. For example, all lawyers know that the word "shall" denotes a mandatory obligation, and that the phrase "reasonable care" means that de-

gree of care which a person of ordinary prudence would exercise in the same or similar circumstances. Thus, when writing the letter, be mindful of your use of common words or phrases that have special meaning to a lawyer but may not, absent explanation, be similarly understood by a non-lawyer.

- As you write your letter, put yourself in the shoes of your non-lawyer client. This will help you write it in a way that will make it under-standable for your client. When editing a draft of the letter, ask your-self, "Have I described this matter in a way that will be understood by my client?" In other words, your goal should be to minimize, as much as possible, any confusion or misunderstanding that your client might have about what you have said in the letter.

[2] Illustration of an Opinion Letter

The following opinion letter is drawn from the *Parkwood Homes v. Delmar Homes* hypothetical used in § 8.02[2]. The letter, written to Parkwood's Chief Executive Officer, is somewhat abbreviated; but the intent here is to merely il-lustrate the principal features of the format and content of most opinion letters as discussed in the preceding subsection. (The footnotes in the letter further highlight some of these features.)

ABLE, BAKER, & CAIN, P.A. Attorneys at Law
104 Southbridge Avenue, Suite 800
Caldonia City, Caldonia 20010 800-424-1000

August 15, YR-0

ATTORNEY-CLIENT PRIVILEGED[14]

Mr. Jack Parkinson Chief Executive Officer,
Parkwood Homes
850 Stimpson Street Caldonia City, Caldonia 20010

Re: Analysis of Options and Recommendation for How to Stop Delmar's False Advertising Campaign Against Parkwood

Dear Jack:[15]

---

14. This heading is included because it is likely that Mr. Parkinson will share the letter with other executives in the Company.

15. Addressing the client by first name assumes that the lawyer has established the req-uisite rapport to do so.

I enjoyed seeing you last week, and I thought our meeting was quite productive. At the end of it, you asked me to analyze certain options we discussed for stopping Delmar's false advertising campaign against Parkwood and to provide you with a recommendation of the best strategy to pursue at this time. This letter does that. It begins with a summary of the facts we know at this point and then discusses the relative advantages and disadvantages of the different options we talked about. The letter concludes with a recommendation that I contact Delmar's lawyer to explore how the companies might resolve this matter informally, whether through a meeting between company representatives or through mediation.[16]

I. SUMMARY OF THE FACTS[17]

Parkwood constructs mobile homes and operates mobile home parks in Caldonia and in fifteen other states throughout the country. The Company's primary competitor in this State is Delmar Homes, which is engaged in the same business and has become quite profitable in recent years. You believe Delmar wants to monopolize the entire mobile-home market in Caldonia.

Last month, one of your Company's employees obtained a promotional flyer being distributed by Delmar to prospective customers of its homes. The flyer states, in part:

> The homes by Delmar beat out Parkwood homes any day! If you want first-rate construction, complaint-free living, and beautiful landscaping, choose Delmar as your first-choice living experience, Parkwood can't give you that and won't give you that. But Delmar will![18]

At this time, we do not know when this flyer was first distributed, how many have been distributed, the names of any persons who have received the flyer, or whether Parkwood's reputation has been damaged by the statements made in the flyer.[19]

Early this month, three of your Company's sales' representatives reported "rumors" that the statements made in the flyer may be repeated in Delmar's forthcoming statewide newspaper-advertising campaign. You anticipate this

---

16. Note how this introduction states the purpose of the letter and how it is organized, and then summarizes the bottom-line opinion.

17. This summary of the facts is relatively brief. If the lawyer's purpose were to have the client confirm the accuracy of the facts, they would be stated in much greater detail.

18. The flyer is quoted verbatim because the actual language is critical to an assessment of whether the statements can be construed as being defamatory.

19. These are important unknown facts.

advertising campaign will begin sometime in the fall, which is the best time of year to solicit sales for mobile homes.

You have told me that, three years ago, Parkwood replaced the roofing on about twenty of its homes in Riverton County in the State after the roofs were damaged in an unusually severe thunderstorm. Two years ago, the siding on about fifty homes in the State had to be replaced due to a manufacturing defect, which was not caused by Parkwood or its construction of the homes. Last year, your Company received about a dozen complaints from homeowners in one of its parks in the State, complaining that Allgood Management Company, which Parkwood hired to maintain the common areas of the park, was not maintaining the landscaping. You have since been assured by Allgood that these complaints have been addressed, and you are not aware of any new complaints.

Because Parkwood caused neither the damaged roofing nor the defective siding and Allgood has corrected any landscaping deficiencies, the statements made in Delmar's flyers are untrue. My understanding is that your primary objective is to stop Delmar from continuing to make false statements about Parkwood, now and in the future.[20]

Delmar is regularly represented in legal matters by Mr. Cecil Burns of Sealey & Burns, LLC, which is located in Caldonia City. I have known Mr. Burns for many years.

II. PARKWOOD'S POTENTIAL OPTIONS & THEIR RELATIVE ADVANTAGES AND DISADVANTAGES[21]

(A) <u>File a Lawsuit Against Delmar for Defamation and Unfair and Deceptive Trade Practices, Seeking Preliminary and Permanent Injunctive Relief, and Damages</u>[22]

To be successful in a lawsuit against Delmar for defamation, Parkwood must prove that (1) Delmar knew or should have known that its statements in the flyer were false; (2) the statements had at least "a tendency" to injure Parkwood's reputation; and (3) the flyer was disseminated to one or more third parties, such a s a potential mobile home buyer. Mere statements of "opinion" (as op-

---

20. This confirms the lawyer's understanding of the client's objective, which is critical to a discussion of relevant options.

21. This section, as it states, sets out all potentially viable options and their pros and cons.

22. The use of sub-headings throughout the letter is designed to make it easier for the client to follow the lawyer's analysis.

posed to statements of fact) are not defamatory. In a claim[23] brought under our Unfair & Deceptive Trade Practices statute, Parkwood must prove all three elements of the defamation claim <u>and</u> that one or more consumers were "misled" by the statements.[24]

Under either claim, within approximately 60 days after filing suit, a judge could consider whether to grant Parkwood a preliminary injunction ordering Delmar to immediately stop making the statements pending a trial of the case, which would not take place until a year or more later. To obtain a preliminary injunction, Parkwood would have to convince the judge (a) that it has a very strong case on the merits; (b) that the Company would suffer "irreparable harm" (i.e., losses that could not adequately be compensated through damages awarded at trial) if the preliminary order were not entered; and (c) that Delmar would not likely be harmed by the order. In addition, Parkwood would have to post a bond with the court (in an amount determined in the judge's discretion) to secure payment of any costs or damages incurred by Delmar on account of the preliminary order if Delmar ultimately were to win at trial. If Parkwood were to win at trial, the judge could enter a permanent injunction, ordering Delmar not to make the statements in the future.

Each claim allows for certain types of damages that may be awarded by a jury. For defamation, Parkwood is entitled to compensation for its "actual damages" (i.e., direct monetary losses, such as lost profits reasonably attributable to the false statements) and "general damages" for injury to its reputation (i.e., loss of good will on account of the false statements).[25] No attorney's fees are recoverable. On the other hand, for a violation of the Unfair and Deceptive Trade Practices statute, Parkwood is limited to receiving compensation for its "actual damages" only, but these damages would be trebled and the judge has the discretion to order Delmar to pay Parkwood's attorney's fees. If the jury renders a verdict in favor of Parkwood on both claims, the Company would have to elect whether it wanted to receive the damages awarded on the defamation claim or those awarded on the Unfair and Deceptive Trade Practices claim.[26]

---

23. The word "claim" is used instead of "cause of action" because the client is unlikely to know what the latter phrase means.

24. Note that the lawyer has chosen to omit any citations to case law or the statute because including citations would add nothing to the client's understanding of the applicable law.

25. Note how the lawyer explains the meaning of these terms for different types of damages.

26. The preceding discussion of the law could be more expansive. Here, the lawyer has limited his discussion of the law to include no more than is necessary for the client to adequately understand the uncertainties and risks associated with the lawsuit option.

Parkwood's chances of prevailing on either claim are, at best, uncertain. A judge might conclude that the statements in the flyer are not defamatory because they are mere expressions of "opinion." On the other hand, it is reasonable to argue that the statements that "Parkwood can't give you … and won't give you … first-rate construction [and] complaint-free living" are not mere opinions, but are false statements of fact. On the Unfair and Deceptive Trade Practices claim, we currently have no evidence that any consumer was "misled" by the statements in the flyer. These uncertainties about being able to prove these claims make it unlikely that a judge would grant Parkwood a preliminary injunction.

Uncertainty also exists about whether Parkwood could recover meaningful damages to justify the expense of lengthy litigation. At this time, we have no evidence of "actual damages," and we have no proof that Parkwood's reputation has been damaged by the statements. Thus, the costs to Parkwood in terms of time, effort, and attorney's fees for going to trial may far exceed any damages awarded by a jury.

Finally, it is reasonable to assume that the mere filing of a lawsuit would not cause Delmar to stop making its statements. Since Delmar has been profitable in recent years and is intent on monopolizing the mobile home market in this State, the company is likely to vigorously defend the suit.[27] In addition to arguing that its statements are not defamatory because they are mere statements of opinion, Delmar will defend on the basis that the statements are true. This means that even if a jury ultimately vindicated Parkwood, the controversy may generate protracted adverse public exposure for Parkwood throughout the litigation process.

(B) Send a Demand Letter to Delmar, Demanding that it Cease its False Statements or Risk a Lawsuit

This option could be executed immediately with little cost and effort. There is no risk of adverse public exposure to Parkwood unless Delmar publicizes the letter (which would be unlikely).

The primary disadvantage of the option is that, by threatening suit, Delmar may react defensively and seek to justify the truthfulness of its statements, if only to itself. As you know, companies react much like people do, and the "take-it-or-leave-it" message of such a demand letter leaves no room for Delmar to "save face," even if the company were inclined to abandon its negative advertising in light of the litigation threat. Therefore, using this option at the outset may quickly escalate the matter into a lawsuit, which carries the uncertainties and disadvantages mentioned above.

---

27. Note how the lawyer sets out the reasons for his assumption.

(C) <u>Develop a Negative Advertising Campaign Against Delmar, or a Positive Advertising Campaign About the Virtues of Parkwood's Mobile Homes</u>

Both of these options will take time and expense to execute, although they are not as time-consuming and expensive as litigation. Neither option is likely to stop Delmar's behavior. If Parkwood engages in negative advertising, Delmar may retaliate by increasing its own negative advertising. If Parkwood engages in positive advertising, any gains to the Company's image may be offset by Delmar's ongoing negative advertising campaign.

(D) <u>Sell Parkwood's Existing Business in the State or "Spin Off" the Existing Operation into a New Company Under a Different Name</u>

These options have the advantage of bypassing the problem with Delmar and disassociating Parkwood's national name from the mobile home business in this State. The advantage of selling assumes the existence of a buyer who is willing to pay a reasonable price for Parkwood's Caldonia business in the face of having to deal with Delmar's highly aggressive and competitive tactics in the future. A sale may also take a long time to execute. Although a spin off of the existing operation into a new company under a different name is less complicated than a sale, a spin off may attract adverse speculation about the true motives for the corporate maneuver; and it may risk providing Delmar with yet another ground for disparaging Parkwood's good name.

(E) <u>Do Nothing and Wait to See the Contents of Delmar's Newspaper Advertising Campaign Before Taking Any Action</u>

This option, by itself, involves no cost or adverse public exposure to Parkwood. If Delmar's newspaper advertisements are not defamatory, Parkwood might decide not to pursue the matter further.

On the other hand, taking no immediate action risks substantial adverse publicity for Parkwood if Delmar's newspaper advertisements repeat the statements made in the flyer. Moreover, in that event, any effort to convince Delmar to voluntarily stop its defamatory statements may be more difficult after Delmar's has already committed itself to a newspaper advertising campaign.

(F) <u>Use Informal Persuasion to Convince Delmar to Stop its Negative Advertising</u>

Under this option, Parkwood would authorize me to contact Delmar's lawyer, Cecil Burns, to explore how the companies might resolve the matter informally. This might be accomplished through a meeting between representatives of the two companies or through an agreed-upon mediation process.

Either method would provide Parkwood with the opportunity to explain the true circumstances surrounding the prior roofing, siding and landscaping problems, which presumably gave rise to the statements made in Delmar's flyer. This may convince Delmar to stop making the statements under the face-saving rationale that they were made due to a "misunderstanding" of the true facts.

This option can be implemented relatively quickly and at modest expense. Because either a meeting between company representatives or mediation would be considered "settlement discussions," the matters discussed in those settings would not be admissible into evidence at a trial.

III. RECOMMENDATION[28]

Based on the discussion above, filing a lawsuit is currently the least desirable option in terms of risk, expense, time, and adverse public exposure. The demand-letter option, at least for now, unnecessarily risks escalating the controversy into litigation. The negative or positive advertising options, as well as the temporary "do-nothing" option, are unlikely to stop Delmar's behavior. Finally, selling or spinning off the existing business essentially bypasses the problem without dealing with it directly.

This leaves the informal-persuasion option. It is low risk, inexpensive and expeditious, and involves no public exposure. It provides a face-saving opportunity for Delmar to stop making its false statements. Moreover, based on my experience with Mr. Burns over the years, I believe he will be receptive to exploring a way in which the matter can be resolved informally, whether in the form of a meeting between company representatives or mediation. Finally, I expect that Mr. Burns will fully advise Delmar about the risks it faces if it continues to make the statements in the flyer, and this may help to induce Delmar to seek an informal resolution of the matter.

In sum, there doesn't seem to be any downside to starting with this option. If it fails, we will at least have more information about Delmar's position and attitude about the matter to better decide what to do next.[29]

Please do not hesitate to contact me if you have any questions about this letter. I otherwise look forward to hearing from you in the near future.[30]

Sincerely,

Marcus G. Able

---

28. As the heading states, this is the lawyer's recommended course of action or strategy for achieving the client's objective.

29. Note how the lawyer in this paragraph and the preceding paragraph explains *why* informal persuasion is the preferred option.

30. This is a simple conclusion to the letter.

§ 8.06 Counseling about Transactional Matters

Many lawyers represent clients in so-called "transactional" matters where the lawyer advises and assists the client about transactions or commitments, such as contracts, real estate matters, wills or estate planning, for-profit or non-profit business incorporations or development, corporate mergers, sales of goods or assets, stock transfers, tax consequences of the foregoing, and the like. Sometimes these services will be rendered to an existing client where the lawyer knows a fair amount about the client's situation, but often that will not be the case. In either event, these types of matters typically do not involve an existing dispute but govern certain obligations between the parties involved. A central objective of this transactional representation is to formalize commitments or arrangements of a client in a way that forecloses a dispute rather than resolves one. Because this area of practice typically operates outside of litigation, some special counseling functions are appropriate in this representation.

[1] Formalize a Transaction That Is Consistent with the Client's Objectives and Aversion to Risk

When advising about and drafting a transactional document, you must have a clear understanding of your client's objectives and sense of risk about the transaction involved. For example, a business client seeking to enter into a contract, a seller or buyer of a home, a testator of a will or a trust, or a person who desires to incorporate or manage the affairs of a business will usually want to simply give legal effect to the transaction without an instrument that seeks to guard against every kind of remote and hypothetical circumstance that might give rise to a dispute about the transaction. The client will often want the transaction effectively consummated, not "killed" by an instrument that turns off the recipient by prolix, protective provisions about what happens when this or that might happen.

This does not mean that you should not, when appropriate, counsel your client about including within a transactional document certain usual or necessary protective provisions that will protect your client in the event of a dispute. This might include, for example, a contract that specifies arbitration as a means for resolving a dispute under the contract. However, too often, some transactional lawyers are tempted to overload the transactional document with complex (and sometimes legally dubious) indemnity provisions or other mandated consequences in the event of certain breaches of the agreement. This attempt at cleverness or craftiness may prevent your client from accomplishing the objective to reach an agreement altogether. In short, the extent to which you prepare a transactional document with provisions that protect your client from unforeseen circumstances must account for your client's objectives in consummating the transaction and your client's aversion to risk—not your own sense of hypothetical risk.

[2] Explore All Circumstances of Your Client's Transactional Situation

When representing a client in a transactional matter, you must not only understand your client's objectives and aversion to risk, but also understand the background of your client's situation and any prior relationship or negotiations between your client and the person or entity with whom your client intends to transact. If you have represented the client in the past, you will sometimes know in advance your client's situation, objectives and aversion to risk. But, if you do not, you will need to discuss these matters in detail with your client, along with any prior dealings or discussions between your client and the other party involved. Those prior dealings or preliminary discussions will be integral to formulating a transaction acceptable to both sides.

In addition, having a complete understanding of your client's situation—such as the nature and operations of the business, the property involved, the economic impacts of the transaction, and the like—will be integral to your counseling about how best to consummate the transaction. These aspects of your client's situation (and the situation of the party with whom your client intends to transact) are essential to proposing a transaction that will be acceptable to all involved. In short, your understanding of these matters is essential to effective transactional representation.

[3] Tailor Your Transactional Document to Your Client, Not Merely to a Form Book

Many transactional documents are prepared from standard "forms" in legal form books or from standard forms developed over time by a law office. These forms are, of course, useful in preparing documents in similar transactions. However, a particular client's situation may require you to advise about and prepare a markedly different transactional document—consistent with your particular client's objectives, aversion to risk, and the special circumstances of your client's transactional situation mentioned above. In sum. whenever you interview and counsel a client in a transactional matter, you should never assume that the objectives and interests of the client are identical to other similarly situated clients. Always remember that each client is unique, which may call upon you to tailor your advice and document preparation to that uniqueness.

§8.07 Counseling the Client as a Deponent

Preparing your client for a deposition requires counseling her about (1) the overall process of the deposition, (2) the substance of her testimony, and (3) how to answer questions. It is unlikely all of these matters can be covered effectively in a single counseling session. Accordingly, you may need to plan for two or three separate sessions (e.g., one session to discuss the overall process of the deposition and the substance of your client's testimony, and another to discuss and practice how to answer questions). Regardless of how you sequence these sessions, all of them should be scheduled close to the actual time of the deposition. That is, if you counsel your client about these matters a week in advance of the deposition, she is likely to forget much of what you discussed by the time the deposition occurs. Thus, plan to conduct your preparation sessions no more than two or three days before the deposition is scheduled. However, make sure you do not conduct the bulk of your preparation on the same day as the deposition because your client may freeze as a result of nervousness. Finally, meet with your client for about an hour right before the deposition begins to discuss or review any last-minute matters.

[1] Discuss the Overall Process of the Deposition

After a deposition is over, most clients will ask you, "How did I do?" or "Did I do alright?" These questions are a manifestation of how most clients feel about a deposition: they are anxious about it. They are worried that they didn't say "the right things," that they may have "hurt" their case, and perhaps even that the deposing lawyer made them "look stupid." Effective counseling about the overall process of the deposition is designed to achieve one primary goal—to reduce your client's anxiety about the deposition so that, at the end of it, you will be able to say to her that she did well because she testified to what she knew as fairly, accurately, and briefly as she could (see subsection [3] below).

In beginning your discussion of the overall process of the deposition, emphasize to your client that the process is designed to be fair to her, and not designed to embarrass, harass, or trick her. Explain to her that:

- You will be sitting next to her throughout the deposition and will not allow her to be harassed or tricked by opposing counsel (which is unlikely to occur in any event);
- You are "in charge" of the deposition and will prevent her from having to answer any improper or unfair questions;
- Along with opposing counsel (and perhaps his client), there will be a court reporter present who will place her under oath and record the entire deposition;
- You will arrange to take periodic breaks during the deposition, and she should feel free to ask for a break if she needs one or wants to talk with you privately for any reason at any time during the deposition;[31]
- After opposing counsel is through asking questions, you will also have the opportunity to ask her questions if you feel this is necessary to correct a matter, clear up any confusion, or have her more fully explain a particular matter; and, if you decide to do to this, you will first talk with her privately about the questions you will ask;
- After the deposition is over, the court reporter will prepare (usually within a few weeks) a verbatim transcript of everything said at the deposition, and she and you will have an opportunity to correct any inaccuracies in the transcript; and
- This overall process of the deposition is designed to be "fair" to her, and you will do everything in your power to ensure that she will be treated fairly throughout the process.

Also emphasize to your client that her sole role in the deposition is that of a *witness* only, not an advocate for her cause. At trial, the only advocates are the lawyers; the judge is the referee; the jury is the decider; the court reporter is the transcriber; and all other participants (including the parties) are witnesses. The job of any witness is merely to tell the "who, what, when, where, which, why, and how" of what he or she knows about the case. You, as her lawyer, carry the entire burden of arguing her case.

---

31. Ordinarily, when a question is pending, the client should answer before conferring with counsel. On the other hand, it is permissible for the client and attorney to confer at any time to discuss whether the question posed implicates a privilege such as the attorney-client privilege. In some jurisdictions, courts have ruled that once the deposition begins, the attorney may not confer with the client except about whether to claim a privilege. *See* Hall v. Clifton Precision, 150 F.R.D. 525 (E.D. Pa. 1993); *see also*, Jean M. Cary, *Rambo Depositions Revisited: Controlling Attorney-client Consultations During Depositions*, Geo. J. Legal Ethics, Vol. XIX, No. 2 (Spring, 2006).

Your client's understanding of her proper role, along with the assurance that she will be treated civilly and fairly, will help to reduce her anxiety and nervousness about the deposition. In addition, in your discussion, let your client openly express her feelings of anxiety. Assure her that most witnesses are nervous about having their deposition taken. But a deposition is not a test, and she should not feel that she needs to be perfect. She, like you and the opposing lawyer, may make some mistakes, but these can be corrected either at the deposition or later on.

Finally, remember to discuss with your client all necessary housekeeping details, such as when and where the deposition will be held. Instruct her not to bring anything to the deposition, such as notes, documents, or anything else. (You will have your file at the deposition if any document needs to be reviewed.) And lastly, talk with your client about what she will wear to the deposition. As a basic rule, her attire should be consistent with the particular image you want her to convey to the opposing side.

[2] Review the Substance of Your Client's Testimony

Invariably, you will be able to forecast the major topics that opposing counsel will cover with your client during the deposition. For example, if lawyer Larry Odden filed a personal injury suit on behalf of Clara Miles against the driver of the pick-up truck, Ronald Smith (*see* §§ 4.10 and 5.10), Smith's attorney is likely to depose Clara about:

- Her personal background (e.g. where she lives and has lived in recent years, her family, when she married Dan, etc.);
- Her educational background;
- Her employment history;
- Everything about how the accident occurred and what happened after it;
- Her non-privileged conversations with the police officer and others about the accident;
- All of her injuries from the time of the accident to date;
- All of her medical treatment;
- Any prior accidents, injuries, or health problems she has had; and
- Her answers to interrogatories, requests for production of documents, and requests for admissions.

In connection with the foregoing, Smith's lawyer is likely to have two primary goals for the deposition: (1) to obtain as much information as possible bearing upon liability and damages, and (2) to evaluate Clara's credibility and overall "jury appeal." Both are critical for trial and settlement purposes.

Based upon your forecast of the major topics that will be covered in the deposition, you should review with your client the substance of her testimony on the most important and sensitive topics, particularly those that directly relate to the disputed issues in the case and the parties' different legal or factual theories on those issues. This includes reviewing with your client important documents, along with her answers to paper discovery. As discussed in subsection [3] below, you should give your client some practice answering questions on particularly important aspects of her testimony.

For example, Larry Odden is likely to review with Clara everything about how the accident happened, her injuries, and how her injuries have affected her from the time of the accident to date. He might review the accident report with her to determine how accurately it describes the accident in light of what she saw, and review the medical reports with her to remind her about her course of treatment. In addition, he might review with her certain answers provided in response to the defendant's interrogatories or requests for admissions.

The purpose of this review is not to have your client "memorize" a story. Rather, it is merely intended to remind your client of the most important aspects of her testimony so that it will be easier for her to give a more complete account of those matters during the deposition. In conducting the review, Larry might simply ask Clara to "describe" or "explain" how the accident happened and then engage her in a discussion about the details in a conversational way. If necessary, he can conduct a more formal practice session with Clara to rehearse answering specific lines of deposition questions on crucial topics as explained in the subsection below.

[3] Discuss and Practice How to Answer Questions

There are five basic rules for answering questions at a deposition:

1. Answer each question fairly, accurately, and briefly.
2. If you don't fully understand the question, say: "I don't understand the question."
3. If you are not absolutely sure about the answer to the question or can't remember the answer, say: "I don't know" or "I don't remember."
4. If an objection is made, don't answer until I tell you to do so.
5. If you are asked "leading" questions, "keep your cool" and answer calmly.

Each of these rules should be explained to your client and illustrated as part of a practice session.

1. Answering fairly, accurately, and briefly.

The old-school approach to answering deposition questions instructs that the client should answer no more than the literal question asked; and, whenever possible, merely answer "Yes" or "No." For example:

> LAWYER: Where were you going before the accident happened?
> CLIENT: To a game.
> LAWYER: To a game?
> CLIENT: Yes.
> LAWYER: What kind of game?
> CLIENT: Basketball game.
> LAWYER: Who was playing?
> CLIENT: I don't know the names of the players.
> LAWYER: I mean, was this a UNC game, a high school game, or what?
> CLIENT: UNC game.
> LAWYER: Who was UNC playing?
> CLIENT: State.
> LAWYER: N.C. State?
> CLIENT: Yes.
> LAWYER: Well, tell me how the accident happened—
> CLIENT: We got broad-sided.
> LAWYER: Can you tell me more about that?
> CLIENT: Yes.
> LAWYER: Please go ahead then—
> CLIENT: Do what?
> LAWYER: Please describe how the accident happened—
> CLIENT: Like I said, we got broad-sided. That's it. That's what happened.

These types of answers illustrate why the old-school approach is a bad one, particularly when taken to the extreme. Although the client has accomplished her attorney's apparent objective of providing as little information as possible to the deposing lawyer, the answers are unnatural, inappropriately glib, and come across as being phony and evasive. Undoubtedly, at trial, the client will give a much more expansive and detailed answer to a question from her attorney on direct examination to explain how the accident happened. If those details were not fairly revealed in the deposition, the opposing lawyer could heavily cross-examine the client on her glib responses to the same question asked in the deposition. In short, any jury hearing the foregoing exchange in the deposition transcript would conclude that the client was either being unfairly evasive at the deposition or was embellishing her testimony at trial, or both. This loss of credibility would severely undermine the client's case.

Moreover, this old-school approach undermines reasonable prospects for settlement. Inasmuch as one of the deposing lawyer's purposes in taking the opposing client's deposition is to assess her credibility and "jury appeal," the performance illustrated above gives a distinctly negative impression about the client. Whether the client's superficial responses are due to her attorney's "tell-nothing" coaching or to the possibility that the client really doesn't know much about how the accident happened, her weak credibility significantly reduces the settlement value of her case.

In contrast, the more appropriate and modern approach to answering deposition questions instructs that your client's answers should be (i) "fair" to the context of the questions asked, (ii) "accurate," and (iii) "brief." Being "fair" to the context of the question simply means being naturally responsive to the unmistakable import of the question, taking into account the particular line of questioning. Being "accurate" simply means to "tell it like it is," and not to embellish the answer in an argumentative way or through the use of "spin." Being "brief" simply means "get to the point" and not digress from the question to gratuitously volunteer information on a different, or even related, matter.[32]

For example, after Larry Odden has explained the foregoing to Clara, he might give her some practice in answering questions fairly, accurately, and briefly in this way:

> L: Clara, let's try out for a little bit what we've been talking about. I'll pretend I'm Mr. Smith's lawyer and I'll ask you some questions in a way that I think he'll ask them. Okay?
> C: Okay. I'm a bit nervous—
> L: You'll do fine. You have a good manner about you. Let your answers flow naturally, truthfully, and just stick to the question asked. Okay?
> C: Okay.
> L: Ms. Miles, where were you going before the accident happened?

---

32. In some circumstances, as where your client has an uncontrollable propensity to ramble, you might otherwise counsel her to try to restrict her answers to "Yes" or "No" answers or to one or two sentences whenever possible. Alternatively, if your client is a highly articulate witness and your primary purpose is to induce a settlement of the case, you might encourage her to be much more expansive in her answers on certain topics.

C: We were going up Franklin Street in Chapel Hill, going to find a place to get some lunch up town; and then we were going to go to the Carolina basketball game. They were playing N.C. State.

L: Now, this accident happened at the intersection of Franklin Street and Estes Drive, is that right?

C: Yes; that's where it happened.

L: Can you tell me how the accident happened?

C: (Pause ...) Well, my husband, Dan, was driving, and I was in the front passenger seat. Our son, Tommy, was in the back seat. Just as we got to the intersection, the light turned yellow. I glanced down for a minute; and then I saw the pick-up truck, coming from the right, and hit us on my side, the passenger side, toward the front of the car. I think I went dizzy for a moment; my head hit the headrest. And then I looked back to see if Tommy was okay and if my husband was okay. (Pause ...). Well, that's how it happened.

L: Very good, Clara. As I say, you have a nice manner. You were natural and poised. I made three short notes that might help you. First, I like the way you paused and collected your thoughts before answering how the accident happened. That's always a good thing to do when you need to.

C: Thanks.

L: My second note, and you may not have realized this, is that you said you glanced down for a "minute" —

C: Oh, really? I meant a "second."

L: I know [laughing]. That's just an example of one of those small mistakes all of us make. As I mentioned to you before, these kinds of things can always be corrected. If Mr. Smith's lawyer had not brought it to your attention, I would have corrected it during my opportunity to ask you questions. If all of us missed it during the deposition, we would have been able to correct it when we reviewed the transcript.

C: I see. Thank goodness.

L: My third note is that you were to the point and brief about how the accident happened. At the end, though, you started talking a bit about getting dizzy, hitting your head on the headrest, and then seeing if Tommy and Dan were okay. Perhaps you stopped at that point because you realized that you were starting to talk about a different topic than how the accident happened, which was the question asked.

C: Yes, I started to realize that. So I stopped.

L: I thought so, and it provides a good example of how you can catch yourself if you start straying from the actual question asked. Mr.

Smith's lawyer might even try to get you to ramble on by being silent after you give an answer or by acting friendly and complimentary towards you. Here again, it is best to catch yourself and leave your answer as it is without going into other matters.

2. Answering, "I don't understand the question."

Tell you client that if there is anything about a question that she doesn't understand, she should say that she doesn't understand or, if appropriate, ask that the question be repeated. If the deposing lawyer asks what she doesn't understand about the question, she should say so if she can. It's not her job to fix the question (e.g., "If you are asking me…, then my answer is.…"). If the deposing lawyer refuses to reframe the question in an understandable way, your client should simply say, "I don't understand."

3. Answering "I don't know" or "I don't remember."

Perhaps the most dangerous thing a client can do in a deposition is to "make up" an answer to a question she knows little or nothing about. Sometimes a client is asked about a matter that one would expect she would know but for one reason or another doesn't actually know or remember. This can tempt the client, who wants to avoid being embarrassed, to construct some form of an answer that is either incomplete or altogether wrong. The danger is that this face-saving effort to be responsive may end up haunting the client at trial when she is cross-examined about the true facts.

Thus, explain this danger to your client. Assure her that she is not expected to remember everything, and that it is not unusual for witnesses to forget matters they once knew or to not know matters that one might expect they would know. In either case, she should simply say, "I don't know" or "I don't remember."[33] If the matter is particularly important and is remembered later, the answer can be supplied as part of a correction to the transcript or an amended answer to paper discovery, or otherwise explained at trial if necessary.

Sometimes the client will know part of the answer to the question or "believe" she knows the answer, but is uncertain. In that event, she should expressly qualify her answer as something she "thinks" to be true or "believes" to be true, but is not absolutely sure. Similarly, if she is asked to "speculate" about a matter or to give an "estimate" or "personal opinion," she should do so if she can but appropriately qualify her answer.

---

33. Generally, the phrase "I don't recall" sounds formalistic or even evasive, and therefore should be avoided unless your client normally speaks this way.

4. Answering when an objection is made.

Explain to your client that during the deposition you might "object" to some of the questions asked. Usually, these will be in the nature of mere "technical" objections that you are obligated to make so that the judge can rule on them in the event the deposition is used at trial. When these types of objections are made, you will nevertheless instruct your client to go ahead and answer the question.

On the other hand, if the deposing lawyer asks a question that invades the attorney-client privilege[34] or persists in asking questions that are unreasonably annoying, embarrassing or oppressive, you will not only object but will instruct your client not to answer those questions.[35] In short, whenever you make an objection, your client should stop whatever she is saying and not answer the question unless you tell her to do so.

5. Answering "leading" questions calmly.

When your client is deposed by counsel for the opposing party, part of the examination may include the use of leading questions (e.g., "Isn't it true that you didn't actually see the accident?" or "You didn't see the accident, did you?"). This form of questioning is invariably irritating and unpleasant for a witness. If your client has had no prior exposure to leading questions, she may become intimidated or angry when she experiences them for the first time.

Thus, you should give your client some exposure to this form of questioning so that she will know "to keep her cool" and to answer such questions calmly, usually with a simple "Yes" or "No." Remind her that because her sole role in the deposition is that of a "witness" and not an advocate for her cause (see subsection [1] above), she should not argue with the deposing lawyer if the pattern of the leading questions appears to distort the truth. If you believe that the use of these questions paints a misleading picture, you will have the opportunity toward the end of the deposition to ask her follow-up questions to have her explain the particular matter or otherwise "set the record straight."

---

34. If necessary review with your client what this privilege means.

35. Under Fed. R. Civ. P. 30(c) and (d), "[a] person may instruct a deponent not to answer only when necessary to preserve a privilege ... or to present a motion ... to terminate or limit [the deposition] on the ground that it is being conducted in bad faith or in a manner that unreasonably annoys, embarrasses, or oppresses the deponent or party."

When giving your client practice in answering leading questions, it is often desirable to have another lawyer in your firm conduct the examination (which need not be long), and then you can comment on your client's performance. For example, Larry Odden (L) might call upon one of his associate lawyers (AL) to question Clara as follows:

> AL: Isn't it fair to say, Ms. Miles, that your health is important to you?
> C: Yes.
> AL: In fact many people would say that their health is "everything"—
> C: Yes.
> AL: It's important not only to you, but to your husband and to Tommy, isn't it?
> C: Yes, I believe so.
> AL: And if you are having problems with your health, the responsible thing to do is to get appropriate treatment, isn't it?
> C: Yes, but I—
> AL: (Interrupting) let me finish if I may, mam. That's true, is it not?
> C: Yes.
> AL: Now, you have told us that you have had continuous pain in your neck and lower back since the accident last February—
> C: Yes, I have.
> AL: You were treated by Sally Byler from February through April 14, isn't that right?
> C: Yes, that's right.
> AL: She's not a medical doctor, is she?
> C: No; she's a chiropractor.
> AL: And after April 14, you didn't seek any further treatment for almost half a year, isn't that right?
> C: Well, I next saw Dr. Wexler at Duke University on October 2.
> AL: Yes; and that's almost six months after April 14, isn't it?
> C: Yes.
> AL: Almost half a year?
> C: Yes.
> AL: Yet, you say you had continuous pain in your neck and back throughout that entire half year—
> C: I did; and that's the truth.
> AL: The fact is, ma'am, you didn't seek any treatment for your continuous pain for almost half a year. That's true, isn't' it?
> C: Yes.

[LARRY NOW COMMENTS ON THE EXAMINATION AS FOLLOWS]:

L: You did an excellent job, Clara. You kept your composure and gave simple, truthful answers. The questions were somewhat unnerving, don't you think?

C: [Laughing] That's an understatement. At one point I had the urge to explain the gap in treatment.

L: Yes; I heard that, but you did well to stop and just answer "Yes" or "No." In light of AL's questioning, let me give you a short example of what I might ask you toward the end of the deposition when it is my turn to ask questions. Okay?

C: Okay.

L: Here goes: Clara, earlier in this deposition you were asked about a gap in your treatment from April 14 to October 2. Do you remember that?

C: Yes.

L: Were you given an opportunity to explain why you received no treatment during that period?

C: No.

L: Please, then, go ahead and tell us why—

C: After I saw Dr. Byler for three months, we ran out of money to pay her. Dan's health insurance didn't cover the treatments. And then when Dan was starting up his new plumbing business, neither of us had any insurance, although we paid on a policy for Tommy. So, I didn't have the money to pay for further treatment.

L: Did there come a time when you were able to obtain health insurance coverage for yourself to pay for further treatment?

C: Yes. In mid September, I found out I had $2000 in coverage for medical payments through my own car insurance, and I used that to pay Dr. Wexler, who was referred to me by Dr. Byler. Since last October, both Dan and I have been able to obtain health insurance, and I was able to pay for physical therapy at Duke for the next three months.

L: Did this treatment help you?

C: Yes. It's helped a lot. My last visit was at the end of December. I'm much better now.

§8.08 Counseling the Criminal Defendant

Representing a criminal defendant is often a particularly arduous and wrenching task. When one or more felonies are charged, your client may face lengthy incarceration—or even execution. A felony conviction carries the loss of certain rights, such as the right to vote, to hold public office, to serve on a jury, to possess a firearm, or to receive certain governmental benefits. Even when only a misdemeanor is charged (e.g., driving while under the influence of alcohol, possession of a controlled substance, or indecent exposure), your client may face public censure, the break-up of his family, or the loss of his job or career. Thus, representing a criminal defendant should be thought of as a grave responsibility.

All the interviewing and counseling techniques discussed in Chapters 3 through 5 are pertinent to representing a criminal defendant. However, because of the special nature of criminal-defense representation, along with the Sixth Amendment's command of effective assistance of counsel and other rights accorded to the accused, this Section discusses three aspects about your role in counseling a criminal defendant: (1) establishing a close relationship of trust and confidence with your client, and the decision-making roles of you and your client; (2) advising about plea bargaining, guilty pleas, and sentencing; and (3) advising about appeals and further post-conviction remedies.

[1] Establishing a Close Relationship of Trust and Confidence, and the Decision-Making Role of You and Your Client

The *American Bar Association Standards Relating to the Administration of Criminal Justice—The Defense Function* ("*Defense Function Standards*")[36] emphasize that you "should seek to establish a relationship of trust and confidence" with your client to the end that your client is completely candid with you about facts that are both incriminating and exculpatory.[37] In this regard, you should not seek "to influence the direction of [your] client's responses" about the facts of the case, such as "advising [your] client at the outset not to admit anything [to you] that might handicap [your] freedom in calling witnesses or in otherwise making a defense."[38] To help obtain candid information from your client, you "should explain the necessity of full disclosure of all facts known to [your] client for an effective defense," and fully explain the attorney-client

---

36. "[The] standards are intended to be used as a guide to professional conduct and performance. They are not intended to be used as criteria for the judicial evaluation of alleged misconduct of defense counsel to determine the validity of a conviction. They may or may not be relevant in such judicial evaluation, depending upon all the circumstances." Defense Function Standard 4-1.1.

37. Defense Function Standards 4-3.1(a) and 4-3.2 and Commentary.

38. Commentary to Defense Function Standard 4-3.2.

privilege.[39] In addition, taking a particularly "caring" approach to your client (*see* § 2.05) is integral to establishing the requisite trust and confidence for effective representation.

Consistent with the trust and confidence established between you and your client, you "should advise [your client] with complete candor concerning all aspects of the case, including a candid estimate of the probable outcome"[40] after you have fully informed yourself on the law and the facts (including conducting any necessary factual investigation and interviewing of witnesses).[41] In being candid, you "should not intentionally understate or overstate the risks, hazards, or prospects of the case to exert undue influence on [your client's] decision as to [what course of action to pursue—whether a plea, trial, or appeal]."[42]

As otherwise provided in Rule 1.2(a) of the *ABA Model Rules of Professional Conduct* (*see* § 6.03), the *Defense Function Standards* differentiate between those decisions relating to the conduct of the case that only your client can make and those decisions that you can make after consultation with your client. Certain decisions relating to the conduct of the case are ultimately for the accused and others are ultimately for defense counsel. Standard 4-5.2 provides:

> (b) The decisions to be made by a competent client, after full consultation with defense counsel include:
>
> > (i) whether to proceed without counsel;
> > (ii) what pleas to enter;
> > (iii) whether to accept a plea offer;
> > (iv) whether to cooperate with or provide substantial assistance to the government
> > (v) whether to waive jury trial.
> > (vi) whether to testify in his or her own behalf;
> > (vii) whether to speak at sentencing;
> > (viii) whether to appeal; and
> > (ix) any other decision that has been determined in the jurisdictionto belong to the client
>
> ...

Strategic and tactical decisions should be made by defense counsel after consultation with the client where feasible and appropriate. Such decisions include

---

39. Defense Function Standard 4-3.1(a).
40. Defense Function Standard 4-5.1.
41. See Defense Function Standard 4-4.1.
42. *Id.*

what witnesses to call, whether and how to conduct cross-examination, what jurors to accept or strike, what trial motions should be made, and what evidence should be introduced.

In connection with those decisions that can only be made by your client, "it is proper for [you] to use reasonable persuasion to guide [your] client to a sound decision ... and to urge [your] client to follow [your] proffered professional advice."[43] Indeed, you "should give [your] client the benefit of [your] advice and experience."[44] However, the ultimate decisions of whether to plead guilty, whether to accept a plea agreement, whether to waive jury trial, whether to testify, and whether to appeal are for your client alone.[45]

[2] Advising about Plea Bargaining, Guilty Pleas, and Sentencing

As defense counsel, you should explore a non-criminal disposition of your client's case in appropriate circumstances.[46] When a plea bargain would clearly be of benefit to your client, the failure to try to negotiate the case may constitute ineffective assistance of counsel.[47] However, for purposes of effective assistance of counsel, you have no duty to enter into plea negotiations when the prosecutor has no desire to negotiate.[48]

For constitutional purposes, a guilty plea is valid if it is entered knowingly, intelligently and voluntarily.[49] This depends upon the competence of the advice you give your client[50] insofar as it affects his knowledge and understanding.[51] That is, a defendant cannot be bound by his decision to plead guilty if he did not receive reasonably effective assistance of counsel. The test of ineffectiveness is whether counsel's representation fell below an objective standard of reasonableness and whether there is a reasonable probability that, but for counsel's ineffectiveness, the defendant would not have pleaded guilty and would have insisted on going to trial.[52] For example, a plea may be involuntary when

---

43. Commentaries to Defense Function Standards 4-5.1 and 4-5.2.

44. Commentary to Defense Function Standard 4-5.2.

45. *Id.*

46. Defense Function Standard 4-6.1(a).

47. *See, e.g.,* Mason v. Balcom, 531 F.2d 717 (5th Cir. 1976).

48. Burger v. Kemp, 483 U.S. 776, 785–86, 107 S.Ct. 3114, 97 L.Ed. 2d 638 (1987).

49. Santobello v. New York, 404 U.S. 257, 92 S.Ct. 495, 30 L.Ed. 2d 427 (1971).

50. United States v. Ramos, 810 F.2d 308 (1st Cir. 1987).

51. *See generally,* Annot. Adequacy of Defense Counsel's Representation of Criminal Client Regarding Guilty Pleas, 10 A.L.R.4th 8.

52. Hill v. Lockhart, 474 U.S. 52, 106 S.Ct. 366, 88 L.Ed. 2d 203 (1985).

counsel grossly and materially misinforms the defendant about the applicable law, the consequences of the plea, or the court's probable disposition. "Under no circumstances should [you] recommend … acceptance of a plea unless appropriate investigation and study of the case has been completed, including an analysis of controlling law and the evidence likely to be introduced at trial."[53]

Throughout the plea bargaining process, you should advise your client of the following:[54]

> (1) His sole right and decision to accept the plea bargain or take the case to trial;
>
> (2) All aspects of the merits of the prosecution's case, your client's possible defenses, potential defense motions, the applicable law, and a candid assessment of the probable outcome of a trial;
>
> (3) The general process of plea bargaining and your particular plea bargaining strategy in the case;
>
> (4) All plea offers made by the prosecutor, what they mean, and their relative merits;[55]
>
> (5) All of the consequences and ramifications of a particular plea, including possible sentences and effects on probation, parole eligibility, immigration status, and the like;
>
> (6) The actual plea-taking process;
>
> (7) Any allocution[56] required prior to the court's acceptance of the guilty plea;[57] and
>
> (8) The processes of taking the case to trial if your client were to choose that option.

The extent to which you should try to persuade your client of the wisdom of pleading guilty in a particular case is a controversial subject. As one commentator has observed:

> Most defendants do not understand our system of justice and cannot be made to understand. They are, in the main, too optimistic: they believe that if their attorneys were willing to fight vigorously on their behalf, they might be acquitted. They suspect, however, that the "legal

---

53. Defense Function Standard 4-6.1(b).

54. *See generally*, Annot. Adequacy of Defense Counsel's Representation of Criminal Client Regarding Plea Bargaining, 8 A.L.R. 4th 660.

55. Defense Function Standard 4-6.2(b).

56. Allocution is the opportunity of the defendant to make a statement to the court in mitigation of sentence.

57. Defense Function Standard 4-8.1 (d).

establishment" (including perhaps their own attorney) is conspiring to deprive them of the right to trial, and even when defense attorneys have the time for patient explanations (as they often do not), defendants may not fully realize the extent of the penalty that our system exacts for an erroneous tactical decision. For these reasons, a Chicago public defender observed, "A lawyer shirks his duty when he does not coerce his client," and this statement suggests a fundamental dilemma for any defense attorney working under the constraints of the guilty plea system. When a lawyer refuses to "coerce his client," he insures his own failure; the foreseeable result is usually a serious and unnecessary penalty that, somehow, it should have been the lawyer's duty to prevent. When a lawyer does "coerce his client," however, he also insures his failure: he damages the attorney-client relationship, confirms the cynical suspicions of the client, undercuts a constitutional right, and incurs the resentment of the person whom he seeks to serve. The defense attorney's lot is therefore not a happy one—until he gets used to it.[58]

While there is no constitutional or ethical requirement that you expressly recommend that your client take a particular course of action, most criminal defense lawyers adopt the position taken by the *Defense Function Standards* that such advice is essential.[59] Of course, however, your advice must be reasonably informed, and any efforts at persuasion must not involve improper threats or coercion.

If your client decides to enter a plea of guilty (or an *Alford* plea, *nolo contendere* plea, or conditional plea),[60] you should fully advise him about the following:

---

58. Alschuler, *The Defense Attorney's Role in Plea Bargaining*, 84 Yale L.J. 1179, 1310 (1974).

59. *See* Commentary to Defense Function Standard 4-5.2.

60. An "*Alford*" plea, named after North Carolina v. Alford, 400 U.S. 25, 91 S.Ct. 160, 27 L.Ed.2d 162 (1970), is a plea of guilty while the defendant nevertheless maintains his innocence, as where he accepts the practical reality that the prosecution's evidence is overwhelming despite his protestations of innocence, or cannot truly say that he committed the offense due to an impairment of his mental state at the time (e.g., due to extreme intoxication or drug use). A "*nolo contendere*" plea is a plea of guilty, meaning "I will not contest it," and may not be used against the defendant in a later civil suit for the same act. A "conditional plea," *see* Fed. R. Crim. P. 11, is a guilty plea that reserves the right of the defendant to appeal the adverse determination of a specified pretrial motion, such that the defendant may withdraw his plea if he prevails on appeal. *See generally*, G. Nicholas Herman, *Plea Bargaining*, Secs. 10:02–10:07 (2d ed. LexisNexis 2004).

(1) All of the terms of any applicable plea agreement to ensure that he understands:

(a) all of its terms and voluntarily agrees to it;

(b) that (e.g., in federal court) if the plea agreement contains a non-binding recommendation about sentencing, the court may reject the recommendation without permitting him to withdraw his plea, and impose a more severe sentence than he may anticipate; and

(c) that (e.g. in federal court) if the plea agreement involves the dismissal of charges or an agreement about a specific sentence, the court may reject the agreement, provide him with an opportunity to withdraw his plea, and impose a more severe sentence than he anticipated.

(2) The contents of the indictment or information to ensure that he understands:

(a) all charges in the case and the elements of proof for each charge;

(b) that by pleading guilty to a felony he will lose certain rights (such as the rights to vote, hold public office, serve on a jury, and receive certain governmental benefits);

(c) the maximum possible penalty and any mandatory minimum penalty;

(d) the effect of any drug quantity involved or other aggravating factors or prior offenses that may affect the maximum and any mandatory minimum sentence (if applicable);

(e) the duration of any authorized or mandatory term of supervised release, and the consequences for violating any conditions of supervised release;

(f) whether probation is available;

(g) any possible forfeiture of property;

(h) whether notice of the conviction must be provided to the victim;

(i) any requirement to pay certain fees; and

(j) any requirement to pay restitution.

(3) The court's particular procedure for accepting the plea—e.g., that the court will place him under oath; and that subject to the penalty of perjury he will be asked certain questions such as his full name, age, education, and whether he has recently been treated for any mental illness or addiction to drugs, or whether he is currently under the influence of any drugs, alcohol, or medication of any kind.

(4) The operation of the relevant sentencing statutes or guidelines to ensure that he understands:

(a) all of their ramifications in his case and an estimate of the applicable sentence;

(b) the availability or non-availability of parole;

(c) the specific sentence to be imposed (if the plea agreement specifies one);

(d) that if the plea agreement does not specify a specific sentence, the court will determine the sentence after a hearing and after reviewing a presentence report or other presentencing-investigation materials;

(e) that (if applicable) the court may depart upward or downward from the sentencing range and may impose a sentence that is less or more severe than the sentence called for by statute or the particular sentencing guidelines;

(f) under what circumstances, if any, the prosecution may appeal the sentence imposed; and

(g) that (if applicable) he has chosen to waive the right to appeal his sentence.

(5) The loss of his rights of:

(a) a trial by jury;

(b) the presumption of innocence and privilege against self-incrimination;

(c) proof of guilt beyond a reasonable doubt;

(d) assistance of counsel at trial;

(e) confronting and cross-examining witnesses; and

(f) the issuance of subpoenas or compulsory process to compel the attendance of witnesses for his defense.

(6) The possibility that the court may ask him questions about his involvement in the offense and/or whether he agrees with the prosecution's summary of the evidence.

When advising your client about sentencing, particularly in connection with his decision about whether to enter a guilty plea, the Commentary to Standard 4-6.2 of the *Defense Function Standards* instructively observes:

> It is also important that the accused be informed that the action of the sentencing judge cannot be definitely predicted. Sometimes an accused who has consented to a particular plea on the basis of discussions between the prosecutor and defense counsel has the misimpression either that the judge is a party to the arrangement or that estimates made by the lawyer are guarantees of what the sentence will be. This situation should be anticipated by defense counsel. If the

lawyer has any doubt about the defendant's complete understanding of the alternatives, the lawyer should seek to clarify the situation, for example, by calling in a relative of the accused or a trusted friend with the defendant's permission.

It cannot be emphasized too much that a crucial factor in plea discussions is the duty of counsel to explain fully to the accused the consequences of a guilty plea in terms of the range of sentences the court can and may impose. Special care must be exercised to distinguish between what a particular judge may do or usually does from what the judge is authorized to do by law. An accused under tension, whether incarcerated or at large, will sometimes not easily distinguish among or remember matters that are clear to the lawyer. Moreover, the "jailhouse lawyer" with whom the accused confers may leave him or her confused by the difference between what is heard in the cellblock and what the defense lawyer says. The need for the accused to understand the range of possible penalties is obvious; without such understanding, a truly intelligent and voluntary choice is not possible.

In addition to the foregoing, whether you are advising your client about sentencing in anticipation of a potential guilty plea or after a judgment of conviction by a jury, you "should also insure that [your client] understands the nature of the presentence investigation process, and in particular the significance of statements made by [him] to probation officers and related personnel."[61] That is, subject to the obligation that your client be truthful in his statements to persons involved in the presentence investigation process, you don't want your client to gratuitously volunteer information that would be harmful for sentencing purposes.

Finally, when there is a right of allocution during the sentencing process, Standard 4-8.1(d) of the *Defense Function Standards* warns that you should be alert "to the possible dangers of making a statement that might tend to prejudice an appeal." The Commentary to that Standard explains the problem in this way:

> In the course of exercising the right of allocution, the defendant may sometimes freely admit the guilt that he or she has, up to the time of verdict, denied; the defendant, for example, may have taken the stand and controverted the evidence by a denial of any participation in the alleged offense. Most judges are not unduly surprised by this, but there are obvious risks involved. Some judges may impose a heavier sentence

---

61. Defense Function Standard 4-8.1(c).

if they believe that the defendant committed perjury at trial. Even more serious perhaps is the fact that the defendant's statement on allocution admitting guilt is part of the record and, if the conviction is appealed, that admission may compromise the appeal, especially if the appeal is based to any degree on insufficiency of the evidence.

The other side of the coin is that if the assumptions underlying the right of allocution are correct, the right is one not to be waived lightly. The more realistic view may be that an accused does not often influence the sentence by his or her own utterances. Nonetheless, because of the risks of a statement by a convicted defendant that might tend to increase the severity of a sentence or prejudice an appeal, defense counsel should be alert to the problem and would be well advised to recommend to the client that counsel make all statements in mitigation or that the client exercise the right of allocution with these hazards in mind.

[3] Advising about Appeals and Further Post-Conviction Remedies

At the outset of your representation, you should establish a clear understanding with your client about whether you will represent him on appeal or in connection with any further post-conviction remedy.[62] As mentioned in Subsection [1] above, "the decision whether to appeal [or pursue some further post-conviction remedy] must be the defendant's own choice."[63]

In counseling your client about pursuing an appeal or some further post-conviction remedy, you should advise him about the relative advantages and disadvantages of those remedies, the extent to which they may be meritorious on the facts of the case, and the probable outcome of seeking such relief. The *Defense Function Standards* summarize these obligations as follows:

> After conviction, defense counsel should explain to the defendant the meaning and consequences of the court's judgment and defendant's right to appeal. Defense counsel should give the defendant his or her professional judgment as to whether there are meritorious ground for appeal and as to the probable results of an appeal. Defense counsel should also explain to the defendant the advantages and disadvantages of an appeal.[64]

---

62. Defense Function Standard 4-3.1(a).
63. Defense Function Standard 4-9.1(b).
64. Defense Function Standard 4-9.1(a).

Appellate counsel should give a client his or her best professional evaluation of the questions that might be presented on appeal.... Counsel should advise on the probable outcome of a challenge to the conviction or sentence. Counsel should endeavor to persuade the client to abandon a wholly frivolous appeal or to eliminate contentions lacking in substance.[65]

Appellate counsel has the ultimate authority to decide which arguments to make on appeal. When appellate counsel decides not to argue all of the issues that his or her client desires to be argued, appellate counsel should inform the client of his or her pro se briefing rights.[66]

After a conviction is affirmed on appeal, appellate counsel should determine whether there is any ground for relief under other post-conviction remedies. If there is a reasonable prospect of a favorable result, counsel should explain to the defendant the advantages and disadvantages of taking such action.[67]

Finally, when counseling your client about the prospects of obtaining relief on appeal or through some other post-conviction proceeding, it may be appropriate to advise him that, as a general rule, pursuing these remedies is usually an "uphill battle." This candid observation is not an overstatement. A convicted client is particularly prone to harboring false hopes about the prospects of succeeding on these types of remedies. Just as he should have no illusions about the vigor with which you will pursue an appeal or other post-conviction remedy, he should have no illusions about your assessment of the ultimate chances of prevailing on those remedies.

---

65. Defense Function Standard 4-9.2(e).
66. Defense Function Standard 4-9.2(g).
67. Defense Function Standard 4-9.5.

Index